Networking Interview Questions

(500 Interview Questions covering Basic, Router, VPN and Firewall)

Other titles of interest......
by SHIVPRASAD KOIRALA

.NET
INTERVIEW QUESTIONS
ISBN : 81-8333-147-5
Pages: 388

SOFTWARE TESTING
INTERVIEW QUESTIONS
ISBN : 81-8333-236-6
Pages: 212

SQL SERVER
INTERVIEW QUESTIONS
ISBN : 81-8333-103-3
Pages: 228

JAVA/J2EE
INTERVIEW QUESTIONS
ISBN : 81-8333-173-4
Pages: 320

NETWORKING
INTERVIEW QUESTIONS
ISBN : 81-8333-243-9
Pages: 216

C# AND ASP.NET
PROJECTS
ISBN : 81-8333-217-X
Pages: 228

Networking
Interview Questions

(500 Interview Questions covering Basic, Router, VPN and Firewall)

by

Shivprasad Koirala
&
Sham Sheikh

BPB PUBLICATIONS
B-14, CONNAUGHT PLACE, NEW DELHI - 110 001

FIRST EDITION 2008 Reprint 2015

ISBN 10 : 81-8333-243-9
ISBN 13 : 978-81-8333-243-9

Distributors:

COMPUTER BOOK CENTRE
12, Shrungar Shopping Centre, M.G. Road,
BANGALORE-560001 Ph: 25587923, 25584641

MICRO BOOKS
Shanti Niketan Building, 8, Camac Street,
KOLKATTA-700017 Ph: 22826518/9

BUSINESS PROMOTION BUREAU
8/1, Ritchie Street, Mount Road,
CHENNAI-600002 Ph: 28410796, 28550491

BPB PUBLICATIONS
B-14, Connaught Place, NEW DELHI-110001
Ph: 23325760, 23723393, 23737742

BPB BOOK CENTRE
376, Old Lajpat Rai Market, DELHI-110006
PH: 23861747

MICRO MEDIA
Shop No. 5, Mahendra Chambers,150 D.N. Rd,
Next to Capital Cinema V.T. (C.S.T.) Station,
MUMBAI-400001 Ph.: 22078296, 22078297

DECCAN AGENCIES
4-3-329, Bank Street,
HYDERABAD-500195 Ph: 24756400, 24756967

INFO TECH
G-2, Sidhartha Building, 96 Nehru Place,
NEW DELHI-110019
Ph: 26438245, 26415092, 26234208

INFO TECH
Shop No. 2, F-38, South Extension Part-1
NEW DELHI-110049
Ph: 24691288

Published by Manish Jain for BPB Publications, B-14, Connaught Place, New Delhi-110 001 and Printed by him at Akash Press New Delhi

Contents of the CD

The contents of the CD accompanying this book will be of great help to you in Networking interviews. The contents of this CD areas follows:

- Sample resumes which will help you in creating a better resume.
- An MS-Excel sheet to guage how much you are ready for Networking interviews.
- Zone alarm installation to practice firewalls (zaZA_Setup_en.exe.)
- A Netcat folder that has the famous netcat tool for port scanning and sending requests to ports for checking security.
- Testnet.zip,TestNet is a simple application to test network connectivity. TestNet is small, simple, and easy-to-use. If you need a way to check your connection from time to time, especially if you are using dial-up, this program might be a great solution.
- Nsaudito_setup.exe, Nsauditor reveals a variety of information, including installed software, users, shares, hot fixes, NetBIOS, drives, RPC, SQL and SNMP information, and open ports. Nsauditor Network Security Auditor is a network security scanner that allows auditing and monitoring remote network computers for possible vulnerabilities, and checks networks for all potential methods that a hacker might use to attack it. Nsauditor is a complete networking utilities package that includes a wide range of tools for network auditing, scanning, monitoring, and more.
- GNS3-0[1].3-win32-all-in-one.exe, the GNS3 application was designed to be a graphical network simulator that allows you to design complex network topologies and to launch simulations on them. Some of the key features of "GNS3" are: It helps in designing high-quality complex network topologies, Emulating Cisco routers, Simulating simple Ethernet, ATM, and Frame Relay switches, Load-balancing between multiple hypervisors.
- tni-setup.exe, Total Network Inventory is a tool that interrogates all computers in a network and reports back with complete information about OS, service packs, hot fixes, hardware, software, running processes, etc., on remote machines.
- BMSetup.zip, BWMeter is a very powerful bandwidth monitor and meter that measures and displays all traffic on your network.

Contents of This Book

- As the name suggests, 'Networking Interview Questions' is meant mainly for freshers as well as professionals who are searching for opportunities in Networking.
- This book covers basics like OSI, IPV4, IPV6, and Subneting in a detailed manner.
- This book also has a complete dedicated chapter on routers, covering the most-asked protocols, such as, RIP, IGRP, EIGRP, OSPF, and BGP.
- Firewall is the most-frequented area during a Networking interview. This book has a full dedicated chapter on firewalls covering concepts such as firewall architecture, NAT, Application gateway, dual home, screened host, and perimeter area.
- No Networking interview is complete without VPN concepts. This book dedicates 60 most-frequently asked questions on VPN covering concepts such as L2F, PPTP, L2TP, GRE, PPP, Tunneling, LAC, LNS, IKE, and ESP.
- There is also a dedicated chapter on protocols covering the most-frequently asked protocols like TCP/IP, UDP, NETBIOS, IGMP, RTP, RCTP, RPC, and a lot more.
- Frequently asked questions on DHCP, DNS, and trouble-shooting are also covered in this book.
- In the CD, we have also provided an interview rating sheet which can be used the learners to judge the extent to which they are ready to face Networking interviews.
- The best part of the book is that other than just Networking interviews, it also dwells on non-technical aspects, such as, creating resumes, conducting salary negotiations, and other vital points (such as, why they want to leave the previous organization?, Where thay see themselves after 3 years, and so on.)

Acknowledgments

This book is dedicated to my kids, Sanjana and Simran, whose play-time has been stolen and given to the creation of this book. I am also thankful to my wife for constantly encouraging me, and also to BPB Publication that gave a newcomer like me a platform to perform. Last, but not the least, i would like to thank my mom and dad for constantly blessing me. I am indeed lucky to have my brother, Raju, who always keeps my momentum preserved. I am also grateful to Bhavnesh Asar who initially conceptualized the idea of this series of books on interview questions. And before I forget, thanks to Shaam for all the effort he has put in. It was his tiresome three months of continuous writing that made sure that we made it in time. Tons of thanks to my reviewers whose feedbacks were an essential tool that helped improve this book.

Shivprased Kopirala

The credit of being a part of this book goes to three persons: my mom, dad, and Mr Shivprased. I mentioned my mom and dad because of all that they did for me and the sacrifices that they made for me, and I mentioned Mr Shivprased because it was he who taught me how to share knowledge through books. I thank him from my bottom of my heart for giving me an role to play in the creation of this book. And above all, I thank the almighty Lord sitting above all of us for showing his presence, and showering his blessings and love in the form of these three persons.

In case you want to get in touch with me, mail at ahteshamax@hotmail.com.

Sham Sheikh

About the Author

Shivprasad Koirala works in a multinational company and has extensive experience in the software industry. He is presently working presently as a project lead, and has, in the past, led projects in banking, travel, and financial sectors. But all in all, he is still a developer at heart working an 8-hour job. Writing is something that he does on the side because he loves writing. The author understands that nobody is perfect. He is, therefore, open to and welcomes any and all comments and criticisms, which can be mailed to shiv_koirala@yahoo.com. The author would like to reassure his readers that all bouquets and brickbats would be received with love and shall be treated with topmost priority.

The author understands that writing an interview question book is a big responsibility. He has tried to cover the maximum number of questions for each the topic in this book. But it is pretty much impossible to cover all questions that can probably be asked. So if any reader comes across any such questions during an interview, that reader is requested to mail it to shiv_koirala@yahoo.com .Who knows, that question can probably secure someone else's job!

Organizational Hierarchy

It's very important during an interview to be clear about what position you are targeting. The questions that you will face depends on the position you are targeting. For example, if you are looking for a Project Manager's position, you will be asked around 20% technical questions and 80% management questions.

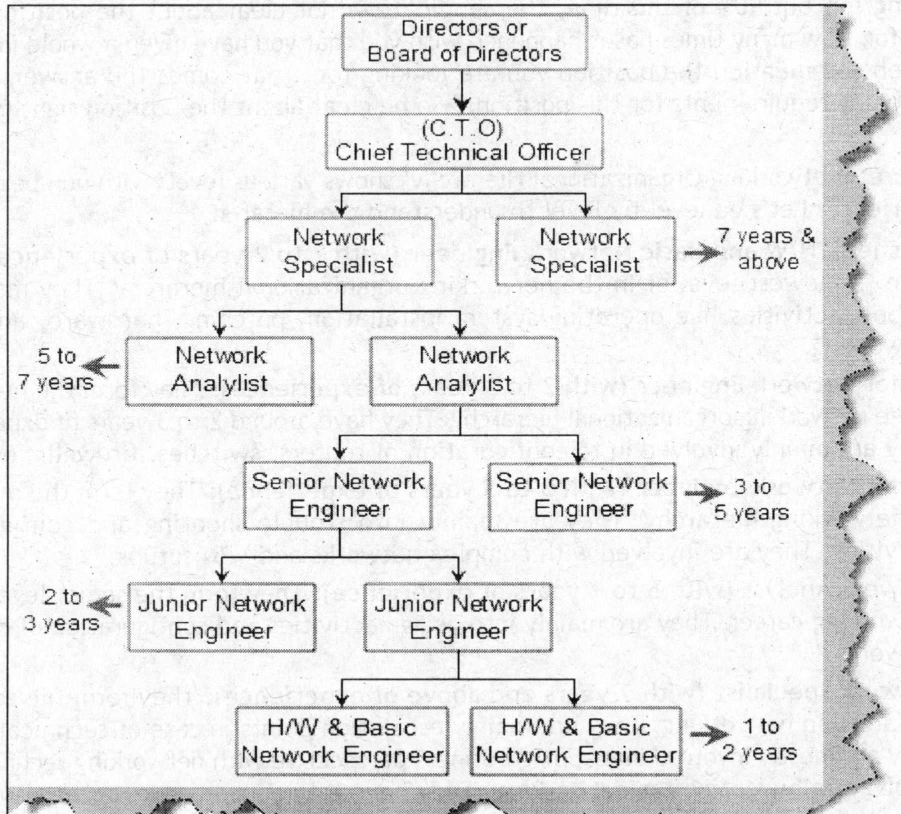

Figure: Networking Organizational Hierarchy

Note: *In small-scale and mid-scale software houses, chances are that they expect a PM to be very much technical. But in big software houses the situation is very much different, interview are conducted according to positions applied for.... Unless the interviewer changes the rule.*

Note: *There are many small and medium-sized software companies that do not follow the hierarchy ahown in the figure above, and have their own* adhoc *way of defining positions in the company.*

So why is the need of hierarchy in an interview? *"Interview is a contract between the employer and candidate to achieve specific goals."*

So, an employer is looking for a suitable candidate and a candidate is looking for a better career. Normally in interviews, the employer is very clear about what type of candidate he is looking for, but 90% of the time, the candidate is not clear about the positions he is looking for. How many times has it happened with you that you have given a whole interview and when you mention the position you are looking for... pat comes the answer, "we do not have any requirements for this position." So be clear about the position right from the start.

The figure, 'Networking Organizational Hierarchy' shows various levels with number of year of experience. Let's go level-by-level to understand the hierarchy.

- **Freshers, H/W and Basic Network Engineer (with 1 to 2 years of experience)**: They form the lowest level of in the networking organizational hierarchy. They mostly do support activities like operating system installation, patching, hardware, and basic networking.
- **Junior Network Engineer (with 2 to 3 years of experience)**: They form the next level in the networking organizational hierarchy. They have around 2 to 3 years of experience. They are mainly involved in to configuration of routers, switches, firewalls, etc.
- **Senior Network Engineer (with 3 to 5 years of experience)**: They form the mid-level of networking hierarchy. They are mainly into trouble-shooting and configuration activities. They are involved with complex networks and VPN setups.
- **Network Analyst (with 5 to 7 years of experience):** They form the senior level in the networking career. They are mainly into design activities and configuration of complex networks.
- **Network specialist (with 7 years and above of experience)**: They form the top level hierarchy in networking. They are mainly escalation points in case of technical issues. They are mostly involved in mapping business perspective with networking technologies. Involved in budgeting for networking. They have a birds-eye view on the day-to-day activities happening in networking.

Guidelines to a Good Resume

Note: *First impression the last impression.*

Note: *A sample resume is provided in the CD.*

Even before the interviewer meets you, he/she will first meet your resume. An interviewer looking at your resume is almost 20% of the interview happening without you knowing it. I was always bad guy at preparing resumes. Now that I am writing a series of book on interviews, I thought that I should devote a section to resumes. You can skip this part if you are confident about your resume. There is no hard and fast rule that you have to follow, but just see if the following points hold true for your resume.

- Use plain text when sending resumes through email. For instance, if you create your resume using Microsoft Word, what happens if the interviewer is using Linux? He will never be able to read your resume. And what if you create your resume in MS-Word 2000 and the interviewer has Word 97? Ouch!
- Always attach a covering letter to your application. It looks traditionally formal and is really impressive. Attach a covering letter even if you are sending your CV through email.

Given below is a check-list of what you should have in your resume:

- Start with an objective or summary, for example:
    - Working as a Network Analyst for more than 4 years. Implemented VPN solutions for large networks.
    - Followed the industry's best practices, and adhered and implemented processes that enhanced the quality of technical delivery.
    - Pledge to deliver the best technical solutions to the industry.
- Specify your core strengths at the top of the resume by which the interviewer can decide whether you are eligible for the position.

For example:

- Looked after the complete networking department independently.
- Played a major role in ISP implementation.
- Worked extensively in Firewall and Router architecture.

- Well versed with ISO procedures.
- Looking forward to work as a Senior Network Analyst.

This is also a good position to specify your objective or position which makes it clear to the interviewer whether he should call you for an interview. For example, if you are looking for senior positions, specify it explicitly. Any kind of certification, such as, CCNA, etc, should be made visible in this section.

- Once you have briefly specified your goals and what you have done, it's time to specify what type of technology you have worked with. For example, CISCO Router, Firewalls, Process (ISO), Supplier Management, etc.
- After that, you can run the interviewer through of your experience (what companies you have worked for, from what date to what date, etc.) This will give an overview of your experience to the interviewer. Now its time to mention all the projects you have worked on till now. This list should be in reverse chronological order, starting with your latest project.

For every project, try to put these things:

- Project Name/Client name (It's sometimes unethical to mention client names; I leave it on the reader to decide.)
- Team strength for each project.
- Time taken for each project.
- Tools, language, and technology used to complete each project.
- Brief summary of the project. Senior people who have vast experience will tend to lengthen their CV by putting in summaries for all projects. Best for all is to just put in descriptions of the first three projects in reverse chronological order, and the rest can be put forth verbally during the interview. I have seen 15-page CVs, but I honestly doubt whether anyone reads them.
- Finally comes your education and personal details.
- If you are trying for onsite postings, do not forget to mention your passport number.
- There are few who try to make their CVs as long as possible. I personally think that a CV should not be more than 4 to 5 pages long.
- Do not mention your present salary in CV. You can talk about it during the HR-round of your interview.
- When you are writing summaries of projects that you have handled, make it effective by using verbs, such as, managed a team of 5 members, architected the project from start to finish, etc.
- Take 4 to 5 photocopies copies of your resume whenever you go for an interview. You may need them.
- Just in case, take at least 2 passport-size photos with you. You may need them too.
- Carry all your current office documents, especially your salary-slips and joining letter.

Salary Negotiation Skills

Ok, the long and the short of it is that we all do it for money! Not everyone maybe, but still, money matters. And salary negotiations are probably the weakest area of the tech-savvy. They DO NOT make good negotiators. I have seen so many who at the first instance will smile and say "Negotiable."

So, keep the following key points in mind when negotiating for money:

- Do a study of what the salary trend is. Have some kind of baseline in mind. What is the salary trend based on the number of years of experience? Discuss things with your friends beforehand.
- Do not mention your expected salary on the resume.
- Let the employer first make an offer. Try to delay the salary discussion till the very end.
- If they ask you how much you expect, come out with a figure that is a little towards the higher end and say that it is negotiable. Remember, never say negotiable on the figure that you actually want, the HR guys will always bring it down. So negotiate on what you want +a little bit extra.
- The normal trend is that they look at your current salary and add a little it so that they can pull you in. Do your homework. Say clearly that my present salary is this much and I expect this much. I will not come down below this.
- Do not talk harshly during salary negotiations.
- It's good to aim high. For instance I want a billion dollars every month, but at the same time, be realistic also.
- Some companies have those little hidden costs attached to the salary. Clarify it, rather than be surprised when you get your first pay packet.
- Many companies add extra performance compensations to your basic, which can be surprising at times. So, ask for a detail breakdown beforehand. It is best to discuss in-hand salary, rather than NET or CTC.
- Find out what the frequency of hikes and appraisals is.
- Take everything in writing, go back to your house and have a look with a cool head. Is the offer worth it? Give it a good thought.
- Do not forget that once you have job in hand, you can always go back to your current employer and negotiate.
- Remember, cribbing about the fact that your colleague is getting paid more than you is highly unprofessional. So be careful during interview, or be sportive, or be a good negotiator in the next interview.

One very important thing is that the best negotiating ground is not the new company that you plan to join, but the old company which you are leaving. So, once you have an offer in hand, go back to your old employees, show them the offer, and only then make your next move. It is my personal experience that negotiating with an old employer is easier than with a new one. Frankly, if approached properly, rarely will anyone will say 'no,' as you have spent quiet some time with them. Just do not be aggressive or egoistic that you have an offer in hand.

Last but not the least, sometime somethings are worth more than money: **JOB SATISFACTION** being one of them. So, if the difference is money is not that much, go for job satisfaction. It is, at times, worth more than money.

Broad Salary Structure

Given below, in a tabular form, is the salary structure in the networking trade. This data is from the perspective of the Indian market. Amounts give below are annual CTCs (Cost-to-Company) of networking personnel according to grade.

Level	Salary range/year (CTC)
H/W & Basic Engineer	75000 to 90000
Junior Network Engineer	120000 to 200000
Senior Network Engineer	300000 to 500000
Network Analylist	500000 to 900000
Network Specialist	900000 and above

Figure: Salary Card for Network Engineers

Interview Rating Sheet

In the CD, we have provided an Interview Rating MS-Excel sheet. This sheet will help you in gaining an insight into how much you are ready for Software testing, JAVA, .NET , SQL Server and Networking Interviews. In the excel sheet, we have eleven sections:

- Guidelines
- JAVA
- Java Results
- .NET
- .NET Results
- SQL Server
- SQL Server Results
- Software Testing
- Software Testing Results
- Networking
- Networking Results

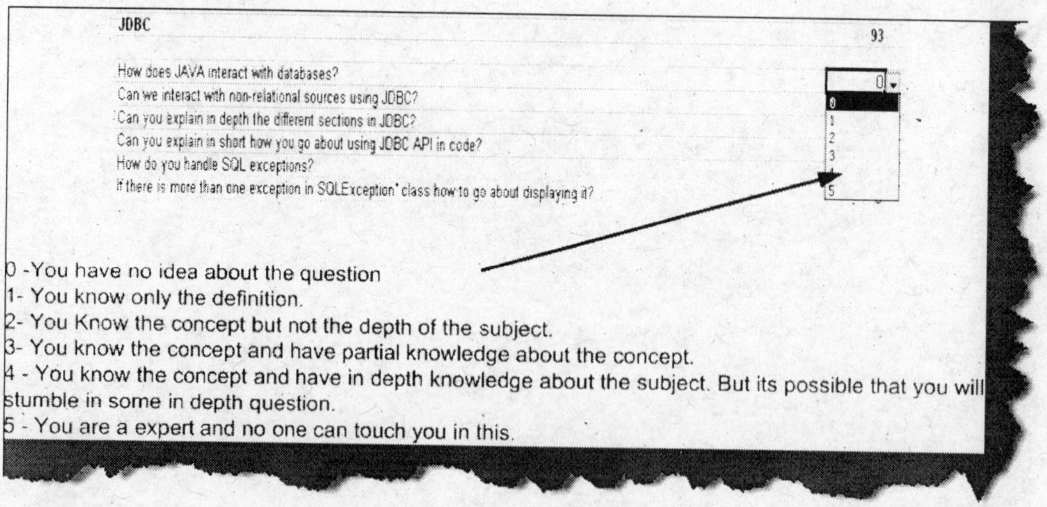

Figure: Rate Yourself

The guidelines-sheet defines the guidelines for rating. For every question asked, you can give rate yourself on a scale of 1 to 5. The following guidelines are to be followed when you rate yourself:

- 0-You have no idea about the question.
- 1-You know only the definition.
- 2-You know the concept but do not have indepth knowledge of the subject.
- 3-You know the concept and have partial knowledge of the concept.
- 4-You know the concept and have indepth knowledge of the subject.
- 5- You are an expert and no one can touch you in this area.

The remaining 10 sections are questions and results. For example, we have the Networking Section and the Networking Results Section. The Networking Section will take in the rating inputs for every question, and Networking Result will show the output. Same holds true for .NET, JAVA , SQL Server and Software Testing.

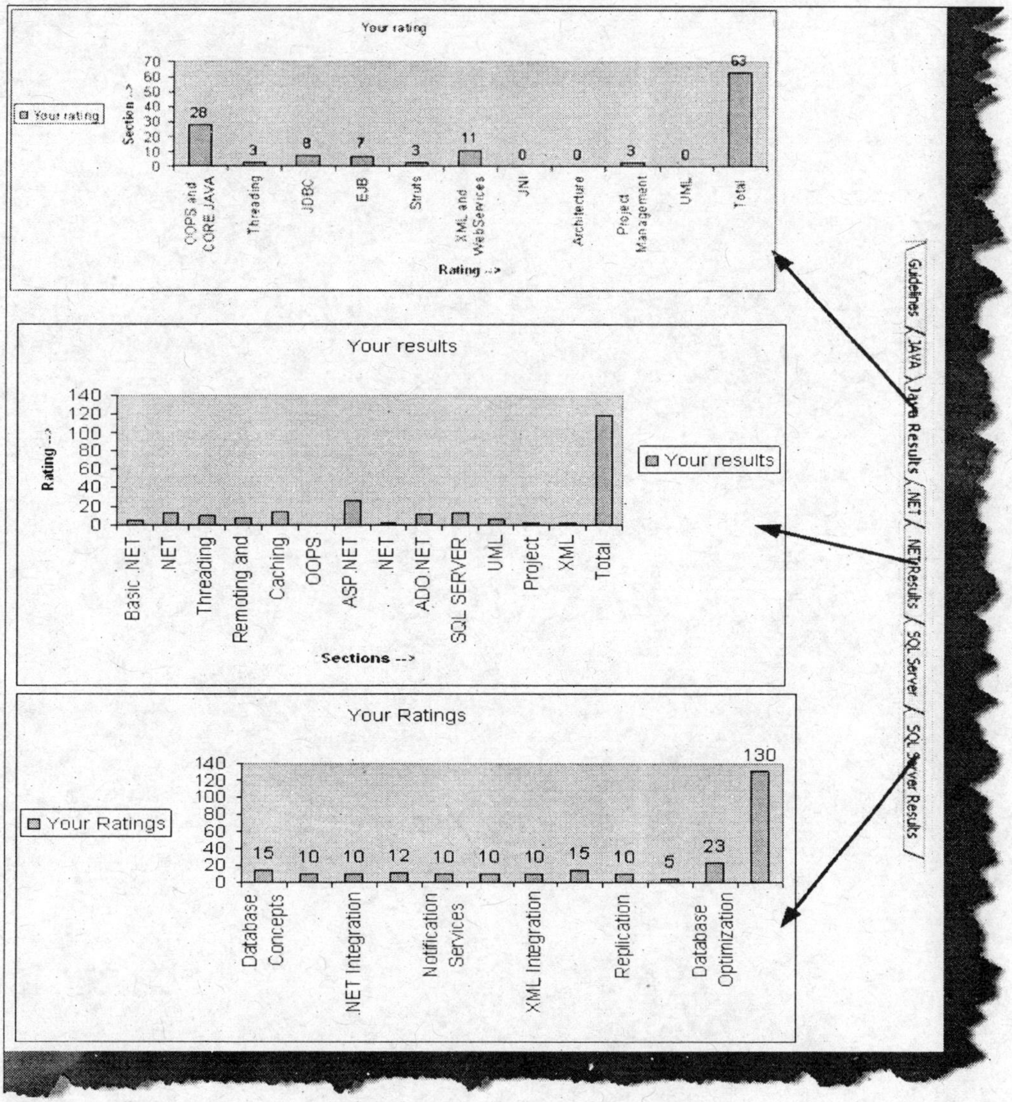

Figure: Overall Rating Values

For every question asked, you need torate yourself. So go through every question and see how good you are. You do not have anyone to supervise you, but remember that at the end of the day it is you who has to clear the interview. So be fair to yourself.

The figure above shows how you have performed in each section, and your overall rating.

Points to be Remembered During Interviews

- One of the first questions asked during an interview is, "Can you say something about yourself?"
- Can you describe yourself and what you have achieved till now?
- Why do you want to leave your current company?
- Where do you see yourself after 3 years?
- What are your positive and negative traits?
- How do you rate yourself in Firewall Implementation on a scale of 1 to 10?
- Are you looking for onsite opportunities? (Be careful do not show your desperation for journeys abroad.)
- Why have you changed so many jobs? (Prepare a decent answer. Do not blame companies and individuals for your frequent changes.)
- Never talk for more than 1 minute straight during an interview.
- Have you worked with OSPF protocol?
- Do not mention client names in your resume. If asked, say that it's confidential. This brings forth qualities, such as, honesty.
- When you make your resume keep your recent projects at the top.
- Find out what the employer is looking for (router implementation or simple Network troubleshooting) by asking him questions at the start of interview.
- Can you brief us about your family background?
- Do you think that you, being a fresher, can really do this job?
- Have you heard about our company? Say five points about our company? Make sure that you read up on the company you are applying in.
- Can you describe your best project?
- Can you work weekends?
- What is the biggest team size you have worked with?
- Describe your current project.
- How much time will you need to join our organization? What's the notice period in your current organization?
- What certifications do you hold? CCNA, CCI, etc,

- Do you have your passport-size photos, final-year marksheet, employment letters from previous companies, last month's salary-slip, passport, and other necessary documents.
- What motivates you the most?
- Why you want to leave your current organization?
- Which type of job gives you the greatest satisfaction?
- What type of environment are you looking for?
- Do you have any experience in Networking Architectures?
- Do you like to work as a team? or as an individual?
- Describe the best project manager you have worked for?
- Why should I hire you?
- Have you ever been fired?
- Can you tell us about a few important points that you have learnt from your past project experiences?
- Have you gone through some unsuccessful projects,? If yes, can you tell us why they failed?
- Are you comfortable relocating? If you have personal problems, say 'no' right at the beginning, or else within two months you may have to read this book again.
- Do you work late nights? The best answer to this is that you can if there is a project deadline. Do not show that it's your culture to work nights.
- Tell us about your special achievements. Here, say something about your best project.
- Do you have any plans of opening your own software company. Beware! do not start pouring out your Bill Gates' dreams, this can create a wrong impression.

How to Read This Book

If you can read English, you can read this book! Just kidding! There are some legends that will make your reading more effective. Every question has a simple tag that rates the question.

These rating are given by the author, and can vary according to companies and individuals.

(B) **Basic Question:** 'Basic Question' means that it is a fundamental question and should be answered. For example, 'ExplainOSI Layers.' Stumbling on these questions will rarely see you pass Networking interviews.

(I) **Intermediate Questions:** These are mid-level questions, and you are expected to answer them if you are looking for a decent position in the company.

(A) **Advanced Questions:** These are advanced level question that are expected when they are looking for specialists in the field.

(P) **Psyche Questions:** These questions do not judge anything in a candidate, but I see it as an attitude problem of the interviewer.

> ***Note:*** *While reading, you will come across sections marked 'Note,' which highlight special points of that section. One advice, do not read this book from start to finish. Go through the index and see which sections you are targeting and revise those.*

Table of Contents

Routers 33

1

Basics

(B) Define Protocol.

Protocols are similar to standards. They set the rules and conventions that define how devices on a network exchange information. Within network communications, protocols define how two devices will carry on their conversation with each other.

(B) Explain the Concept of OSI Layers.

OSI stands for 'Open system Interconnection' (OSI). Let us understand why OSI has come into the picture. Until the year 1970, there existed lot of proprietary custom protocols. So if one network had to communicate with another network, it was a big issue.

For instance in the '70's, Custom Protocol Figure,' we have two networks, one which stands on DECnet protocol and the other on SNA (System Network Architecture) protocol. If we want to connect these two networks, then the networking device should be aware of both these protocols. Till 1970, there existed many such custom protocols which made it extremely difficult to enable such kind of cross-protocol communication.

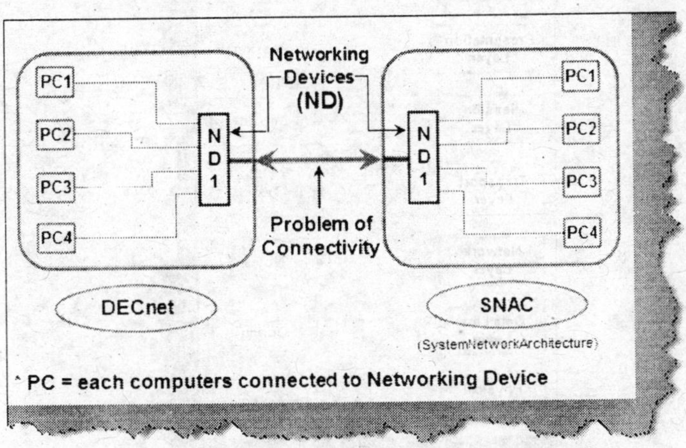

Figure: 70's Custom Protocol Figure

One of the major problems of these custom protocols was that the hardware and the devices for networking were also tied up to those protocols. So, in short, if an organization decided to change a protocol then it had also to change its networking devices, and *vice versa*. There was tight bonding between the networking devices and protocol.

> **Note:** *In some cases, we still remember organizations that changed their protocol because the hardware was very costly. This tight bonding between network devices and the protocol was a major issue.*

With the above discussed issues and problems, a need for a unified networking protocol was very essential. This gave birth to OSI, and as the name explains itself, it was, 'Open System Interconnection.' In short, this protocol was designed to define a standard protocol for network communication.

> **Note:** *It took 7 years to develop the OSI model, i.e., 1977 – 1984.*

(B) Explain the Different Layers in the OSI Model.

> **Note:** *Almost 60% networking interviewers will ask this question.*

There are seven layers in the OSI model:

- Application Layer
- Presentation Layer
- Session Layer
- Transport Layer
- Network Layer
- Data-Link Layer
- Physical Layer

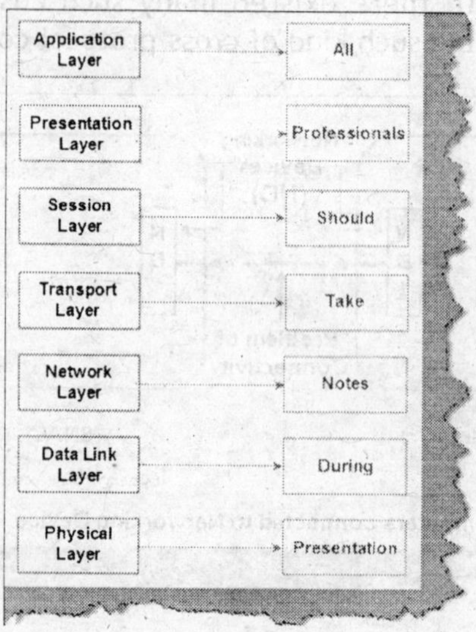

Figure: OSI Trick

> ***Note:*** *You can remember all the above seven layers using the mnemonic, 'All Professionals Should Take Notes During Presentations.' Well, everything is fair in love and an interview. Figure 'OSI Trick' shows the trick to remember them with ease.*

(B) Explain the Application Layer in the OSI Model.

The Application Layer is the topmost layer of the OSI model. It provides network access to application and to users. The Application Layer provides services with which users can access all types of networks. So applications and users use these services to communicate with devices and remote applications. As shown in the figure, 'Application Layer,' you can see how applications and users interact with the application layer protocols, such as, HTTP, FTP, etc.

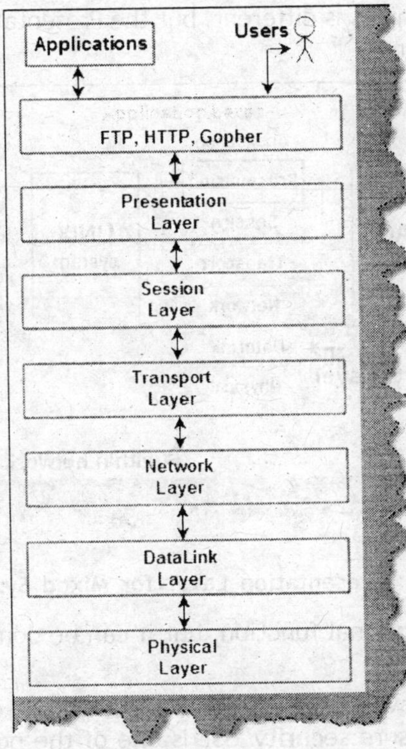

Figure: Application Layer

(B) Explain the Presentation Layer in the OSI Model.

The Presentation Layer is sixth from the top. It is the least used layer as compared to others. The main function of this layer is the presentation of data. Now, let's understand what exactly it functions. There are situations when data sent from one system to another system has to be viewed in a different way. Presentation Layer handles the following functionalities as shown in the figure, 'Presentation Layer Functions.' Translation is the main function of the Presentation Layer, the other functions are rarely used.

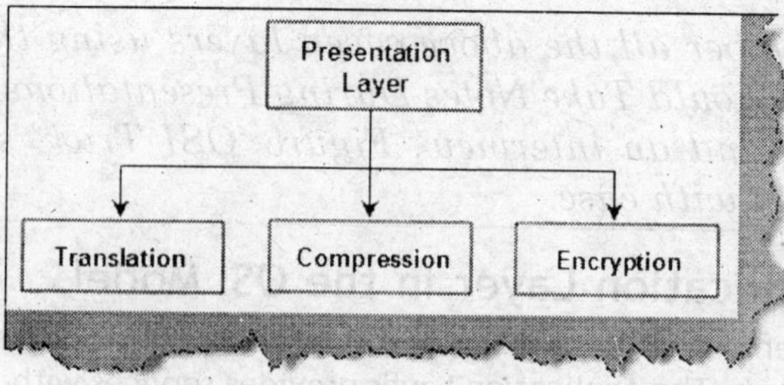

Figure: Presentation Layer Functions

Translation: In a network, there can be many types of computers. For example, as you can see in the figure, 'Presentation Layer for Mixed Systems,' we have two different types of systems in the same network, one is the MAC machine and the other is a UNIX machine. Character set in both machines is different, but the Presentation Layer hides the differences between these two machines.

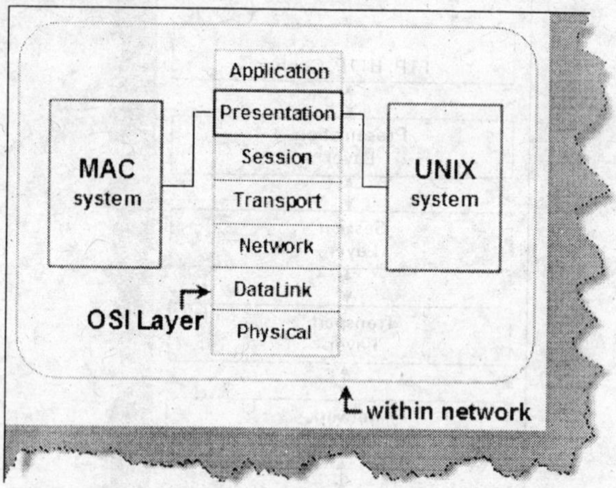

Figure: Presentation Layer for Mixed System

Compression: This is an optional function, but it can be done by the Presentation Layer to improve performance.

Encryption: While data travels down the security stack, we can use the Presentation Layer encryption function to ensure security. SSL is one of the popular encryptions used in the Presentation Layer.

(B) Is it Compulsory that Compression, Encryption, and Translation Functions will be used During Communication?

If we look at the functionalities of the Presentation Layer, it is not a compulsory layer. For instance, if we have different types of computers, then we will need the translation function. If we want encryption, then we will need encryption functionality and same holds true for compression. So the Presentation Layer can be completely eliminated during communication if we do not have different computers and if we do not need encryption and compression.

(B) Explain the Session Layer in the OSI Model.

The Session Layer defines how two computers establish, synchronize, maintain, and end a session. Ok, so now what does that mean? The following are roles which the Session Layer plays:

Session Check Points, Adjournments and Termination:

TCP acknowledgment (ACK) packets are regularly passed between clients to identify the last packet that was received. TCP waits for the transmission of an ACK packet until a timeout is reached or a number of packets equal to the TCP data is sent. This delay increases the efficiency of the protocol and makes checkpoints. At any point, TCP can start transmission from the previous checkpoint if a failure occurs. Though not commonly employed, TCP sessions may be adjourned by setting the TCP window to 0 bytes. This informs the sending host that no buffer is available to hold transmitted data and halts communications without losing the connection. TCP provides a means for both graceful and immediate session terminations. Graceful session terminations occur by sending a finish (FIN) flag that is subsequently acknowledged by the recipient. Immediate session terminations occur by using packets with the reset (RST) flag set.

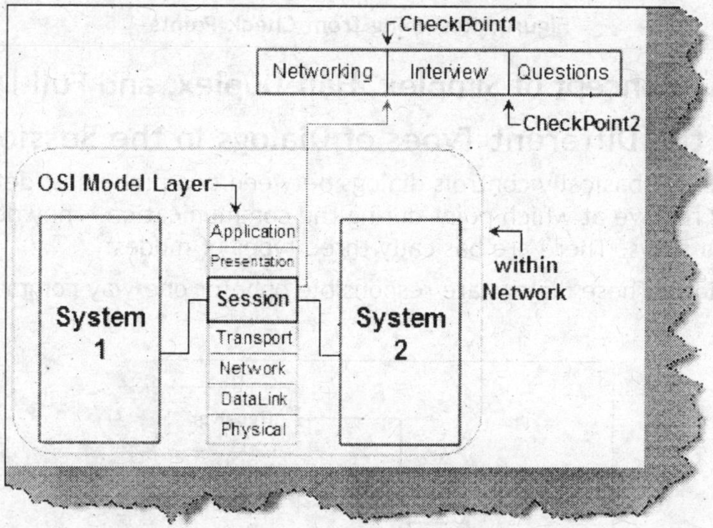

Figure: Checkpoints on the Datagram

Consider the figure, 'Checkpoint on the Datagram.' Let's say we have systems 1 and 2. System1 wants to send data 'Networking Interview Questions.' So, the Session Layer makes checkpoints on the datagram as shown in the figure.

Figure "Resuming from Check Point" shows how the check points will work. As said previously, there are two check points. So, let's say the first packet communicated is 'Networking,' and while sending the second packet 'Interview,' there is a network failure. System1 keeps trying, when the network is restored, it starts transmitting from CheckPoint1. This helps to utilize bandwidth in a very efficient way.

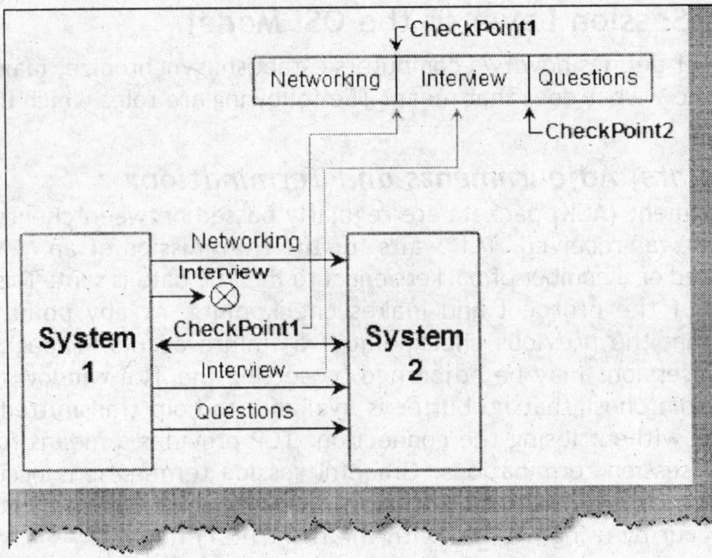

Figure: Resuming from Check Points

(B) What is the Concept of Simplex, Half-Duplex, and Full-Duplex dialogs?

(B) What are the Different Types of Dialogs in the Session Layer?

The Session Layer basically controls dialogs between two processes, determining who can transmit and receive at which point during the communication. They determine direction in which data flows. There are basically three types of modes:

Simplex Dialogs: These dialogs are responsible only for one-way communication and data transfer.

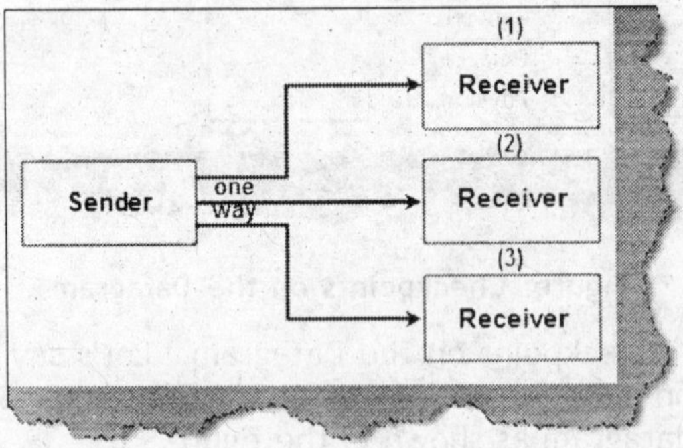

Figure: Simplex dialogs

For example, like a radio station that only sends signals to the receiver but does not receive data from those receivers. So basically you can analyze the same like one transmitter and many receivers as shown in the figure 'Simplex Dialogs.' So, the transmitter only sends signals and receiver receives the same, but signals are not sent from the receiver to the transmitter. In one sentence, the data is sent one-way.

Half-Duplex Dialogs: In these dialogs, data is transferred in only one direction at a time. But here data can travel bi-directionally, unlike simplex dialogs where data transfers from only the sender to the receiver. In simple words either the data is send from the sender to the receiver or vice versa but not both at the same time. So basically either only the sender is sending data, or only the receiver is receiving data. The figure 'Half-Duplex Dialogs' explains the concept in a more clear fashion. Device A sends 'Message A' and then device A sends a signal saying that it has finished transmitting (Over and Out.) Device B then sends 'Message B' and once 'Message B' is sent, Device B sends an acknowledgement that it is done, and gives chance to Device A for communication.

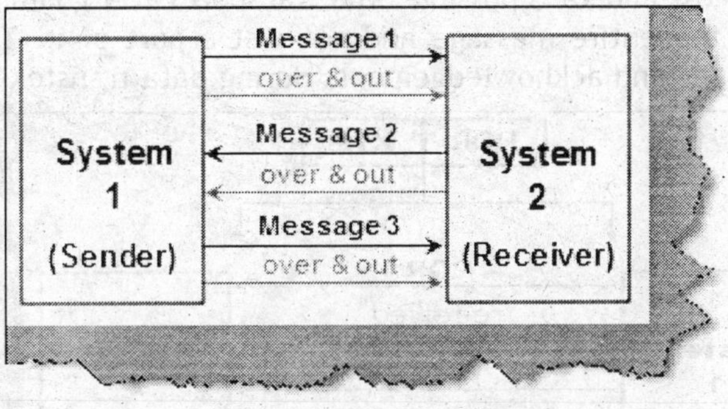

Figure: Half-Duplex Dialogs

For instance, radio operators converse on the same communication channel. When one operator has finished transmitting, he must release his transmit key so that the other operator can then take over.

Full-Duplex dialogs: This dialog channel is one of the most sophisticated and efficient ways of data communication. It permits two way simultaneous data transfers by providing each device with separate communication channel. For instance, voice telephones use this kinds of dialogs. So, in this communication mode none of the parties have to wait and communication happens simultaneously. Figure 'Full-Duplex Dialog' shows how two-way simultaneous communications happens in the same communication channel and between different devices.

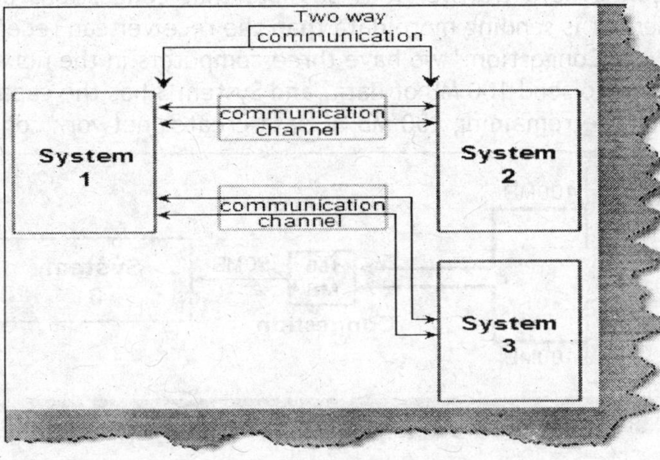

Figure: Full-Duplex Dialog

(B) Explain the Transport Layer in the OSI Model.

(A) Explain the Concept of Congestion.

The Transport Layer sits between the Network and Session Layers. It is responsible for delivering messages between the network hosts. Given Below are the main services provided by the Transport Layer.

Ensuring no Loss of Data.

While transferring data, it is possible that we have network congestion, connectivity issues, etc, due to which loss in data is possible. The Transport Layer guarantees end-to-end, error-free, delivery of the entire message and not just a part of it. This is guaranteed by a series of handshakes and acknowledgements during data transfer.

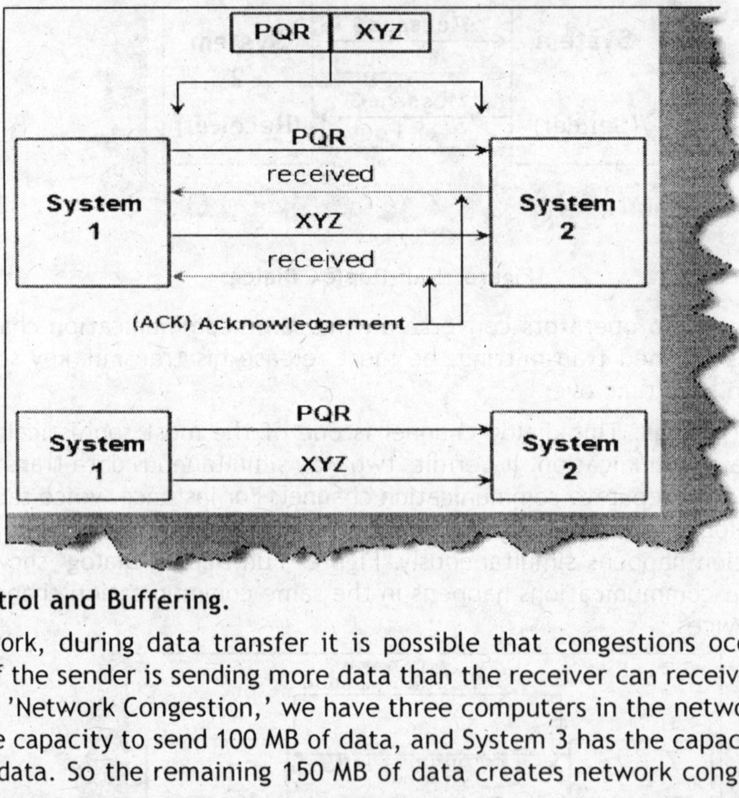

Flow Control and Buffering.

In a network, during data transfer it is possible that congestions occur. This normally happens if the sender is sending more data than the receiver can receive. For example, in the figure 'Network Congestion,' we have three computers in the network. Systems 1 and 2 have the capacity to send 100 MB of data, and System 3 has the capacity to receive only 50 MB of data. So the remaining 150 MB of data creates network congestion.

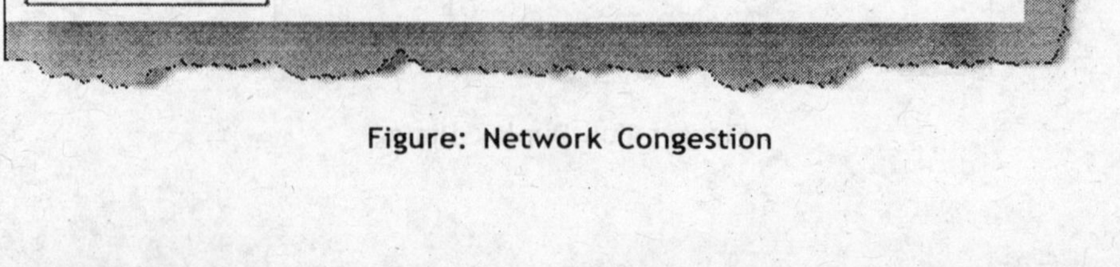

Figure: Network Congestion

The above scenario is handled by the Transport Layer using three methods of flow control:

- Buffering
- Multiplexing
- Parallelization

In buffering, the receiver system has memory allocated. Any data first sent is collected in this temporary memory and then processed. If the buffer is full receiver sends a 'No Ready' flag to sender asking it to hold data transfer. Multiplexing and parallelization are better ways of handling congestion than buffering.

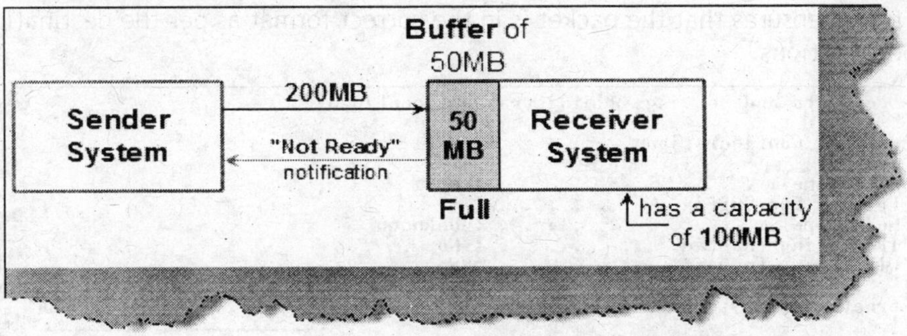

Figure: Buffering System

Multiplexing and parallelization is left to end readers to read up on.

(I) Explain the Network Layer.

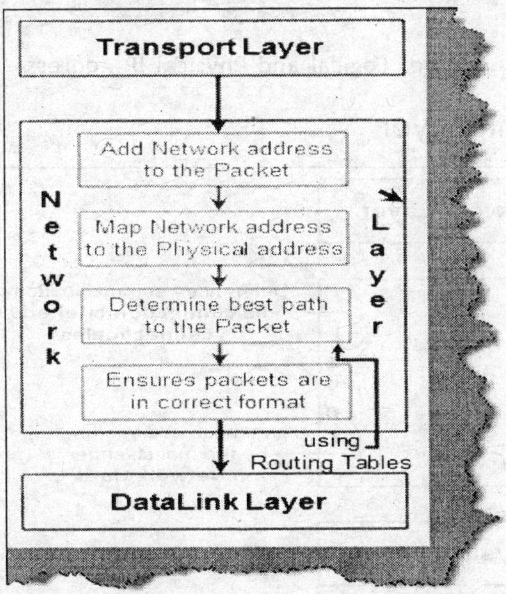

Figure : Network Layer in Action

The Network Layer is responsible for delivering the packets. A Network Layer knows where to deliver the packets using the logical address called the network address or the IP address.

Figure 'Logical and Physical IP Address' shows the Logical Address (i.e., IP Address) and Physical Address (i.e., MAC Address). You can see the same using the IPCONFIG command in Windows operating system.

The Network Layer performs the following functions to deliver the packets:

- The network address is added to the packet received from the transport layer.
- It then maps the logical address (i.e., IP Address) to the physical address (i.e., MAC address.)
- It determines the physical path using the routing tables.
- It finally ensures that the packet is in the correct format as per the destination networks specifications.

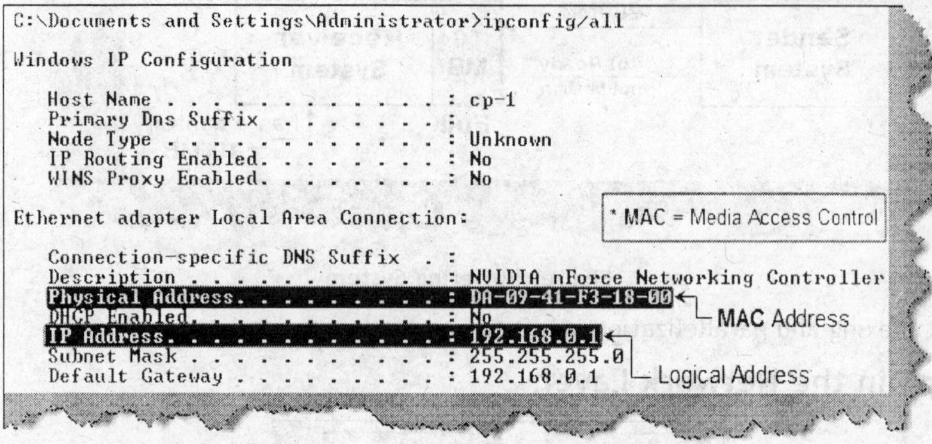

Figure: Logical and Physical IP Address

(B) Explain Data Link Layer

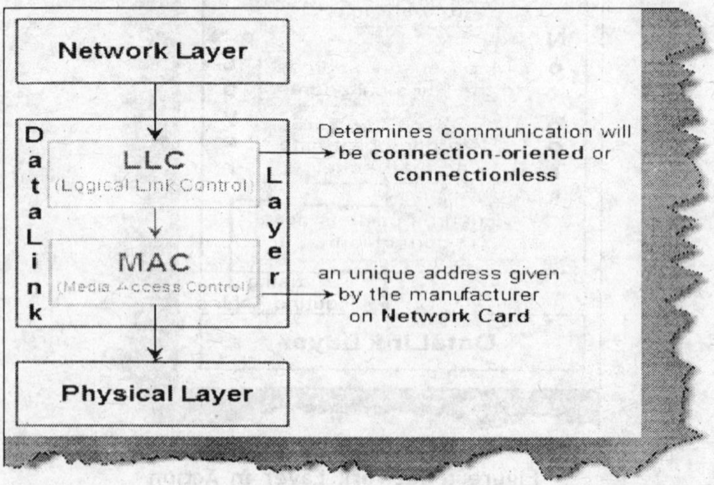

Figure: Data Link Layer in Action

Data Link layer connects the network layer and the physical layer. As shown in figure 'Data Link Layer in Action,' there are two layers in Data link LLC and the MAC layer.LLC decides whether the communication is connectionless or connection oriented. MAC layer adds the destination and source physical address to the frame.

The MAC layer is responsible for connection with the physical media. The LLC layer bridges the MAC layer to the top-level protocol. Connection-oriented service checks that a message arrives correctly. This increases reliability, but that comes at a cost, i.e., performance is decreased.

(B) Explain Physical Layer.

The Physical layer forms the lowest part of the OSI model. This is the layer where data is physically moved across the network interface. Many people think that Physical layer means the actual network hardware, which is not the actual case. All hardware have some kind of relation with the Physical layer to send data. But the hardware can use the Data Link layer as well. For example, an Ethernet network uses Physical and Data Link layers. The Physical layer deals with actual 1's and 0's that are sent over the network. Repeaters and hubs operate at the Physical Layer level. Following are the functions of the Physical layer:

Hardware Specifications: Details of operation of cables, connectors, wireless radio transceivers, network interface cards, and other hardware devices are generally a function of the Physical layer (although also partially the Data Link layer, layer 2.)

Encoding and Signaling: The Physical layer is responsible for encoding and signaling functions that transform the data from bits that reside within a computer or another device into signals that can be sent across the network.

Data Transmission and Reception: After encoding the data appropriately, the Physical layer actually transmits the data, and of course, receives it. Same is true for wireless.

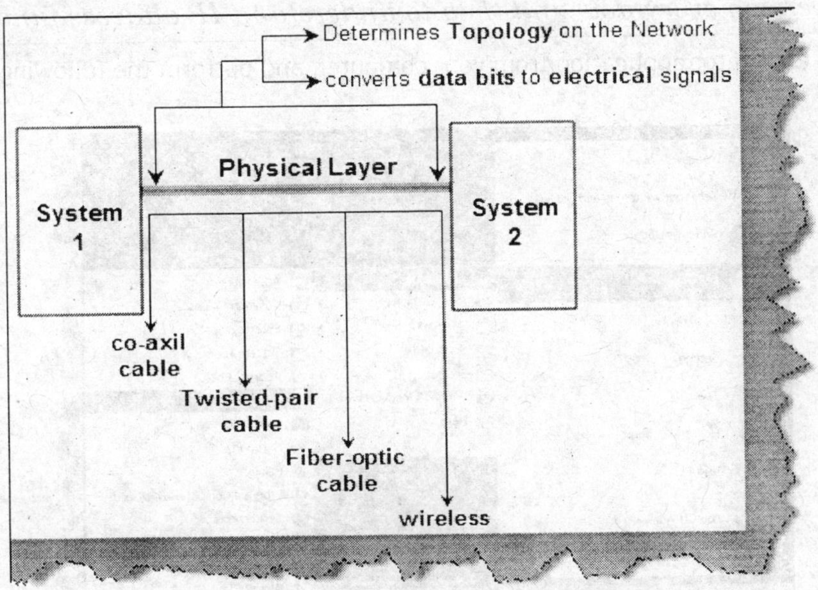

Figure: Physical Layer of the OSI Model

Topology and Physical Network Design: The Physical layer is also considered the domain of many hardware-related network design issues, such as, Local Area Network (LAN) and Wide Area Network (WAN) topology.

(B) Explain What an IP Address is.

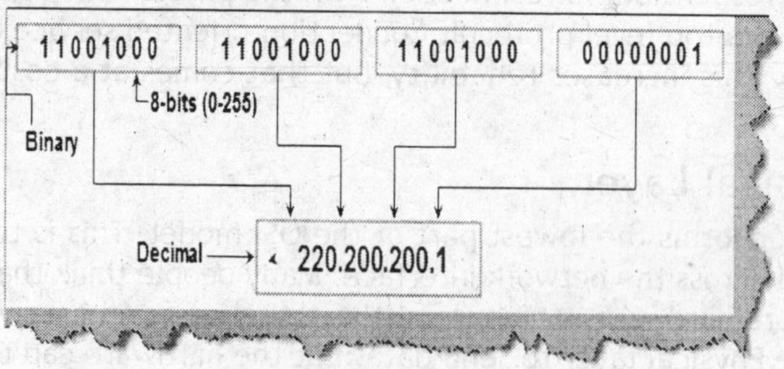

Figure: IP Address 32-Bit

An IP address is a 32-bit binary number that can be expressed in binary, hexadecimal, or decimal form. An IP address helps identify a device uniquely in a network. You can see from the figure 'IP Address 32-Bit' how an IP address in decimal gets converted to binary.

Note: *In the next question, we will see how to convert decimal to binary.*

(B) How do you Convert Decimal Numbers to Binary Numbers?

Note: *This is not an interview question as such. Just that we need to understand the fundamental of how to convert decimal to binary. You will need this conversion every now and then to understand IP address fundamentals.*

Open the Calculator application from your computer, and perform the following simple steps:

Step 1:

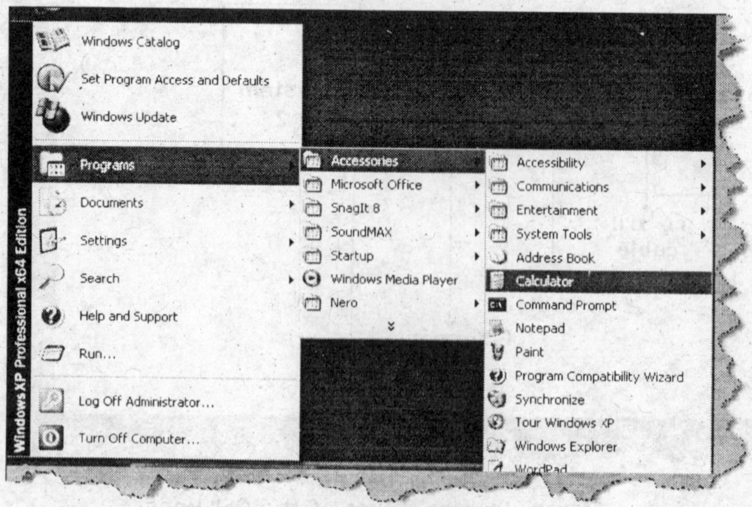

Figure: Open calculator

There are two ways to open 'Calculator':

- Press the Window-marked Key and keeping it pressed, press 'R,'

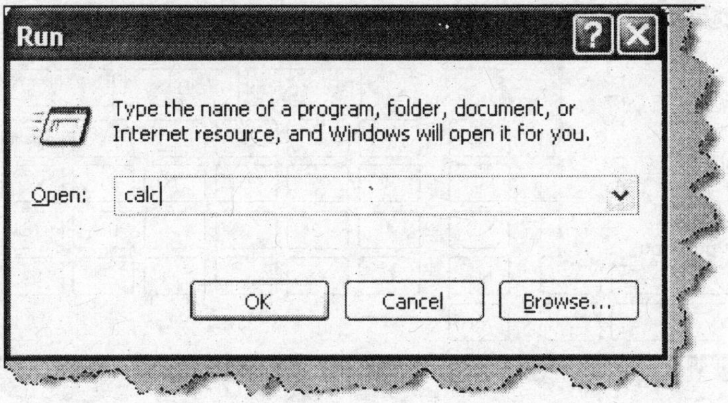

Figure: Run Calc

after opening the **RUN** window type "calc" and then press Enter. You will observe the following screen:

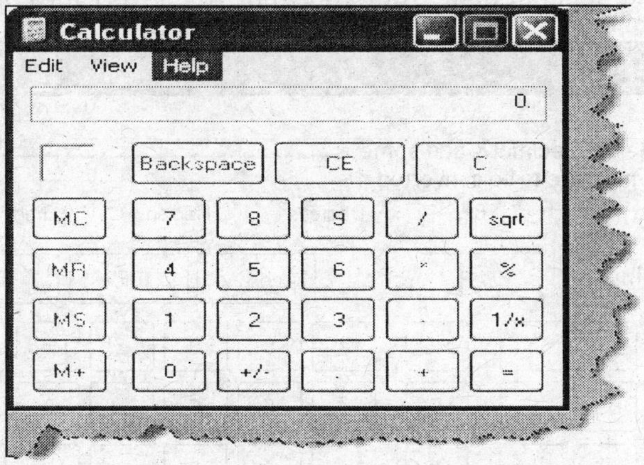

Figure: Calc

OR

- Click Start->Programs->Accessories->Calculator, you will be prompted with the 'Run' screen.

Step 2:

- After opening Calculator, click 'View' and then 'Scientific', you will see the following screen:

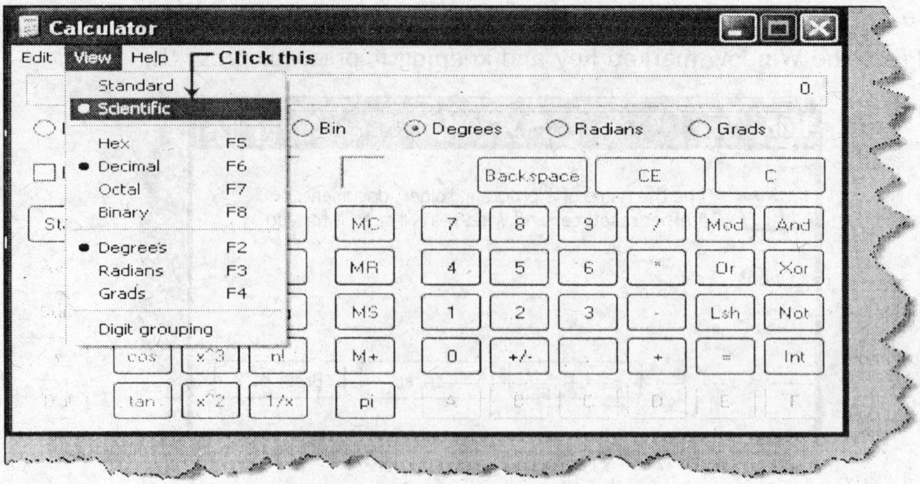

Figure: Scientific Mode

Step 3:

Now key in the decimal digits that you want to convert into binary, e.g., **190.**

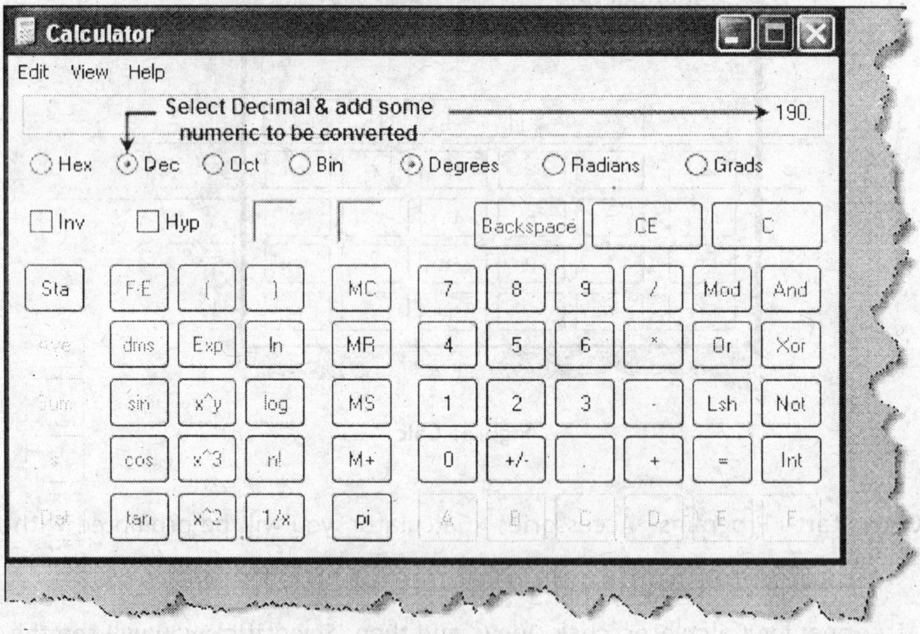

Figure: Select Decimal

Now to see the converted form of Decimal to Binary, select 'Bin' and you see the converted form of Decimal as follows:

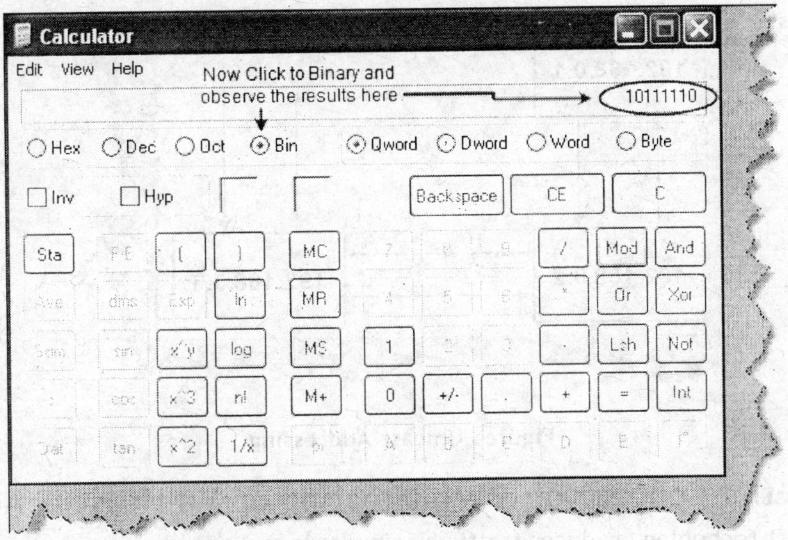

Figure: Binary Results

(B) How Many IP addresses Can Come in IPV4?

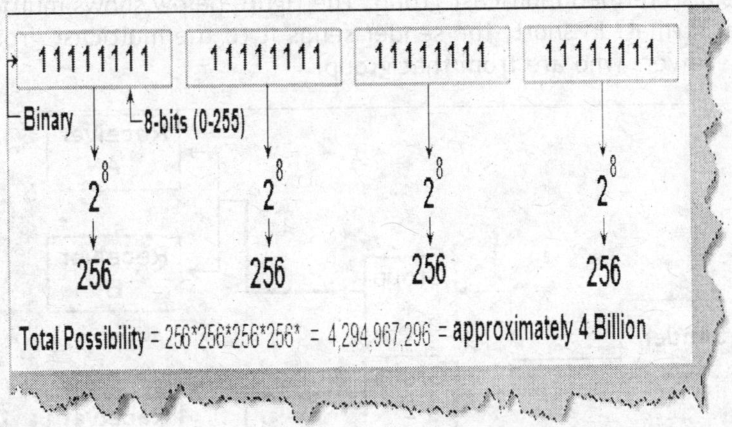

Figure: IP Address Capacity

As the name itself suggests, IPV4 it's a 32-bit binary number as shown in the figure, 'IP Address Capacity.' The maximum capacity of an 8-bit number is 0-255, i.e., 256. So the total number of possibilities is 4 billion. We can, therefore, have 4 billion IP addresses in IPV4.

(B) Explain the Concept of Unicast IP Addresses.

Unicast IP addresses uniquely identify a host in a network. The data received by Unicast is received and processed by a single host. Given below is the pictorial presentation of 'Unicast Addressing.' Hosts are identified uniquely in the network and as you can see, no IP address is duplicated between the three host. As you can see from the figure, data is received and processed by a single host only.

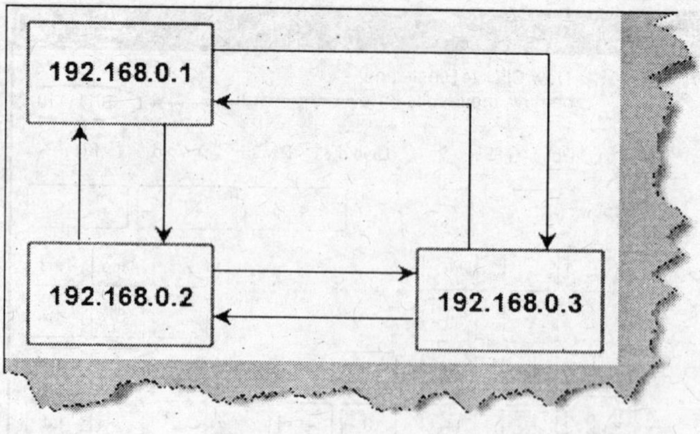

Figure: Unicast Addressing

(B) Explain the Concept of IP Multicasting or Multicast IP Address.

IP multicast technology reduces traffic by simultaneously sending stream of information to thousands of recipients at one go. Some of the practical implementations include video conferencing, stock quotes, software distribution, etc. Multicast is based on the concept of groups. So basically, a multicast IP address represents particular hosts in a network. This group is also termed multicast group. The figure below shows multicast fundamental in a pictorial format. In short, the sender sends it to the multicast group, which is then sent to all receivers who are from that group.

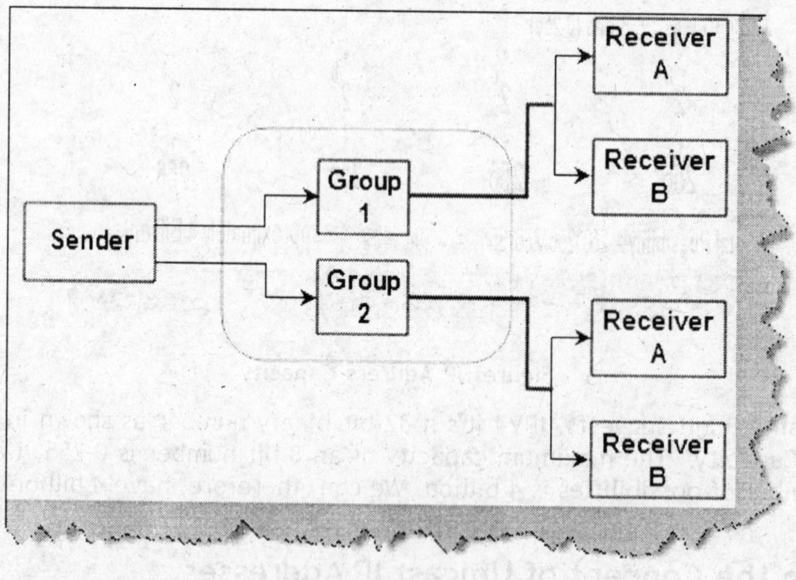

Figure: IP Multicasting

(I) How Many Types of Subnet Classful Networks are There?

There are three different types of subnet classful networks as shown in table below:

Class	Subnet mask
A	255.0.0.0
B	255.255.0.0
C	255.255.255.0

Figure: Classful Subnet Types

(A) What are the IP Address Ranges for Public and Private IP Addresses?

The classification tree given below shows how IP address ranges are assigned class wise and categorized according to public and private IP addresses.

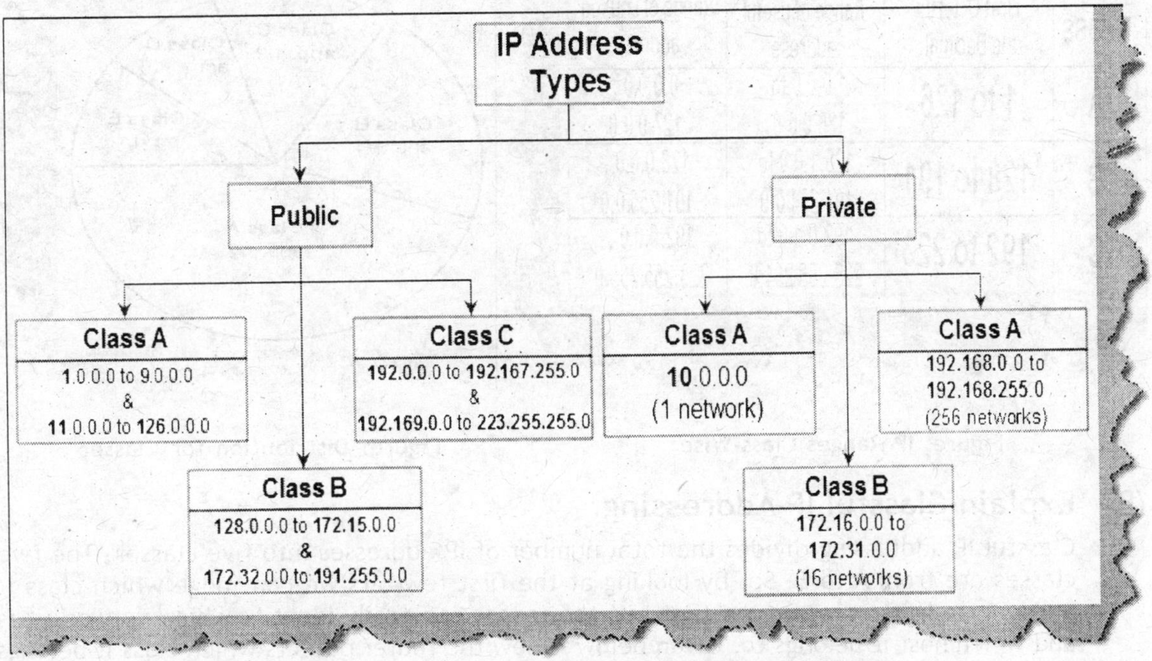

Figure: IP Address Range Classification

(B) Why do we Need Classes and How Many Types of Classes Exist?

Organizations comes in different sizes and so the number of IP addresses varies according to the organization size. So the developers of internet devised a system to divide the number of IP addresses into different classes. Some classes can be used by small organizations having small networks, while others can be used by large organizations. There are five classes: Class A, Class B, Class C, Class D, and Class E.

Class A: This is basically unicast (please refer for Unicast fundamentals in the previous question) addressing very large organizations with thousands and millions of hosts to connect to the internet.

Class B: This is again unicast addressing for medium-sized organizations that are anticipating hundreds or thousands of host to connect to the internet.

Class C: This is again a unicast addressing scheme for organizations that have more than 250 hosts to connect to the internet.

Class D: This is used for IP multicasting (please refer to multicasting in the previous question.)

Class E: These IP addresses are reserved for experimental purpose by designers of the internet.

(B) How are IP Addresses Distributed Between Different Classes?

The table given below shows how the IP address range distribution takes place for classes A, B, and C.

Class	First Octet in the Decimal	Range of useful address	Range of unused address
A	1 to 126	1.0.0.0 to 126.0.0.0	0.0.0.0 , 127.0.0.0
B	128 to 191	128.1.0.0 to 191.254.0.0	128.0.0.0 , 191.255.0.0
C	192 to 223	192.0.1.0 to 223.255.254.0	192.0.0.0 , 223.255.255.0

Figure: IP Ranges Class-Wise

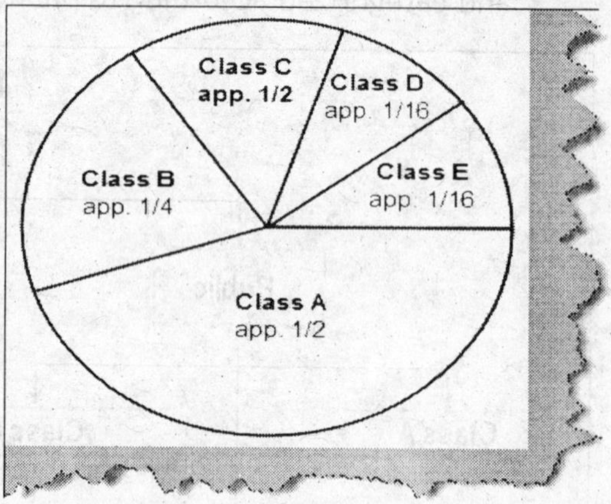

Figure: Distribution for Classes

(B) Explain Classful IP Addressing.

Classful IP addressing divides the total number of IP addresses into five classes. The five classes are from A to E. So, by looking at the first few bits we can judge which class it belongs to. Depending on the first bit, the router can easily identify which network it is and which host it belongs to. Given below is how the router detects which class it belongs to from the first few bits of the IP address. The flow goes something as shown below:

- If the first bit of the IP address is '0,' then it's Class A and if the value is not zero it moves to the next step to check the value of the second bit.
- If the second bit is '0,' then its class B. If the value is not '1,' then it moves to the next step to check the third bit, and so on.

The figure 'Diagram of Address Detection' shows how the class is decided for a classful IP address.

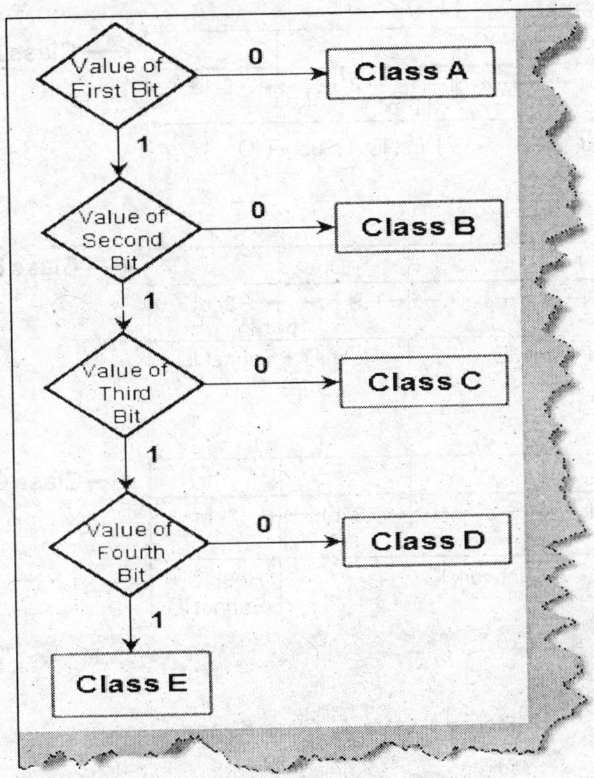

Figure: Diagram of Flow of Address Detection

A classful IP address is made up of two parts: the 'Network' part and the 'Host' part of the IP address. What varies is the size of the network for every class.

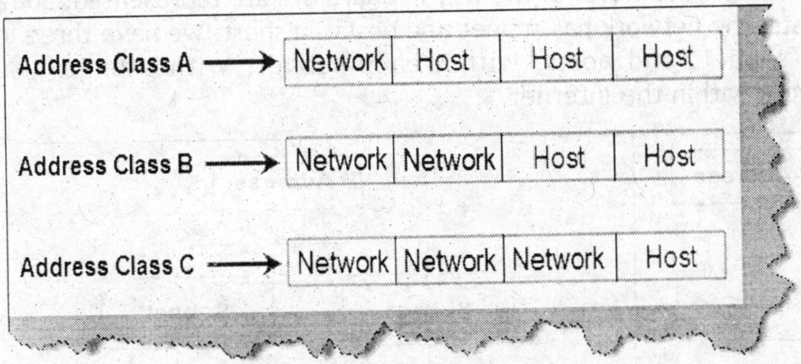

Figure: Classful IP Addressing

Figure 'Class A, Class B, and Class C' shows how the length of network ID varies. For Class A we have 8 bits of network ID, for Class B we have 16 bits, and for Class C we have 24 bits. The more the number of network bits, the less the number of hosts.

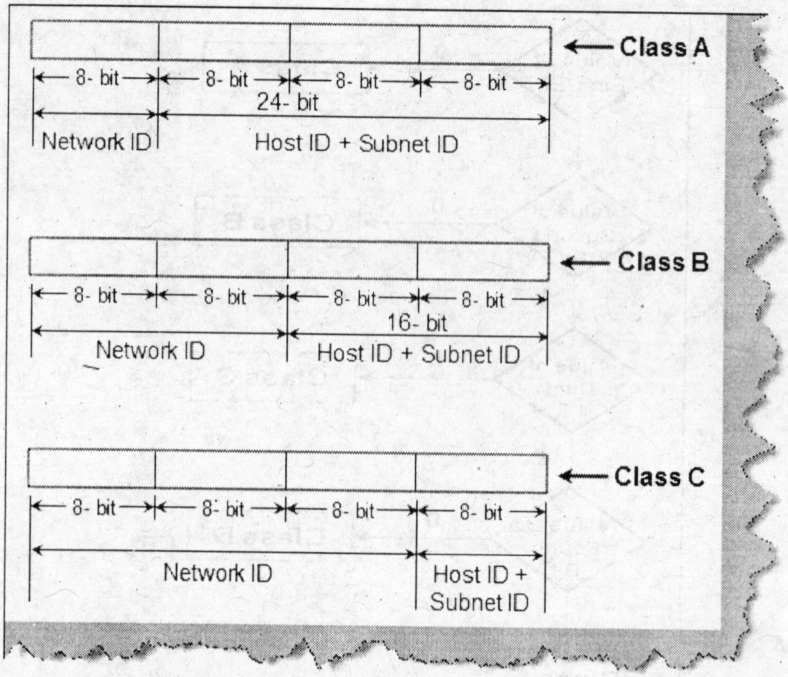

Figure : Class A, Class B, and Class C

(A) Explain the Concept of Subneting.

As we saw in the previous question, there are only two levels of hierarchy, i.e., the first is the network and the second is the host. So fundamentally, each organization is represented by a network identifier and hosts that are directly added to that network. Subnet addressing adds more hierarchical level to the way IP addresses are represented. So rather than directly having hosts, the network has subnet and hosts. In short, we have three levels of hierarchy: network, subnet, and hosts, within each subnet. With subnet, you have your own internetwork within the Internet.

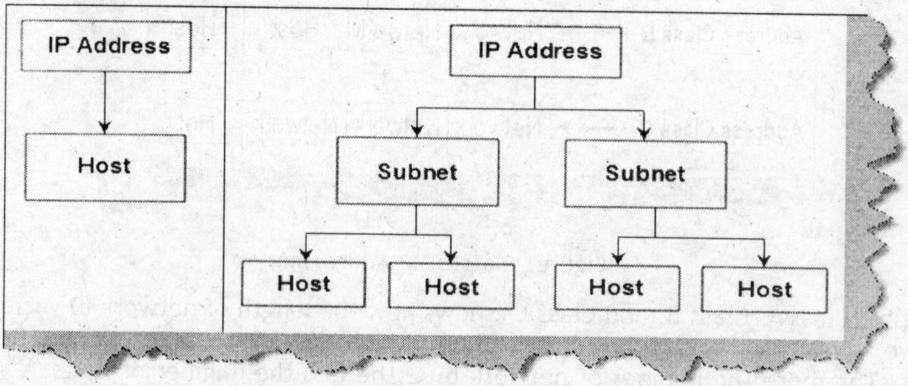

Figure: Network Diagrams for Hierarchy

(I) What are the Advantages of Using Subneting?

Below is the list of advantages of having subneting:

- Using subnet, we can logically organize the network with actual physical structure of the company. For instance, you logically group computers which belong to the accounting department and the purchase department separately.

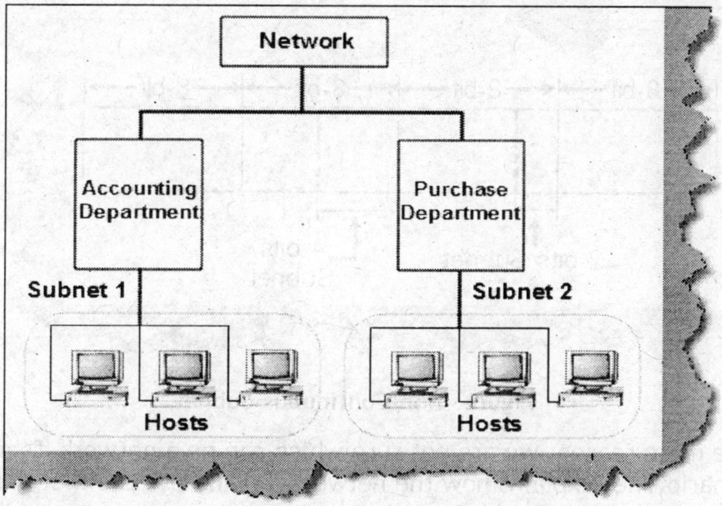

Figure: Mapping with Physical Structure of the Company

- All external entities connect to the subnet. So the internal hosts are completely isolated from an external entity like the Internet. For the rest of the Internet, your organization is just one big, flat network. This also means that any changes made to the internal structure are not visible outside the organization.

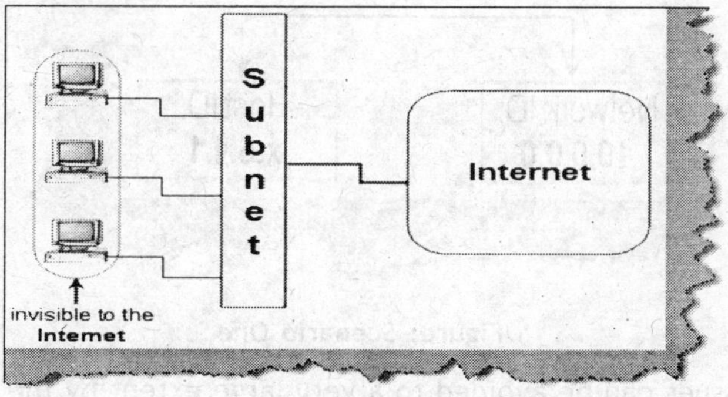

Figure: Invisible to the Internet

- We do not need new IP addresses. We can use small blocks of Class C.

(B) If the Host has a Subnet ID, Why Do We Need a Subnet Mask?

This is a really tricky question. If the IP address has a subnet address, why do we need a separate subnet mask? Firstly, we can assign subnet IDs in a non-continuous fashion if necessary. This means that you can assign subnet in between the network addresses as shown in the figure 'Non-Continuous Subnet .' We have 2 bits of subnet in the second 8 bit and 4 bit in the third 8 bit. In such kind of scenarios, to find the subnet will not be efficient. Subnet mask ANDING process is efficient and faster. ANDING process is explained in the next question.

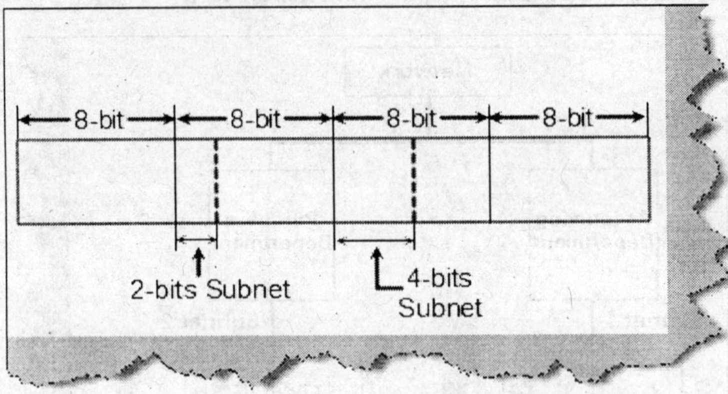

Figure: Non-Continuous Subnet

There is one more reason, we are not sure which can be a network ID and which a host ID. Figure 'Scenario One' explains how the network ID can form the first part of the IP address and the other bits can form the host ID.But then it is very much possible that the first 2 bytes form the network ID, and the rest the host ID.

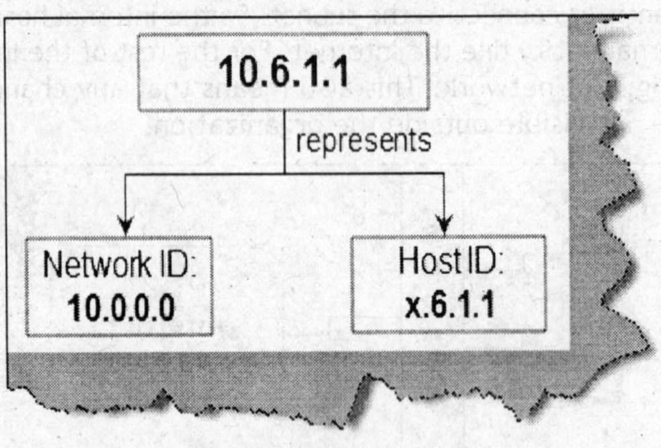

Figure: Scenario One

So, the above issues can be avoided to a very large extent by the ANDING process.

(I) How is Network Address Calculated From the Subnet?

Figure 'TCP/IP Properties' shows the Subnet mask and the IP address. The IP address is the host IP and below the IP address is specified the Subnet mask. Network address is obtained by ANDING the Subnet mask and the IP address of the host.

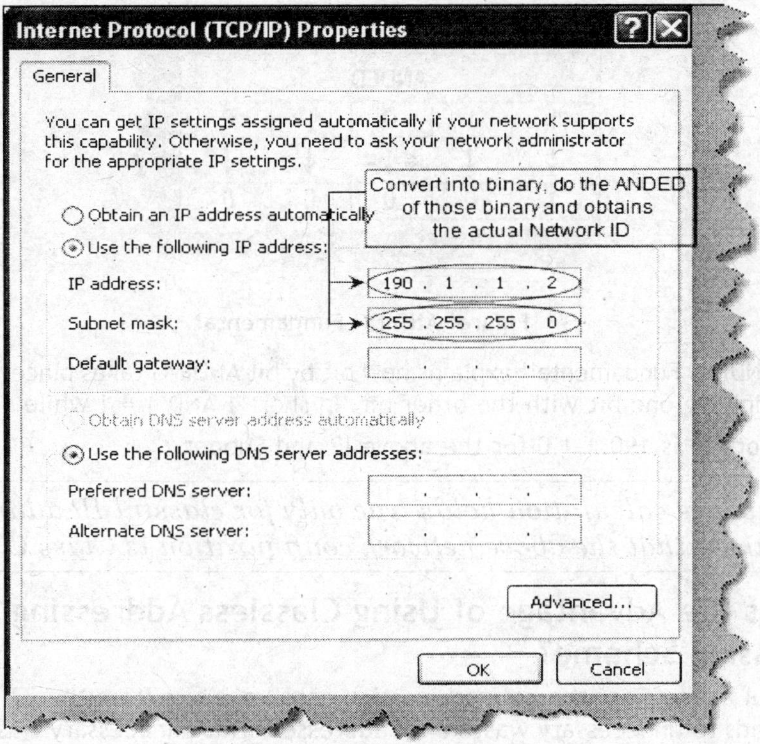

Figure: TCP/IP Properties

Let go step by step and see how the ANDING process will work. First let's convert the host IP address and the subnet IP address to binary.

Address	190	.1	.1	.2
Binary	10111110	00000001	00000001	00000010
Subnet	255	.255	.255	.0
Binary	11111111	11111111	11111111	00000000
Anded	10111110	00000001	00000001	00000000
Network IP	190	.1	.1	.0

Figure: Conversion of IP's to Binary Format

> **Note:** *In the previous question we have explained how we can convert a IP address into its binary format.*

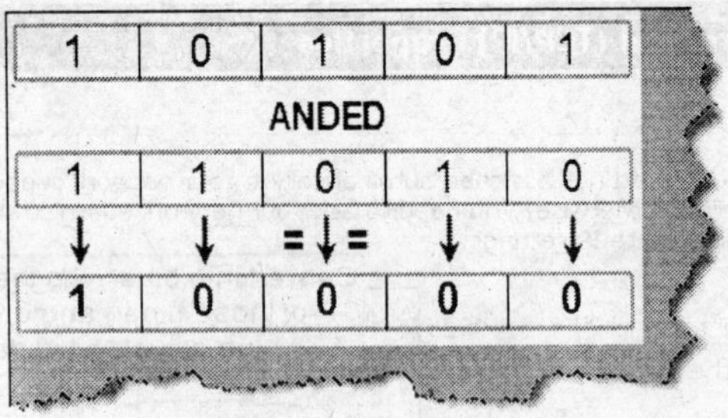

Figure: ANDING Fundamental

Figure 'ANDING Fundamental' explains how bit by bit ANDING takes place. ANDING is nothing but multiplying one bit with the other bit. In short 1 AND 1 = 1 while 1 AND 0 = 0.

So, network IP is 190.1.1.0 for the above IP and Subnet.

> ***Note:*** *The above calculation holds true only for classful IP addresses. We had assumed that the above network configuration is Class C subnet.*

(B) What is the Advantage of Using Classless Addressing Over Classful Addressing Scheme?

In classful addressing, the network portion consumes bits from the 32-bit address itself, which leads to unnecessary waste of IP addresses. This unnecessary waste of IP addresses is avoided in classless addressing scheme.

(I) Explain the Concept of CIDR.

(I) Twist: Explain Superneting.

CIDR stands for Classless Inter-Domain Routing. It is a method by which we do not need Class A, Class B, and Class C to identify an IP address. So, it is represented as xxxx.xxxx.xxxx.xxxx/Prefix. Where 'Prefix' is the number of bits used to identify a network. For instance, below is a class A IP address and an 8-bit size is assigned for the network information.

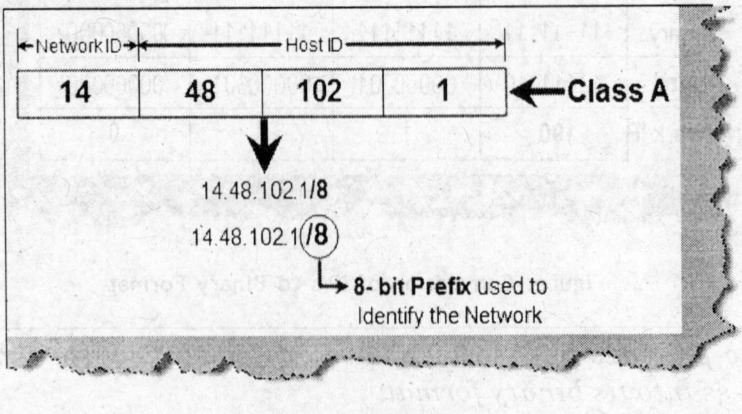

Figure: CIDR Prefix

The Prefix in short also defines the mask in subnet. For instance, Class C subnet has a prefix of 24 because of 24 bits, i.e., 3 bytes of the IP address are used to store network information.

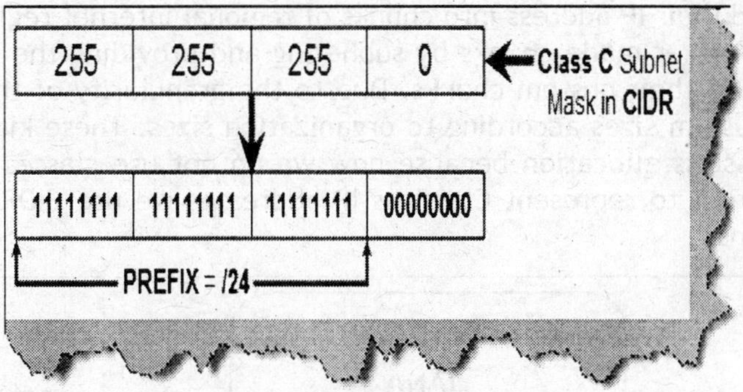

Figure: Subnet Mask in CIDR

But as the name suggests, Classless does not have to represent class as such. The above example was given from the perspective of how Class A and Class B is represented using CIDR. Figure 'CIDR Without Class' shows IP address representation which is split in to 12 bit of network information and 20 bits for host information. These type of splits do not represent Class A, B, or C networks. But as was said previously, CIDR was meant mainly to represent network in a classless fashion. So the below example is represented by IP Address/ 12.

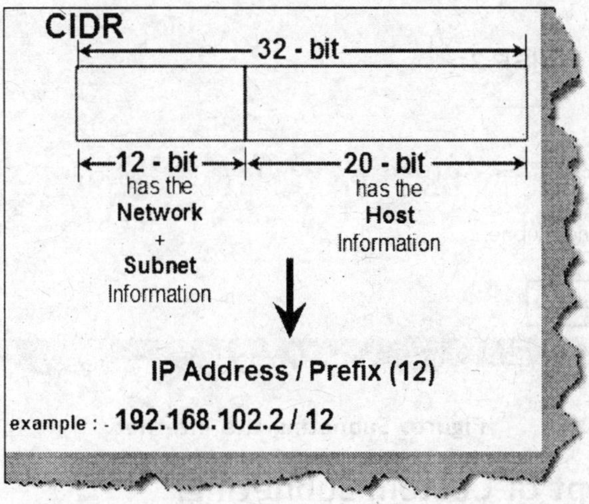

Figure: IP Address/Prefix

CIDR is based on a concept called a superneting. In short, superneting means subneting the Internet. In brief, you subnet all the IPs into small pieces and distribute those small pieces to the organization according to their size and requirement. For instance, Class B has 65534 hosts while Class B has 254 hosts. Now consider an organization that has 300 hosts which is very much the size of a med-sized organization. In order to fulfil their requirement of 300 hosts, they will book Class B which has 65534 hosts which means wastage of 65234 hosts. In short, we needed some kind of mechanism using which we could have customized the size of IP addresses according to the size of the organization. In order to achieve the same, creators of the Internet decided to subnet the internet IP addresses, i.e., nothing but superneting. So the IP address distributors, i.e., IANA as shown in figure below, subneted their IP address into chunks of regional internet registers.These internet registers then further made chunks by subneting and providing the same chunk to ISPs. ISPs further made their custom chunks. Due to the granularity of the break-up, we can now allocate custom sizes according to organization sizes. These kinds of allocation are also called Classless allocation because now we do not use classes to represent the IP notations. In order to represent Classless IP addresses we use CIDR as discussed in the previous sections.

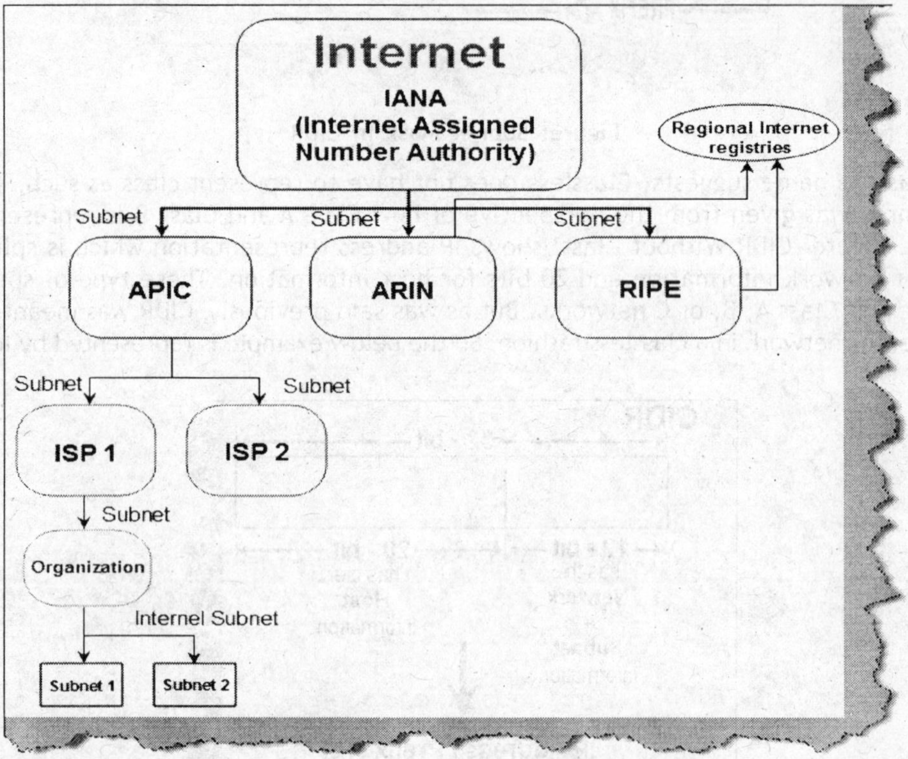

Figure: Subneting the Internet

(I) Explain Concept of Custom Subneting.

In custom subneting, you allocate subnet bits and host bits depending on your network requirements. The diagram below shows how we have customized by assigning 5 bits to the subnet and 11 bits to the host id. Customization of subnet is very essential because the number of hosts vary from organization to organization and also according to logical classifications.

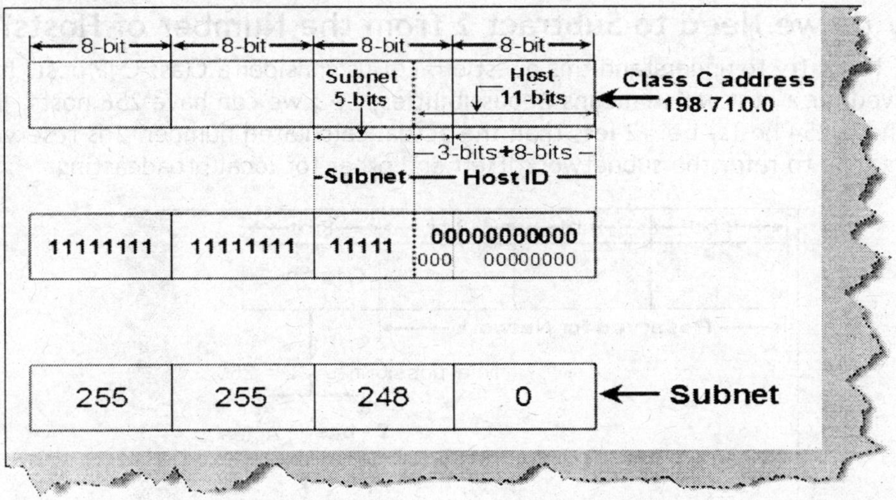

Figure: Custom Subneting

(A) What is the Implication of Increasing and Decreasing Subnet Bits?

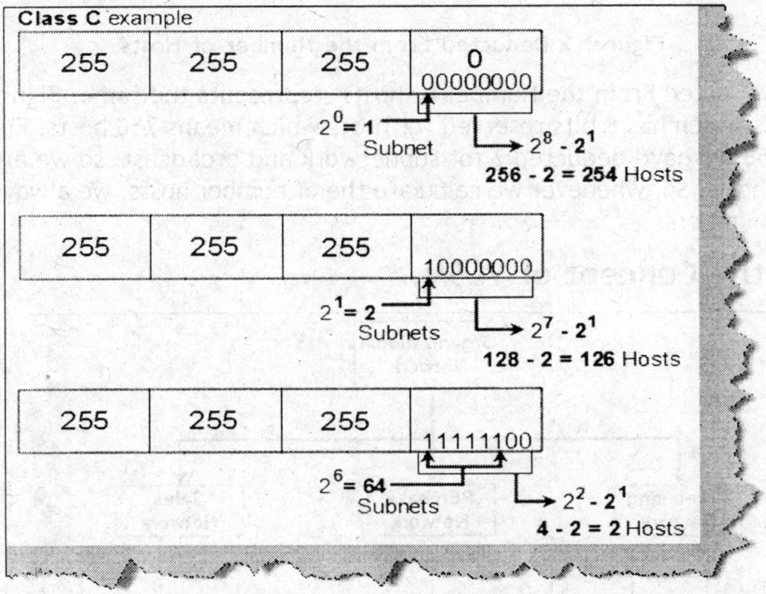

Figure: Increase and Decrease of Subnet

Figure 'Increase and Decrease of Subnet' shows the effect on number of hosts. If we give 0 bits for the subnet, we have one subnet that can have 254 hosts. If we give 1 bit to the subnet, we can have two subnets with 126 hosts each, and so on. In short, the more bits we assign to the subnet, the more subnets with less number of hosts we have.

(I) Why do we Need to Subtract 2 from the Number of Hosts?

First, let us try to understand this question. Let us consider a Class C IP host. It has 8 bits reserved for a host which means 2^8 possibilities, i.e., we can have 256 hosts. But we can only have 254 hosts, i.e., 2 less than the actual calculated number. 2 is reserved for two things, one to refer the subnetwork itself and other for local broadcasting.

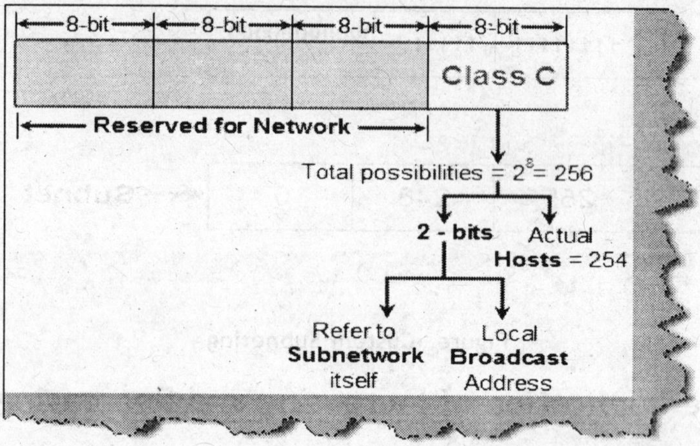

Figure: 2 Deducted From the Number of Hosts

Figure "2 Deducted From the Number of hosts' represents the same. Figure shows a Class C IP address which has 8 bits reserved for hosts which means 256 hosts. Further, from this figure of 256 we have deducted 2 for subnetwork and broadcast, so we are left with only 254 actual hosts. So, whenever we calculate the of number hosts, we always deduct 2 from the actual numbers.

(I) Explain the Concept of VLSM.

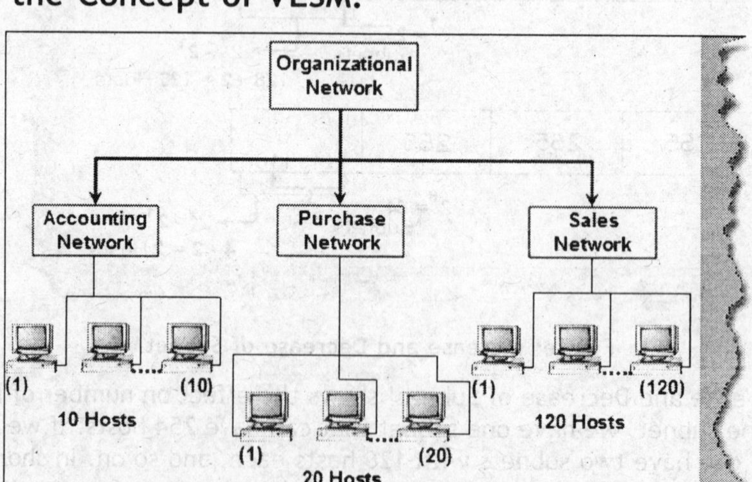

Figure: Practical Networking Scenario

VLSM stands for 'Variable Length Subnet Masking.' In order to understand VLSM, we need to understand the issues with traditional subneting. Let us take a practical example of an organization as shown in the figure 'Practical Networking Scenario.' In this organization, we have three departments: Accounting, Purchase, and Sales. In the accounting department, we need ten hosts, in purchase ten, and in sales 120.

Let's assume that we are going to use Class C IP addresses. So according to the requirements we need 3 subnets for Accounting, purchase and sales. So we use 2 bits for subnet, i.e., 2^2, by which we can get 4 subnets Yes, we know what you are thinking, one subnet is unused. But that's fine because of the way binary number works this has to be excused. As we have assumed, it is Class C and we will have only 6 bits for the hosts. In short, we will have 62 hosts per Subnet. To make this understanding a bit more clearer, figure 'Distribution with Traditional Subneting' explains a lot. So 24 bits are taken to represent network information, i.e., network ID. 2 bits for the subnet, by which we can have 4 subnets. We are then left with 6 bit, i.e., 62 hosts. We have distributed all the subnets with 62 hosts each. But the sales department need 120 hosts. So there's the problem of equal distribution of hosts across subnets.

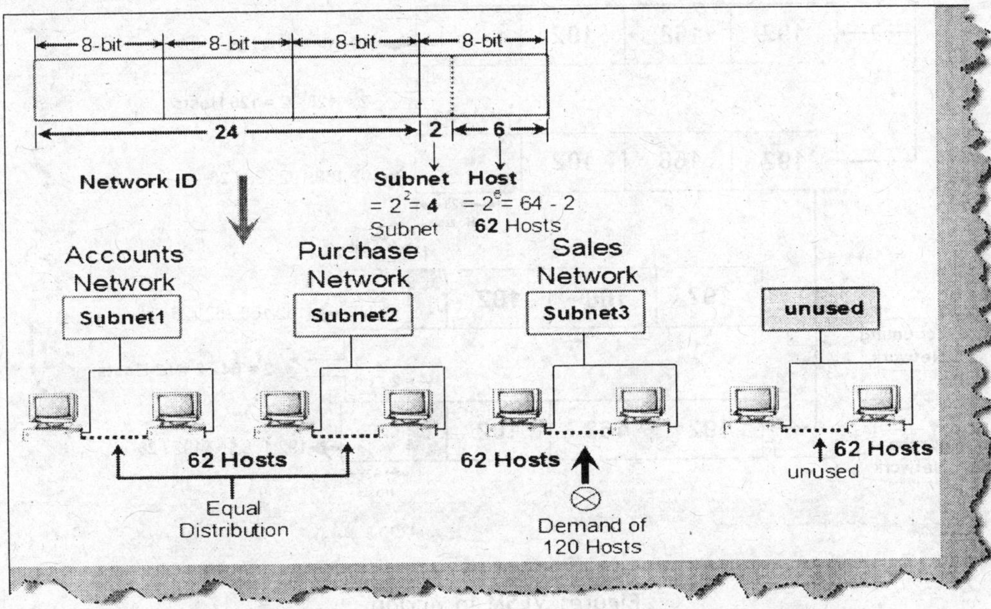

Figure: Distribution With Traditional Subneting

The solution is through VLSM. We subnet the subnet, thus cutting the IP addresses as needed. Let's understand how VLSM can fit practically into the above organization. Figure 'VLSM in Action' is the pictorial representation of the same. Here, we are using CIDR notation to represent the allocation. In the previous question, we have looked into what CIDR is. So at the top level, we have the main IP address, Class C: 192.168.102.0/24. 24 here says that 24 bits are reserved for the network ID. 24 bits lead to a total of 254 hosts and our requirement is 10 hosts (for accounting,) 20 hosts (for purchase,) and 120 hosts (for sales.) So, 254 hosts is not a proper classification.

In order to have the above classification, we divide the network into two further sections by assigning 1 bit to the subnet. With 1 bits assigned to the subnet, we have 2 subnets (2^1 = 2, i.e., 0 and 1.) So with 1 bit assigned to the subnet, we are left with only 7 bits for the host. With 7 bits we have 2^7, i.e., 128-2 = 126 hosts. Now we have two subnets of 126 hosts each. We need 120 hosts for sales, so we can use one subnet for the sales network. But we have still two more classifications, 10 Hosts for accounting and 20 hosts for purchase. So we again break one of the subnets further by assigning two bits to the subnet which results in 2 more subnets with 62 hosts each. With 62 hosts we can now assign to the accounting and purchase networks. In short, VSLM is breaking subnets further into subnets which can then be customized according to organizations.

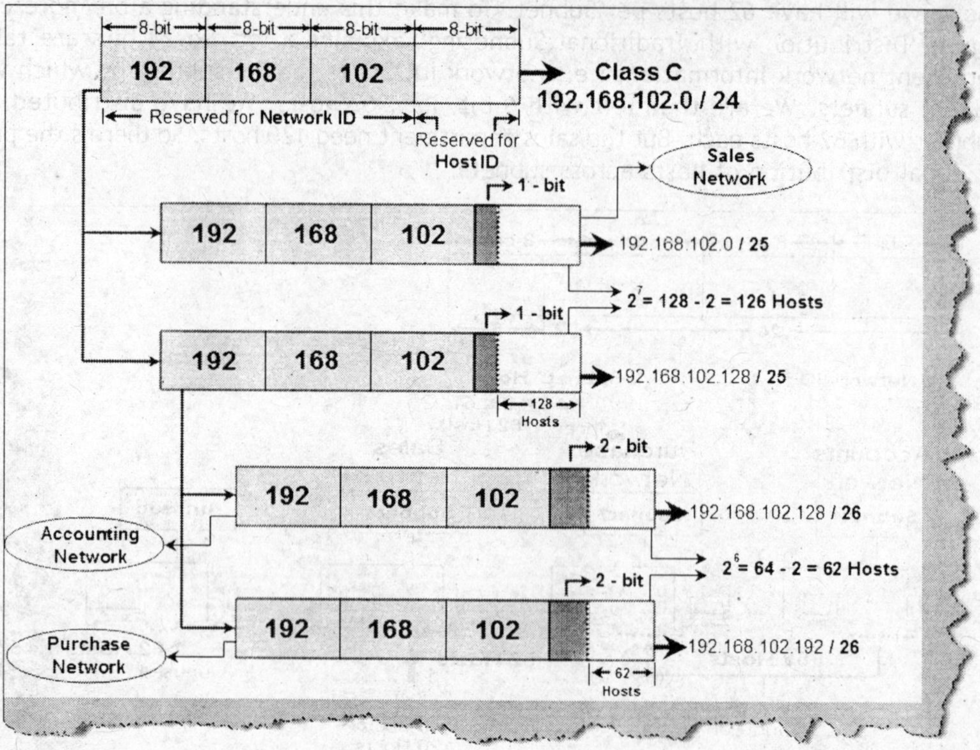

Figure: VLSM in Action

(I) Explain IP Packets in Detail.

IP manages how packets are delivered to and from servers and clients.

The IP header appears as follows:

Each field contains information about the IP packet that it carries. The descriptions in the following sections should be helpful.

Version Number

The version number indicates the version of IP that is in use for this packet. IP version 4 (Ipv4) is currently in widespread use.

Header Length

The header length indicates the overall length of the header. The receiving machine then knows when to stop reading the header and start reading data.

Type of Service

Mostly unused, the Type of Service field indicates the importance of the packet in a numerical value. Higher numbers result in prioritized handling.

Total Length

Total length shows the total length of the packet in bytes. The total packet length cannot exceed 65,535 bytes, or it will be deemed corrupt by the receiver.

Identification

If there is more than one packet (an invariable inevitability,) the identification field has an identifier that identifies its place in line, as it were. Fragmented packets retain their original ID number.

Flags

The first flag, if set, is ignored. If the DF (Do Not Fragment) flag is set, under no circumstances can the packet be fragmented. If the MF (More Fragments) bit is turned on (1), there are packet fragments to come, the last of which is set to off (0).

Offset

If the Flag field returns a 1 (on), the Offset field contains the location of the missing piece(s) indicated by a numerical offset based on the total length of the packet.

Time to Live (TTL)

Typically 15 to 30 seconds, TTL indicates the length of time that a packet is allowed to remain in transit. If a packet is discarded or lost in transit, an indicator is sent back to the sending computer that the loss occurred. The sending machine then has the option of resending that packet.

Protocol

The protocol field holds a numerical value indicating the handling protocol in use for this packet.

Checksum

The checksum value acts as a validation checksum for the header.

Source Address

The source address field indicates the address of the sending machine.

Destination Address

The destination address field indicates the address of the destination machine.

Options and Padding

The Options field is optional. If used, it contains codes that indicate the use of security, strict or loose source routing, routing records, and time stamping. If no options are used, the field is called padded and contains a 1. Padding is used to force a byte value that is rounded.

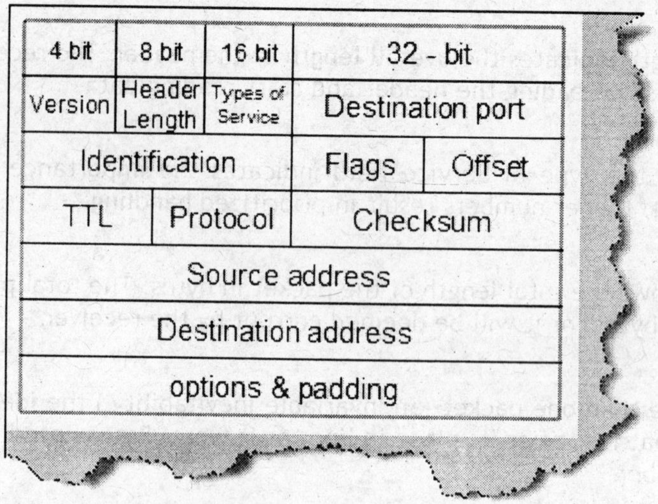

Figure: Internet Protocol

2

Routers

Note: *We will first try to understand a few concepts, sucha as, DPU, fragmentation, MTU, Hubs, Repeaters, and Switches. Then we will slowly move towards router concepts.*

(B) Explain the Concept of DPU, Segments, Datagram, Frame, and Packet.

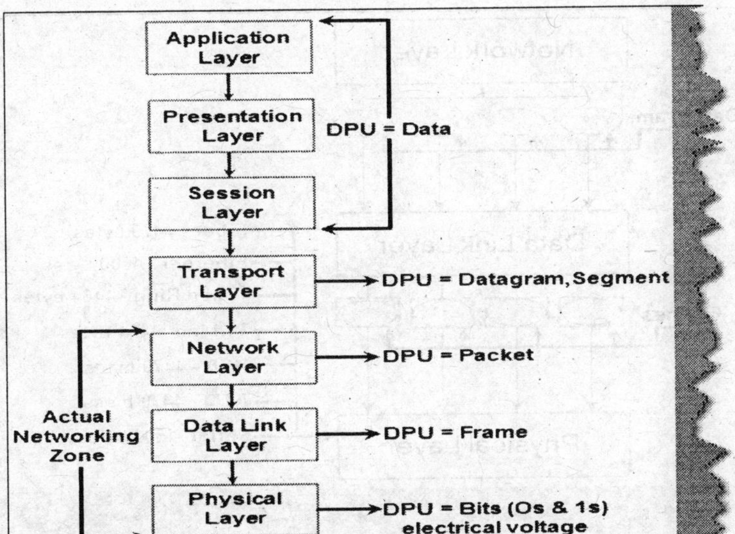

Figure: DPU in Different Layers

Before everything else, we need to first understand the concept of DPU. DPU stands for 'Data Protocol Unit.' DPU is nothing but a chunk of data. DPU is known by different names depending upon which layer it currently is in. Streaming data is broken in small logical chunks so that it can be managed properly. Layers 1 - 4 (Transport, Network, Data Link, and Physical layers) are actually networking layers which mean that all the networking happens in these layers. In these layers, the DPU is known as 'Segments.' In all the upper layers (Application, Presentation, and Session leayers) DPU is known as 'Data.' The data stream is broken in to small chunks and segments, and this process is called 'Segmentation.'

In the Network layer, DPU is called 'Datagram' or 'Packet.' The difference between segments and packets is that packets contain source and destination addresses.

In the Data Link layer, DPU is called 'Frame.' Frame contains the entire data passed from the previous layer, but it also adds extra information for error detection. This extra information is called 'Checksum.'

Finally, in the Physical layer, the frame is converted into electrical radio signals, which can then sent across hardware medium.

(I) What is IP Datagram, Fragmentation, and MTU?

When data is sent using IP the higher layer data which is in form of IP ,datagram is broken down into frames. In order to make sure that data is transported on the physical network, this conversion is essential. The underlying physical network can be fiber, Ethernet, token ring, ATM, etc. Each physical network will have its own frame format, with each format having its own limitation of data which can be sent on a single frame. As shown in the figure 'IP Datagram and the Physical Layer,' fiber has 4470 bytes, Ethernet has 1500 bytes, and so on. This data size capacity is called an MTU, i.e., 'Maximum Transmission Unit.' So, in short, if the IP datagram packet is more than the frame's data size, the physical device cannot deal with the same.

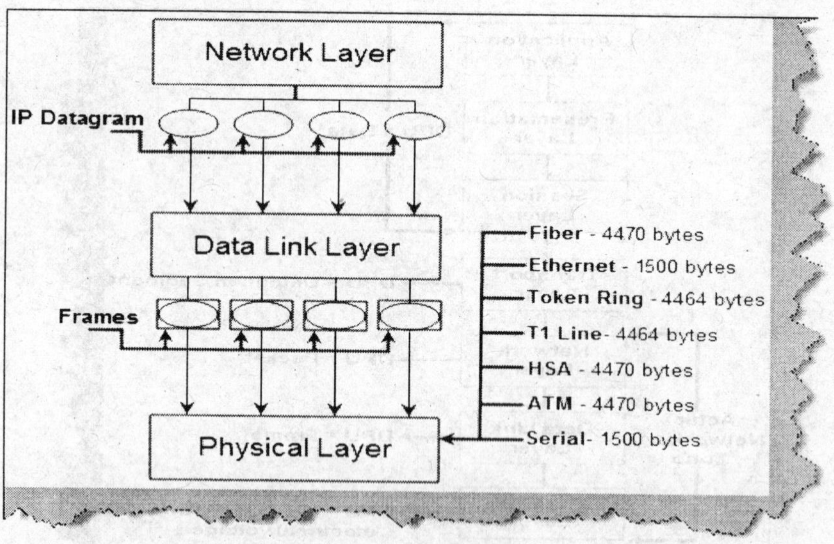

Figure: IP Datagram and the Physical Layer

Ok, now that we know what the problem is, how do we solve the same. As said before, MTU decides the size of the frame which can be transmitted over the physical network. So, when the IP layer receives a message which needs to be transmitted, it computes the size of the IP datagram and adds 20 bytes to the IP header. It then looks at the physical layer and the MTU of the physical layer. If the IP datagram packet size is more than the

MTU, it fragments (splits) the same so that data can fit in the frame size of the physical layer.

(B) Explain in Detail With Examples How Data Fragmentation Works

Let us try to understand the question with a sample IP datagram packet. Figure 'Multi-Stage Data Fragmentation' explains the concept in a more detailed manner. From device A, an IP datagram packet of 10000 bytes is passed. The first physical layer till router 1 has MTU capacity of 3300 bytes frame. In order that 10000 bytes fits in the frame, the IP datagram is further split in to 4 sections, i.e., three sections of 3300 bytes and 1 frame of 100 bytes. You can see the four blocks between Device A and router 1. Note the 100 bytes frame. From router 1 to router 2, the MTU capacity is 2000 bytes per frame.-So again, the data is fragmented in five pieces of 2000 bytes each. You can see the five blocks of frame in between routers 1 and 2. From router 2 to router 3, the MTU capacity is 3300 bytes per frame. But it does not reassemble the frame just because the MTU size is bigger than the previous layer. It just transmits as is with the same block classification. You can see from the figure, 'Multistage Data fragmentation' how the blocks are still five blocks and not less.

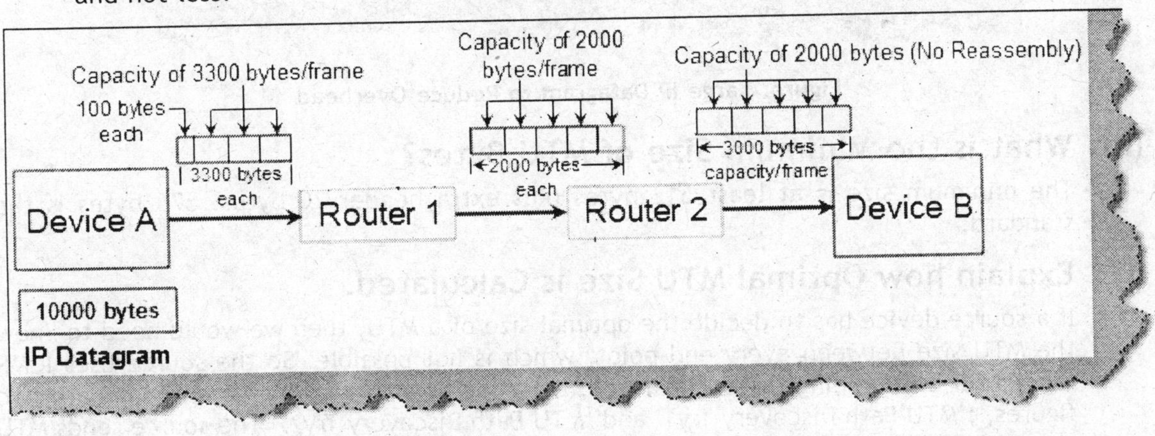

Figure: Multi-Stage Data Fragmentation

(I) Larger the IP Datagram, Lesser the Overhead: True or False?

The above statement is absolutely true, larger the IP datagram, lesser is the overhead. Let's understand how this works. Refer to the figure, 'Large IP Datagram to Reduce Overhead' for a clearer understanding. Consider a scenario where the source wants to send 10,000 bytes of data. Let's take a first scenario that this data has to go over a physical layer that has MTU of 3300 bytes. With every IP datagram, there are 20 bytes of extra header information. So when the data fragmentation happens for an MTU size of 3300 bytes, there is 80 bytes of extra overhead information as shown in the figure. For every fragment, there is extra 20 bytes of header information. Now lets consider a scenario where we need to send the same data over a physical layer the MTU size of which is 5000 bytes, LOL only 40 bytes of overhead information. In short, larger the IP datagram size, lesser the overhead.

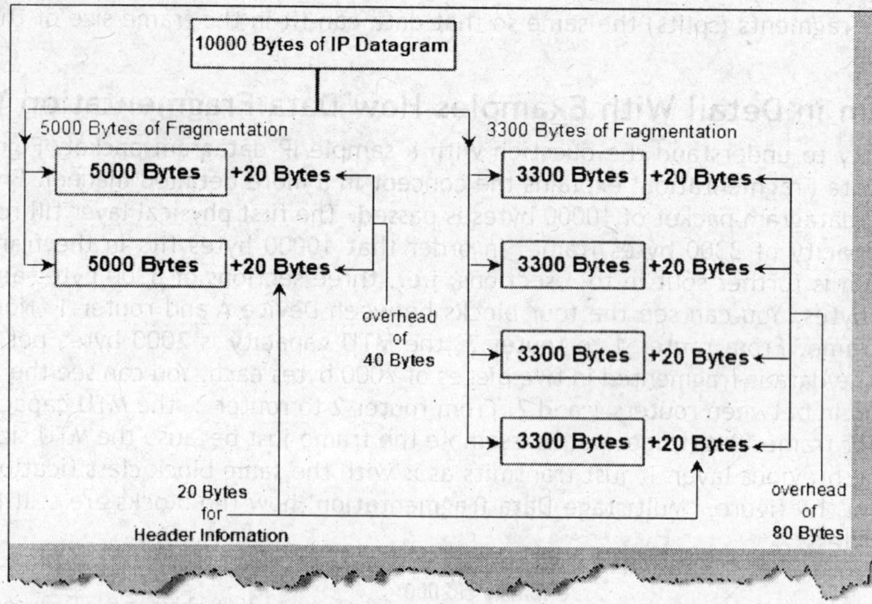

Figure: Large IP Datagram to Reduce Overhead

(B) What is the Minimum Size of MTU Bytes?

The minimum size is at least 512 bytes plus extra header 20 bytes. 576 bytes is the standard.

(I) Explain how Optimal MTU Size is Calculated.

If a source device has to decide the optimal size of a MTU, then we would need to know the MTU size between every end point, which is not possible. So the source uses ICMP replies for determining the optimal size. Let's see how this works. Given below are two figures, ;'MTU Path Discovery Try1' and 'MTU Path Discovery Try2.' The source sends MTU size of its local physical link. If that fails, then the source re-adjusts the MTU size and tries again. For instance, in the figure 'MTU Path Discover Try1,' the source first sends the IP datagram with a size of 2000 bytes per frame which is the size of it local physical link. The source IP datagram is 10000 bytes per frame which is divided in five frames that is 2000 bytes per frame. But the next physical link from router 1 to router 2 is of 1000 bytes MTU size. But the source has sent the IP datagram with the DF (Do not Fragment) flag set, which means the IP datagram will not fragment. So the IP datagram cannot move ahead and sends an error back in form of ICMP packet saying 'destination unreachable.'

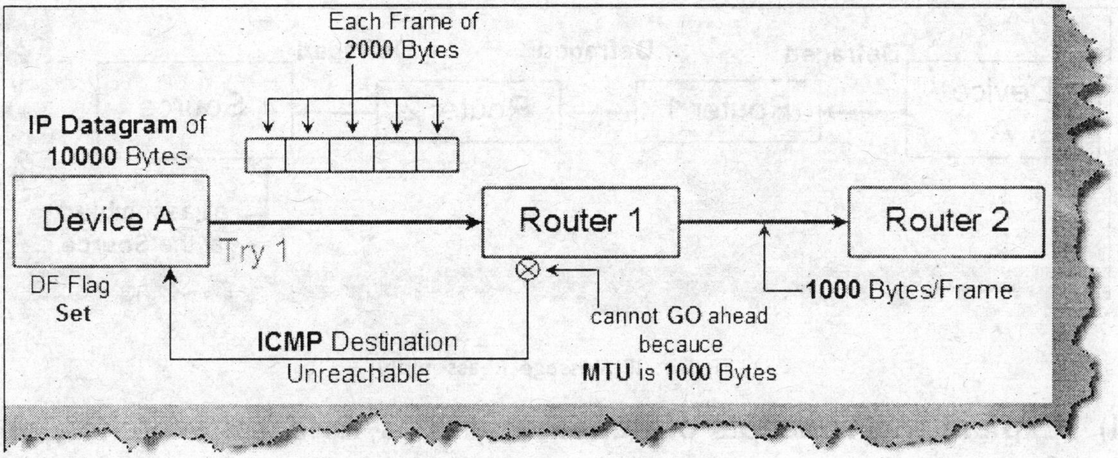

Figure: MTU Path Discovery Try1

Now, the source tries for the second time with 1000 bytes defragmentation. This time the datagram is able to reach router 2 because the MTU size fits across all paths of the physical network.

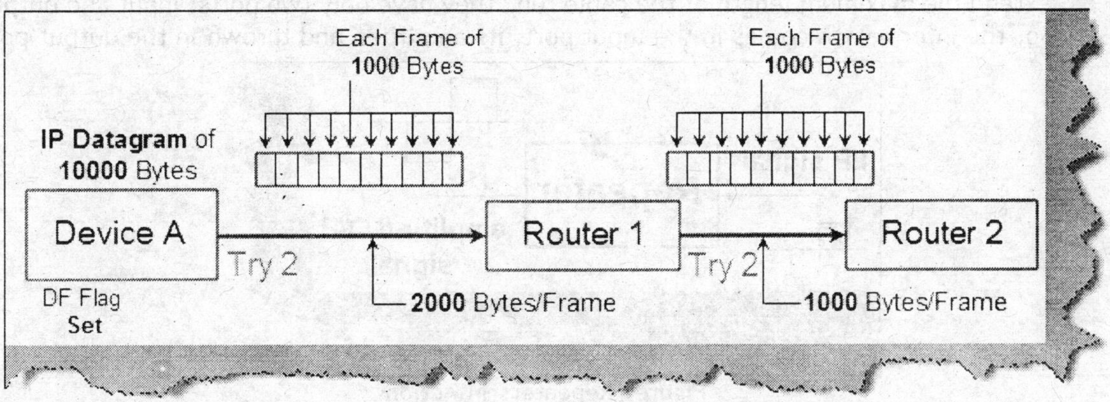

Figure: MTU Path Discovery Try2

(I) How Do the IP Messages Finally Reassemble?

Depending on the MTU capacity, of the physical layers, routers can defrag the IP datagram. Defrag can happen at multiple places. Finally, the fragmented datagram is reassembled at the source.

> ***Note:*** *No reassembly happens of the IP datagram in between. It only happens at the source.*

Figure 'IP Message Reassembly' shows how the IP datagram is split in between the router transmission. But the final reassembly only happens at the source.

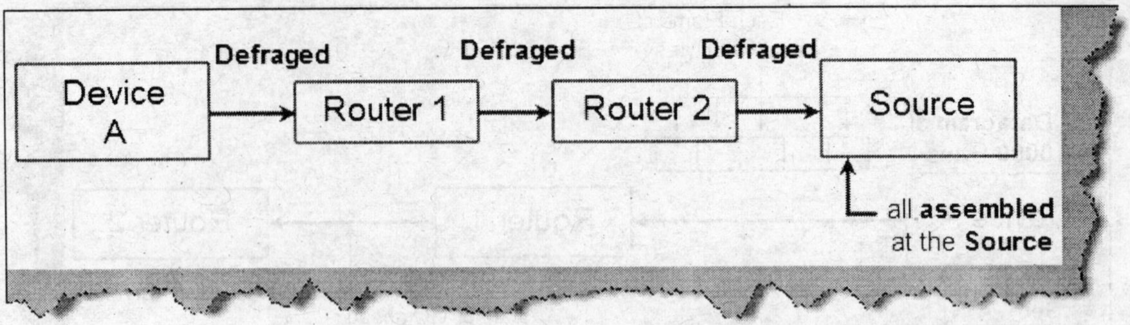

Figure: IP Message Reassembly

(I) Explain the Concepts of Repeaters, Hubs, Bridges, Switches, and Routers.

Repeaters are mostly associated with Physical layers. They do not have the intelligence to examine the frame information or the header information. They just amplify the electrical signals. In short, it makes no decisions on how the frame is forwarded, it just takes the frame, creates a copy of it, and forwards it along the way. Repeaters are mostly used to extend the maximum length of the cable run. They have only two ports: input and output. So, the information comes in the input port, its amplified and thrown in the output port.

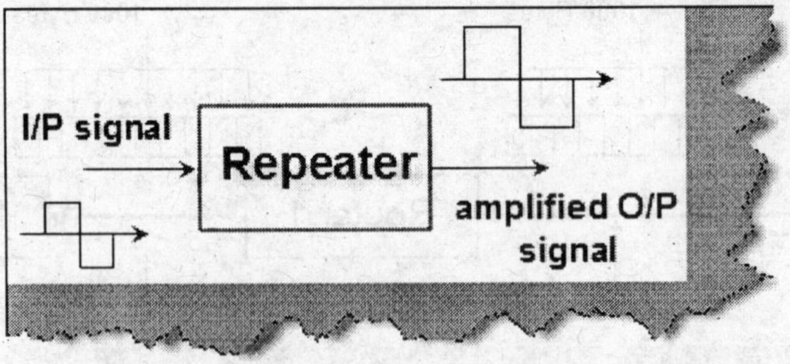

Figure: Repeaters in Action

Hubs are built on the same concept as repeaters, only that thay have more than one port. In short, it's a multi-port repeater. So a signal sent at any one port in the hub is forwarded to all other ports. Again, no examination of the frame is done, neither is any intelligent decision made; only the signal is forwarded along the way. Hubs are normally deployed on small LANs to provide connection to network nodes. But because the data is sent to all nodes, a huge bandwidth is compromised.

Bridges are different from hubs and repeaters in the sense that they have ability to interpret frame data information. Frame contains information like the MAC address of destination as well as source, and also the check suminformation. And because frames have the ability to read these information, bridges are capable of making intelligent decisions on how to forward packets. Bridges builds a table in memory which records the MAC addresses and ports. So when the bridge receives a frame, it directs the traffic to the destined MAC address and port only, thus increasing bandwidth performance. Bridges have only one input and output port each.

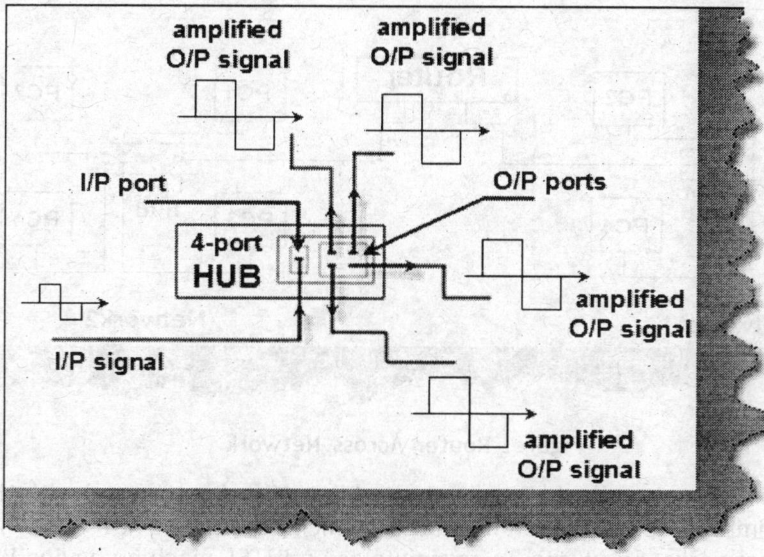

Figure: HUB in Action

A Switch is same as the bridge, which means it can also read frames but it goes one step further than bridges, it has multiple ports. So depending on the source and destination MAC addresses, it sends data to the particular computer rather than to the whole world.

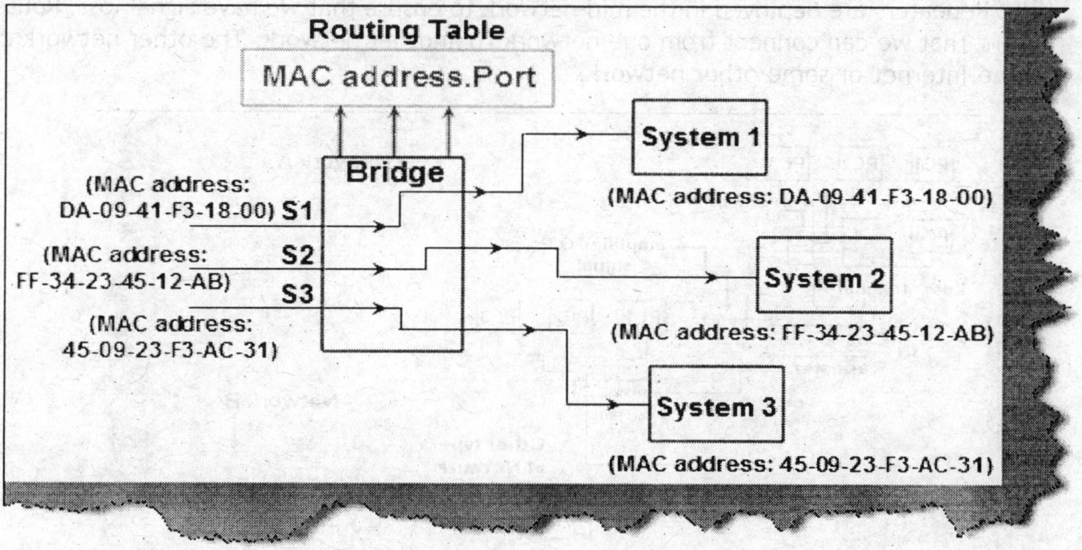

Figure: Switch and Hub Concept

Router is a device which forwards packets between networks. Hubs and switches can only forward packets between single networks. You can see in the figure below how hubs are used to connect internal computers, and how router connects different networks.

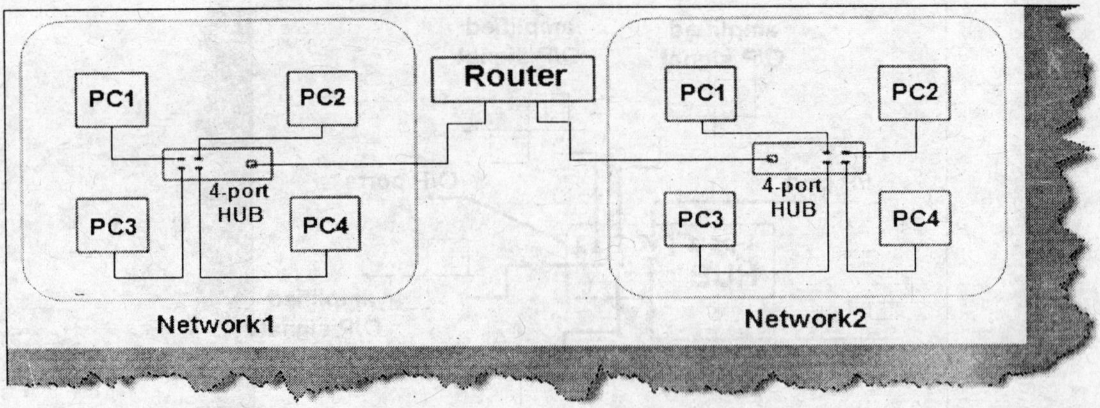

Figure: Router Across Network

Router deals with network addresses only, and hence, are associated with Network layers. A router is simply a computer running a code which determines how and where to forward packets to networks. So, it can be as simple as an INTEL machine having Windows Server operating system or complex as with a specialized operating system, such as, the CISCO router.

Let's summarize the relationship between Bridges, Hubs and Routers using the figure below. In the figure, we have two networks: A and B. Network A has seven computers which are further grouped in 4 and 3 computers. The computers grouped together are connected using HUB. Repeaters are deployed in the mid-network to ensure that we have signal loss. Routers ensure that we can connect from one network to another network. The other network can be the Internet or some other network.

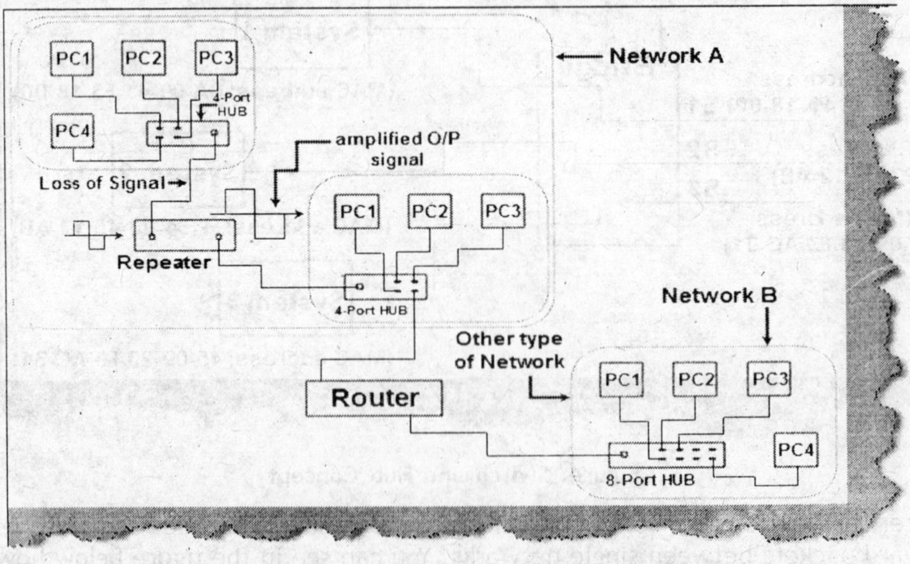

Figure: Relationship Between Bridges, Hubs, and Routers

(I) On What Layers do Routers, Switches, Bridges, and Hubs operate?

The figure below answers the question.

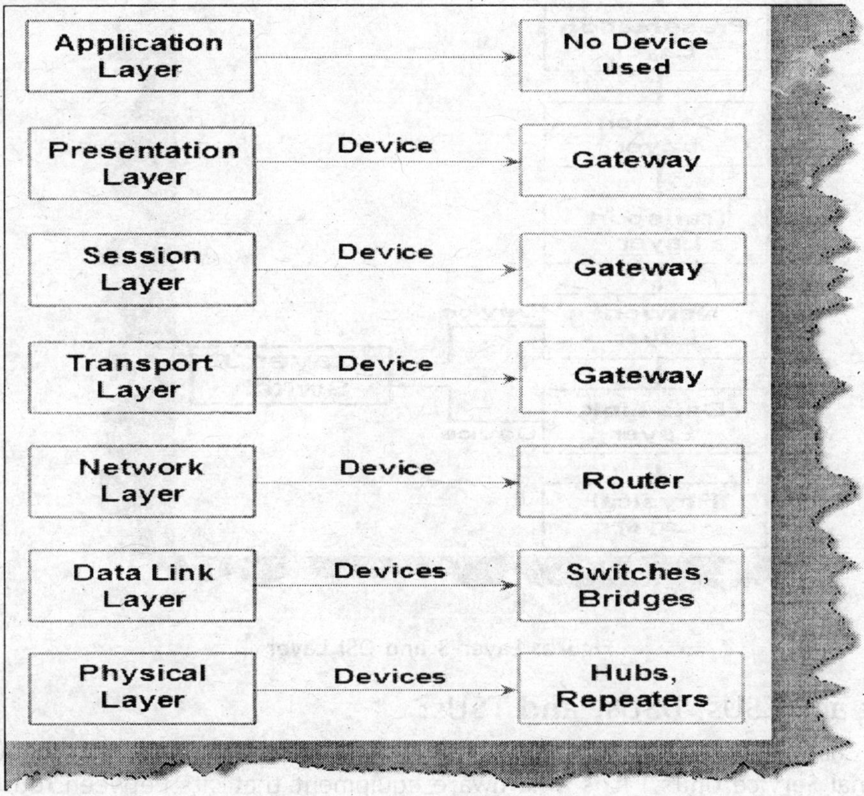

Figure: OSI and Hardware. Relationship

(I) Explain the Concept of Layer-3 Switches.

A layer-3 switch is a hybrid device. It combines the function of switches and routers in one box. So, it has the ability to operate at both levels: Data Link and Network. Figure 'Layer3 and OSI Layer' shows the how Layer-3 combines the functionality and how it operates at the two OSI layers. Layer-3 switches operate on the Network and Data Link layers.

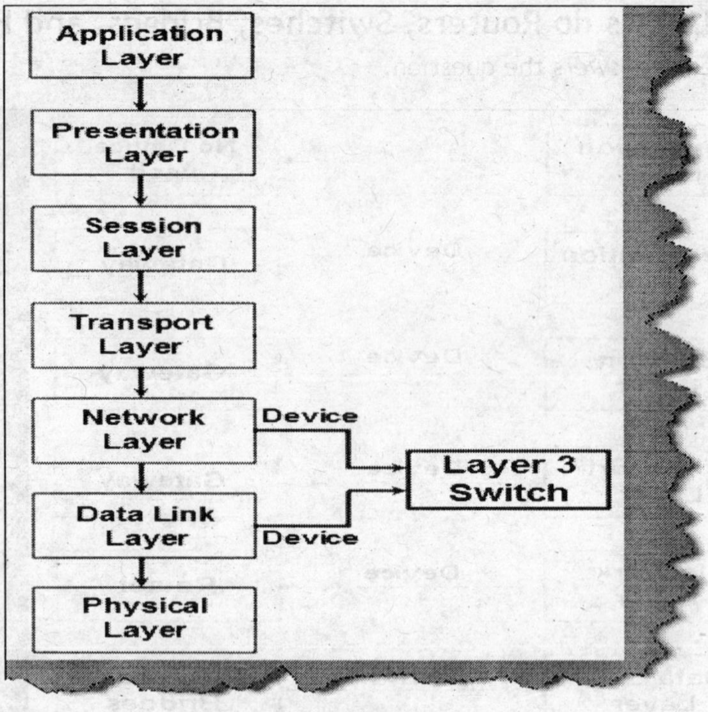

Figure: Layer-3 and OSI Layer

(I) What are CSUs, DSUs, and TSUs?

CSUs (Channel Service Units) and DSUs (Data Service Units) are also known as TSUs (Terminal Service Units.) It is a hardware equipment that sits between routers and the WAN network which can be T1. Even though T1 is a digital line, the signaling methods used by telecommunication companies differ a lot. So CSUs and DSUs condition the signal received from the router and make it compatible according to the WAN network technology provided by the phone companies. Telecommunication organizations plug in their connection in to RJ-45 Jack as shown in the figure 'CSUs and DSUs in Action.'

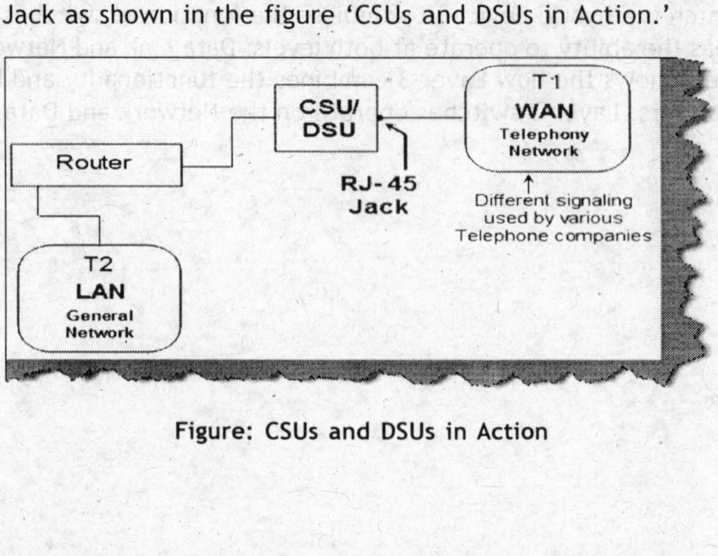

Figure: CSUs and DSUs in Action

(I) What are the Basic Components of a Router?

Routers can be a simple computer which has code that determines where the packets can be forwarded. So routers can be a simple computer with Windows Server, or it can be complex with specialized operating system, such as, CISCO. But there are some basic components which will always remain fix irrespective how you implement the router fundamental. The following components form the main sections of routers:

Processor: Processors' make and speed vary according to the volume of packets to be handled, and the complexity of filtering required. So heavier the volume of packets, better the processor speed should be.

Operating System: The heart of any router is its operating system. Normally, vendors have their own proprietary operating system. For example, CISCO routers have their own operating system called Cisco IOS (Internetwork Operating System.) Cisco IOS has gone through lot of version updates but the core remains the same. In short, if you can configure one CISCO router, you can configure any.

Memory: Routers use different memory for different functions. There are basically two types of memory: volatile and non-volatile. Volatile memories are those which store information temporarily, in case of device rebooting, the data is lost. Non-volatile memory is complete unlike volatile memory. Table 'Memory Allocation According to Router' shows different memory allocations:

Table: Memory Allocation for Routers

Type of memory	Where is it used
RAM/DRAM	Active program and operating system instructions, the running configuration file, routing tables
NVRAM	Start up files
ROM	POST, bootstrap, and startup/power-up utilities (usually limited version of), Cisco IOS
Flash	Cisco operating systems (IOS).

RAM memory is volatile and faster than non-volatile memory. Information from non-volatile memory is copied into the volatile memory for faster execution. Memory data like route tables are stored in volatile memory because these data is referred with high frequency.

Network interface: Without the network interface, you cannot connect to the external world. There are two types of network interfaces: WAN and LAN.

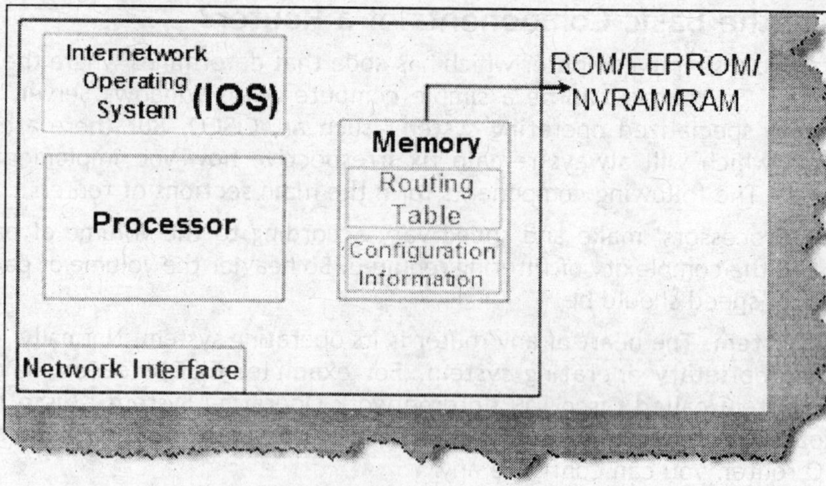

Figure: Different Components in a Router

Figure 'Different Components in a Router' shows what a CISCO router is made up of.

(B) Explain WAN and LAN Interfaces in Routers.

(B) What are DB-15, DB-60, and RJ-45 in CISCO Routers?

WAN interface makes it possible to connect to WAN links such as modem or digital lines like T1. WAN links on CISCO is nothing but a female serial port DB60 as shown in the figure 'RJ-45, DB-15 and DB-60 in Routers.'

LAN interface connects the router to one or more networks. The interface is in the form of a DB-15 female connector or the RJ-45 Jack. RJ-45 is not used for connection but for programming. In short, you can connect a terminal to this jack and program it using TELNET.EXE.

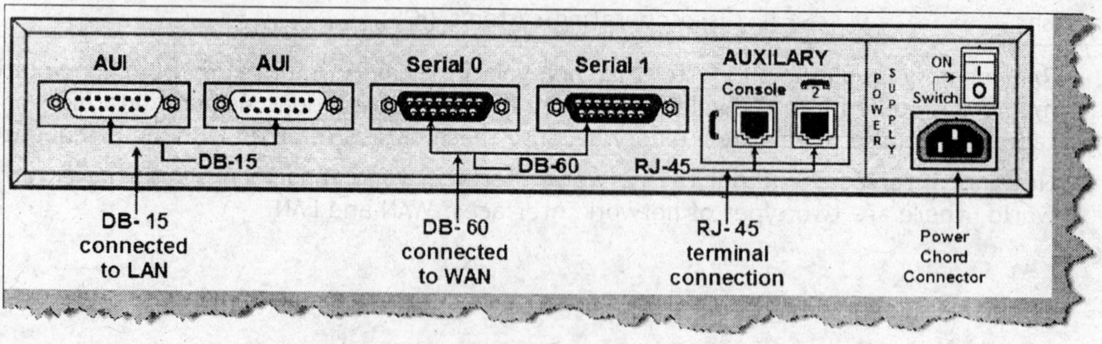

Figure: RJ-45, DB-15, and DB-60 in Routers

(B) Explain the Concept of TTL.

(B) Explain the Concept of ICMP Packets.

IP datagrams travels across networks and from one router to another. To ensure that these datagram do not move endlessly in a loop within the network, TTL came into the picture. TTL field has time value in seconds. When the IP datagram packet passes through a router, the value is decreased by one second. When the TTL value becomes zero, the router destroys the datagram packet which voids the datagram to move endlessly around the network. Figure 'TTL in Action' shows how TTL works. So for instance 'Data 1' is sent with 2 seconds of TTL. In router 1, 1 is subtracted from the TTL, so it becomes 1 second. Data 1 then goes to router 2, and the TTL becomes 0. When router 2 sees the value 0, it destroys the packet and sends an ICMP packet with a 'Time Exceeded Message' error message. Now, let's look at data 2. It has sent the data with a TTL value of 3 seconds. Each router Deducting 1 from the value in each router, it can easily reach the destination.

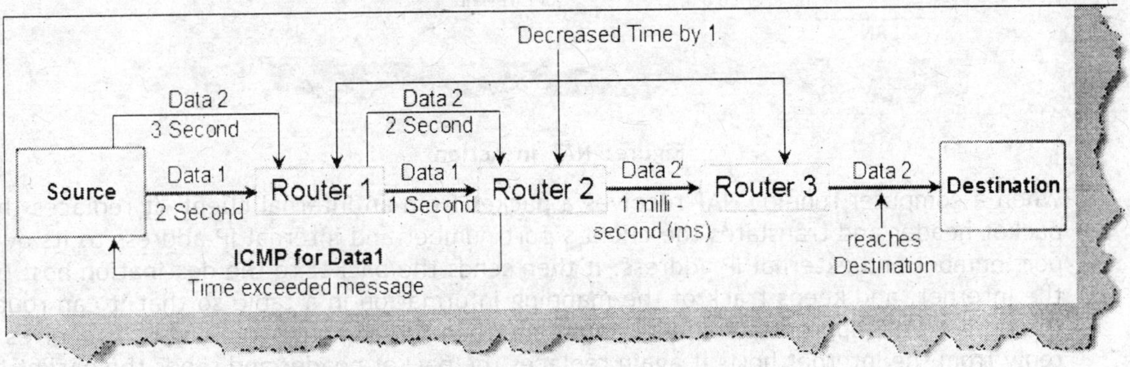

Figure: TTL in Action

(B) Which Operating System Does CISCO Have?

CISCO routers have their own operating system called Cisco IOS (Internetwork Operating System.)

(I) Explain the Concept of NAT.

Internet is growing at an exponential rate. So small, medium, big, and even personals need public IP addresses to connect to the Internet. The Internet protocol has two version, one is the IPV4 and the other is IPV6. IPV4 is supposed to allow 232, i.e., four billion addresses. Already 80 % of the addresses are used till date. But the growth of the Internet is very much exponential. So sooner or later all these addresses will get used. So there are two options, using IPV6 or NAT. NAT is a temporary fix until IPV6 is implemented in full-fledged manner. With NAT, we can share large number of hosts with lesser number of public IP addresses.

NAT is a hardware device, i.e., either a firewall or a router which sits between groups of computers and the Internet as shown in the figure below. The device, i.e., the firewall or the router has a public IP address and its mapped to all the other computers in the local network. Thus, we have only one IP address for a group of computers. In the diagram 'NAT in Action,' we have three computers and one router or firewall, which does the NAT for us. Now whenever we get any request, NAT reads the destination and the port and sends it to the particular address itself. When any data needs to go to the Internet, NAT changes the IP address and sends it accordingly.

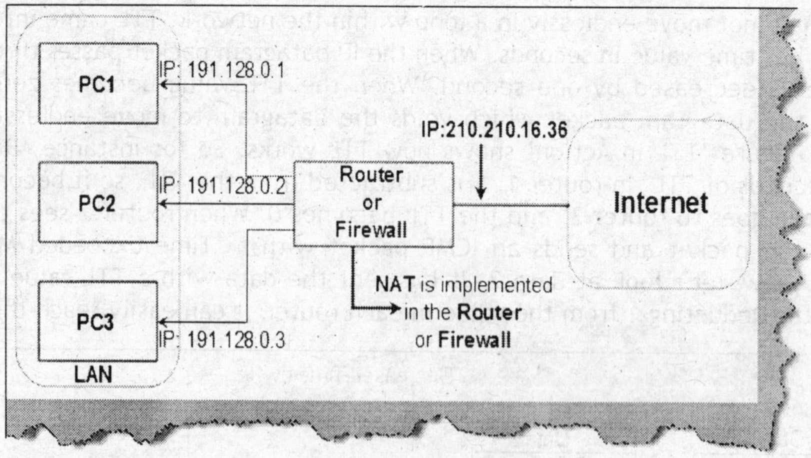

Figure: NAT in Action

When a computer running NAT receives a packet from an internal client, it replaces the packet header and translates the client's port number and internal IP address to its own port number and external IP address. It then sends the packet to the destination host on the Internet, and keeps track of the mapping information in a table so that it can route the reply to the appropriate client computer. When the computer running NAT receives a reply from the Internet host, it again replaces the packet header and sends the packet to the client. Both the client computer and the Internet host appear to be communicating directly with each other.

(B) How is NAT Implemented?

NAT is implemented either on the router or on the firewall.

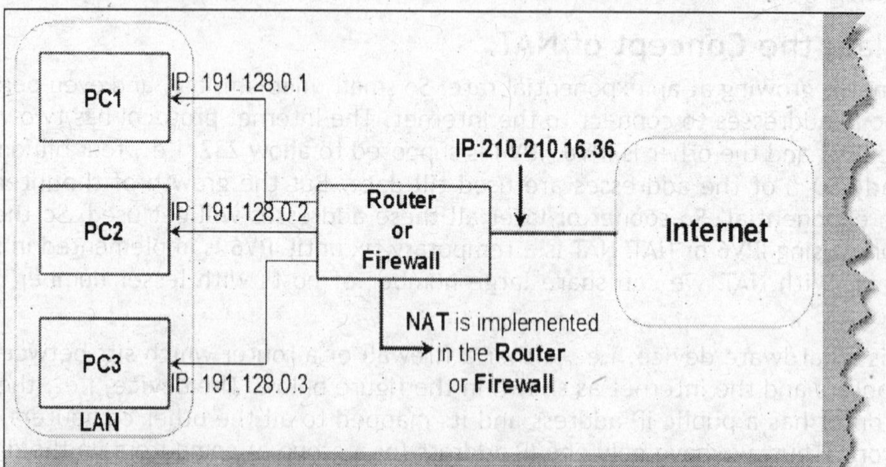

Figure: NAT Implementation

(I) Explain how NAT Actually works.

The figure below defines how NAT actually functions. In the figure below, we have two computers which are in the Local Area Network, and they are assigned private IP addresses: 192.168.0.1, 192.168.0.2 and 192.168.0.3, respectively. The router or the firewall (210.210.25.166) implements NAT which sits between the Internet and the internal LAN. As shown in the figure, there are six steps that take place when any data passes through NAT, let us understand these six steps in a more detail manner.

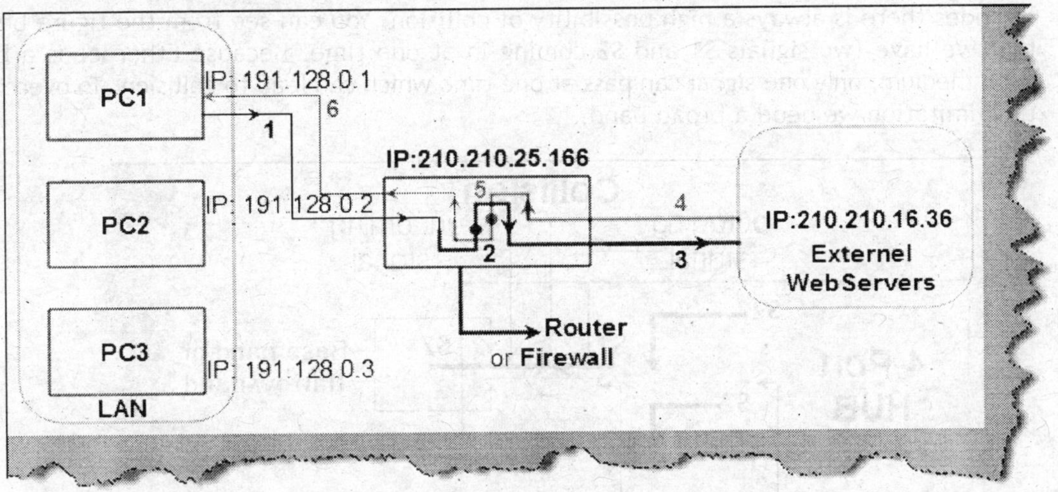

Figure: Six Steps for NAT

Step 1: An internal LAN computer wants to send data to external web servers. Figure 'Six steps for NAT' shows the same in a pictorial format. '191.128.0.1' wants to connect to the '210.210.16.36' external server. The client computer sends a packet to the computer running NAT. The packet header indicates that the packet originates from port 1074 on the computer with the IP address 192.168.0.1, and has a destination of port 80 on '210.210.25.166' (this is the NAT computer IP.)

Step 2: The computer running NAT changes the packet header to indicate that the packet originates from port 1563 on host '210.210.25.166,' but does not change the destination. The computer running NAT then sends the packet to the Web server over the Internet.

Step 3: The external Web server receives the packet and sends a reply. The packet header for the reply indicates that the packet originates from port 80 on '210.210.16.36,' and has a destination of port 1563 on host '210.210.25.166.'

Step 4: The computer running NAT receives the packet and checks its mapping information to determine the destination client computer. The computer running NAT changes the packet header to indicate a destination of port 1074 on '210.210.25.166,' and then sends the packet to the client. The source of the packet remains as port 80 on '210.210.16.36,' which is the IP address of the Web server.

(I) Why Do Collisions Occur in HUBS and Repeaters?

(I) Explain the Concept of Collision Domain.

Hubs and repeaters work on single collision domain architecture. Hubs are deployed on smaller Ethernet LANs to provide connection to network nodes. Ethernet is a base band medium which means only one signal can go at a time. So at any instance, if there are two signals transmitted, there is huge probability of collision which degrades performance further. Ethernet is based on single collision domain architecture, an increase in the number of nodes there is always a high possibility of collision. You can see from the figure below that we have two signals S1 and S2 coming in at one time. Because Ethernet is a base band medium, only one signal can pass at one time which can lead to collision. To overcome this limitation we need a broad band.

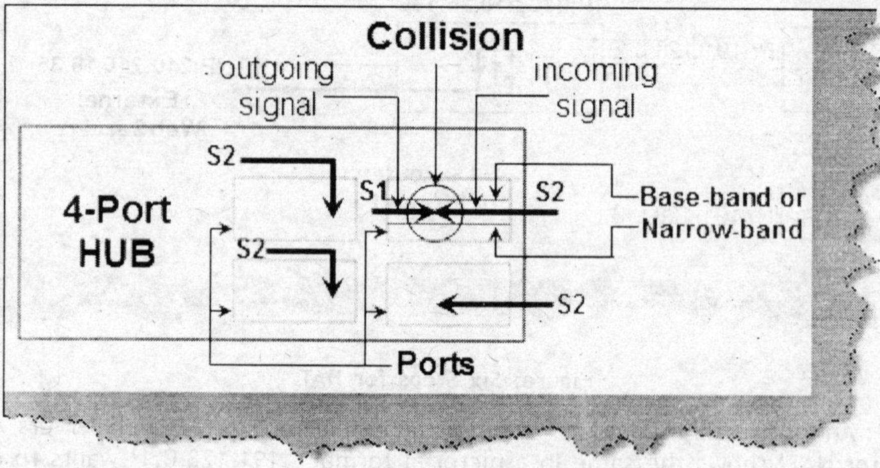

Figure: Collision

(B) What is the Concept of Routing Tables?

Routers are responsible for forwarding traffic from one host to another. So basically, router analyzes the IP address and decides the next hop. The question now is, how does the router know where the datagram should go? This information is stored in a Routing Table. Every record in the routing table is called 'Routing Entry.' It is like a link list that says what the next hop for a particular destination is. So each time the router gets an IP datagram, it evaluates and sends it accordingly looking at the IP routing table. Fewer the entries, faster the data will reach the destination.

Let's understand how routing table works actually. Figure 'IP and Routing Tables' explains the same in a pictorial format. Every router has a routing table that says what the next hop is says for destination xyz. In this figure, we have four routers that are interconnected. Router2 connects 198.x.x.x network, Router3 connects 192.x.x.x. network, and Router1 connects to Router4 which in turn connects to 191.x.x.x. We will look at the Router3 routing table. If any host from 192.x.x.x network sends a datagram the destination of which is 198.x.x.x, router3 will forward the same to router2 by looking at the routing table entries. Same holds true for 196.x.x.x. If a datagram packet has to be sent to 191.x.x.x, then the next hop is to 196.x.x.x because router1 is directly connected to 191.x.x.x and not router3. When router1 gets a datagram which needs to be sent to 191.x.x.x, it just looks at its routing table and forwards the same to router4. Router4 then looks at its table which says this can be directly sent to host and acts accordingly.

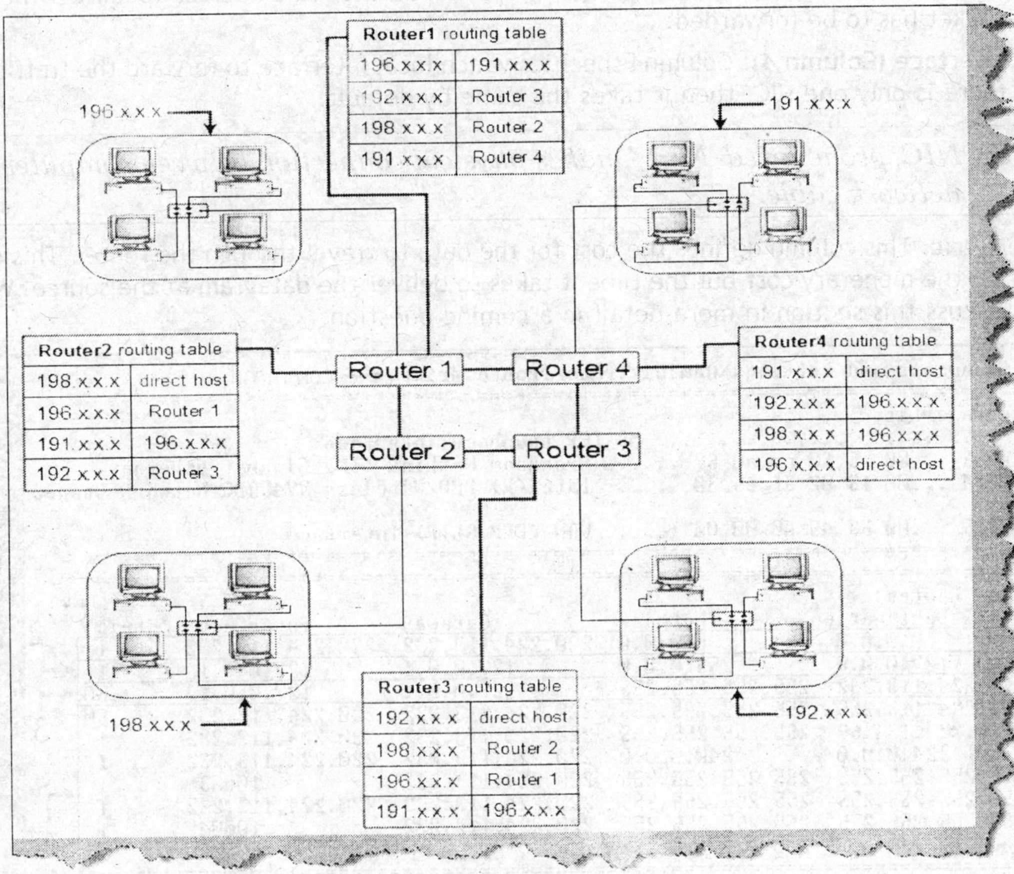

Figure: IP and Routing Tables

(I) What is the Use of Route Prints?

This question is answered in the next question.

(I) Explain in Detail What a Routing Table Looks Like.

We had seen in an earlier question how routing tables work. Routing tables are stored in the host itself. So let's view routing table data contained at the host. In order to view the routing table data, do the following (this is applicable only to the Windows operating system.) Go to command/DOS prompt by typing 'cmd' in 'run' and enter command 'Route Print.' Once the command runs successfully, you should see an output similar to the figure 'Router Print Output.' The output in the figure is route table of that host. Let's try to understand the output step by step. The main section is the active routes section. We will be concentrating more on this section. In active routes, we have five columns Network Destination, Netmask, Gateway, Interface, and Metric.

Network Destination (Column1): This column lists every network the host has.

Network Mask (Column2): The function of network mask is similar to subnet mask. It helps us identify the network portion of the IP address.

Gateway (Column 3): This is the gateway's IP address. This address specifies where the packet has to be forwarded.

Interface (Column 4): Column4 specifies which local interface to forward the traffic to. If there is only one NIC, then it takes the same by default.

> ***Note:*** *NIC, pronounced 'Nick,' makes physical connection between computer and network cable.*

Metric: This column defines the cost for the data to travel through the router. This cost is not the monetary cost but the time it takes to deliver the datagram at the source. We will discuss this section in more detail in a coming question.

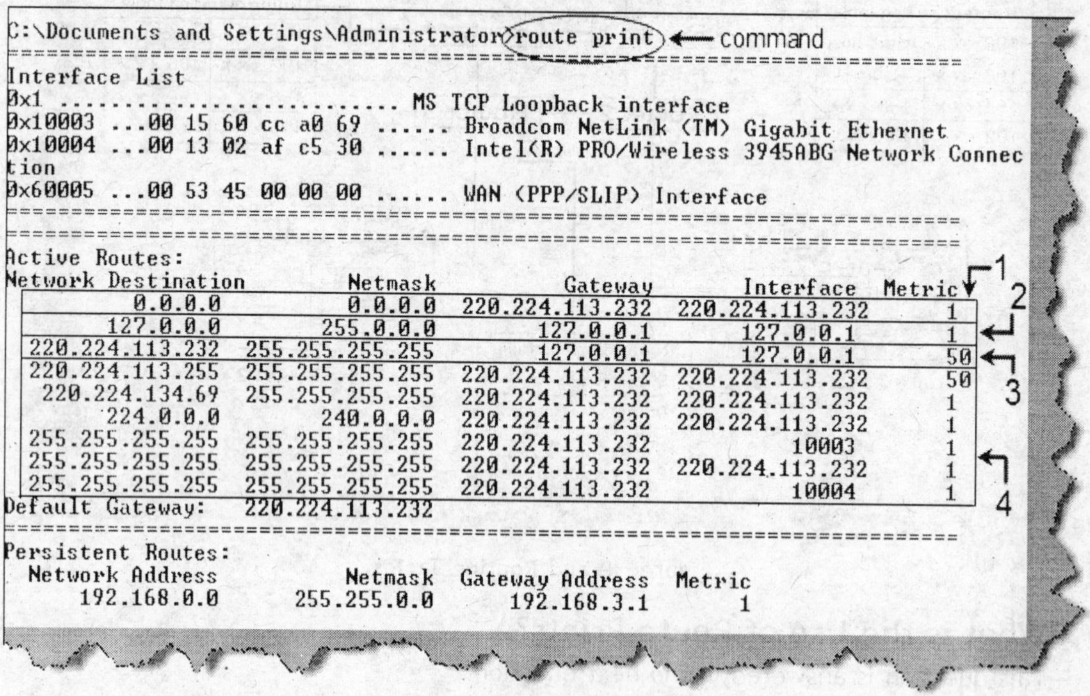

```
C:\Documents and Settings\Administrator>route print
===========================================================================
Interface List
0x1 ........................... MS TCP Loopback interface
0x10003 ...00 15 60 cc a0 69 ...... Broadcom NetLink (TM) Gigabit Ethernet
0x10004 ...00 13 02 af c5 30 ...... Intel(R) PRO/Wireless 3945ABG Network Connec
tion
0x60005 ...00 53 45 00 00 00 ...... WAN (PPP/SLIP) Interface
===========================================================================
===========================================================================
Active Routes:
Network Destination        Netmask          Gateway       Interface  Metric
          0.0.0.0          0.0.0.0  220.224.113.232  220.224.113.232       1
        127.0.0.0        255.0.0.0        127.0.0.1        127.0.0.1       1
  220.224.113.232  255.255.255.255        127.0.0.1        127.0.0.1      50
  220.224.113.255  255.255.255.255  220.224.113.232  220.224.113.232      50
   220.224.134.69  255.255.255.255  220.224.113.232  220.224.113.232       1
        224.0.0.0        240.0.0.0  220.224.113.232  220.224.113.232       1
  255.255.255.255  255.255.255.255  220.224.113.232            10003       1
  255.255.255.255  255.255.255.255  220.224.113.232  220.224.113.232       1
  255.255.255.255  255.255.255.255  220.224.113.232            10004       1
Default Gateway:   220.224.113.232
===========================================================================
Persistent Routes:
  Network Address          Netmask  Gateway Address  Metric
      192.168.0.0      255.255.0.0      192.168.3.1       1
```


Figure: Route Print Output

Now let's understand every row in active routes. We have marked the rows for explanation. We have four rows. Let's go through these roes step by step.

Row 1: This row defines where to send packets for IP datagram for which no specific route is defined. This row is also called the default gateway, default route, or gateway of last resort.

Row 2: Row 2 defines the loopback address. Loopback addresses are used for testing purposes. By pinging the loopback IP address, we can check whether the local IP stack functions properly or not. Figure 'Loopback' shows details of the same.

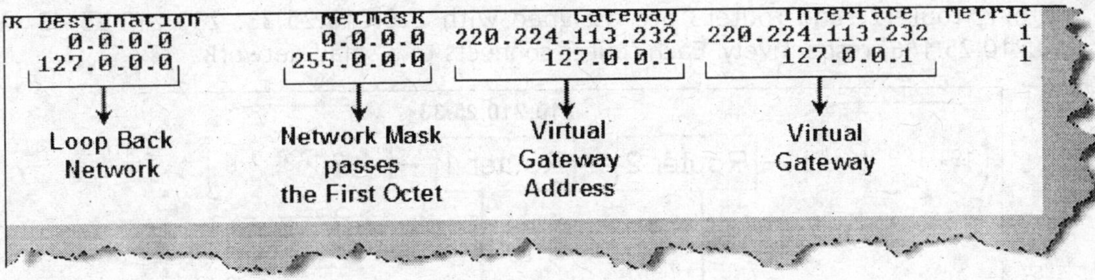

Figure: Loopback

So column1 is the loopback network. Column2 is the network mask which allows the first octet to pass. Thus, it exposes network address 127. Column3 represents a gateway virtual address which actually maps to the IP address of the workstation. Column4 is again a fictitious address through which packets are sent out.

Row 3: This row specifies the actual IP address of the host. You can also notice we have a netmask 255.255.255.255. This will help us pass all four octets and reveal the actual IP address.

Row 4: From row 4 onwards, all the rows indicate the broadcast information for multicasting. If you look at the netmask, i.e., 255.255.255.255, it means all hosts on all networks. It allows all bits to be passed through.

(B) How Can You See Route Tables on the Router?

On the router command prompt, type the command given below. This will display the route table configuration.

```
show ip route
```

(B) Explain the Concepts of Static and Dynamic Routing.

Static and dynamic routing are the methods by which we can populate route tables. Manually entered route paths are called static routes. Dynamic routes are routes which a router learns from other routers by using protocols RIP (Routing Information Protocol,) IGRP (Interior Gateway Routing Protocol,) EIGRP (Enhanced Interior Gateway,) etc.

(B) When Should Static and Dynamic Routes be Used?

Static routes are added manually by hand. It is the best solution when we have small networks, and the networks do not change very often. When we say change, we mean new hosts, and networks are not frequently added or removed. While dynamic route are best suited when the network structure is very dynamic. Dynamic routes use network resources to learn where all hosts are, and the structure of the network.

(I) How do you Configure Static Routes on a Router?

As explained in the previous question, static routes are route paths that are added manually. Let us consider a small network as shown in the figure 'Sample Network for Static Routes.' We have three routers interconnected, i.e., router1, router2, and router3. All routers, i.e., router1, router2, and router3 are assigned with 210.210.25.33, 210.210.25.43, and 210.210.25.166, respectively. Each router connects to a small network.

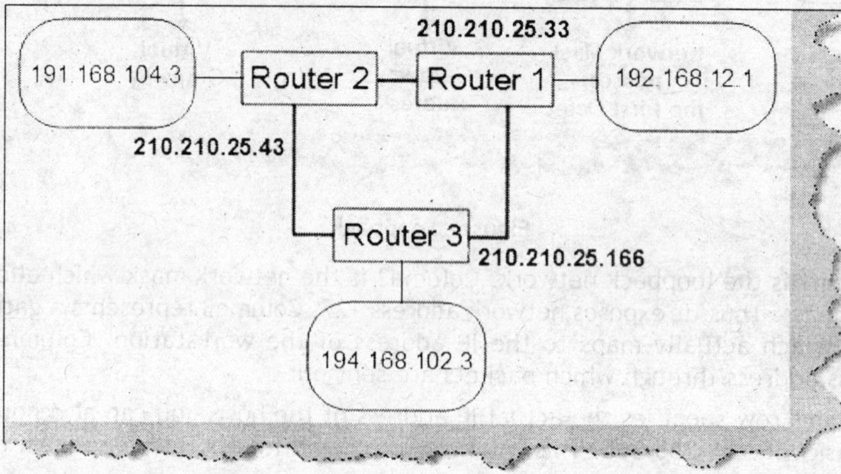

Figure: Sample Network for Static Routes

Static routing is added by using the 'IP Route' command. In order to add static routers, we first need to enter the configuration terminal by using the command 'config-term.' Once we are inside the config-term, we can then add static routes by using the 'IP Route' command. Given below is the command of IP router. The first element is the destination host. Destination host is the host where the datagram has to finally reach. The second column is the subnet mask to get the network. The third column is the 'Next Hop' for this destination host. Next hop is like saying if you get this destination host, then this is the next hop.

IP route << Destination host >> <<Subnet mask>> << Next Hop>>

Router # config-term	Destination Host	Subnet Mask	Next HOP
Router - 1 (config)# IP route	191.168.104.3	**255.255.255.0**	210.210.25.43
Router - 1 (config)# IP route	194.168.102.3	**255.255.255.0**	210.210.25.166
Router - 2 (config)# IP route	192.168.12.1	**255.255.255.0**	210.210.25.33
Router - 2 (config)# IP route	194.168.102.3	**255.255.255.0**	210.210.25.166
Router - 3 (config)# IP route	192.168.12.1	**255.255.255.0**	210.210.25.33
Router - 3 (config)# IP route	191.168.104.3	**255.255.255.0**	210.210.25.43

Figure: Commands for Static route

In the figure below, we have used IP route to assign static route to the above sample defined in figure 'Sample Network for Static Routes.' You can easily understand the commands and map the same to how it fits into the above sample network. Once done, you can view the same using the 'show ip route' command. Below is a command which is actually executed on the router. So for every destination network, we define the next hop attribute which defines the router which connects to the network.

(B) Explain Static Default Routes.

A static default route is also called the 'gateway of last resort.' When no match is found in the route table for a destination, a router will drop the packet and send ICMP 'destination unreachable' message to the sender. Gateway of last resort or static default route says that when we do not find destination in the route table, we use the static default route table. Let us try to understand this with a small example. Consider the small network shown in figure 'Static Default Route.' We have three routers: router1 (210.210.25.177,) router2 (210.210.25.178,) and router3 (210.210.25.179,) and they have 192.168.102.7, 192.168.112.15 and 192.168.114.13 hosts, respectively connected. One of the important things to be noted is that router2 connects to both router1 and router3. So router2 is a good candidate for 'Gateway of Last Resort' or 'Static Default Route.'

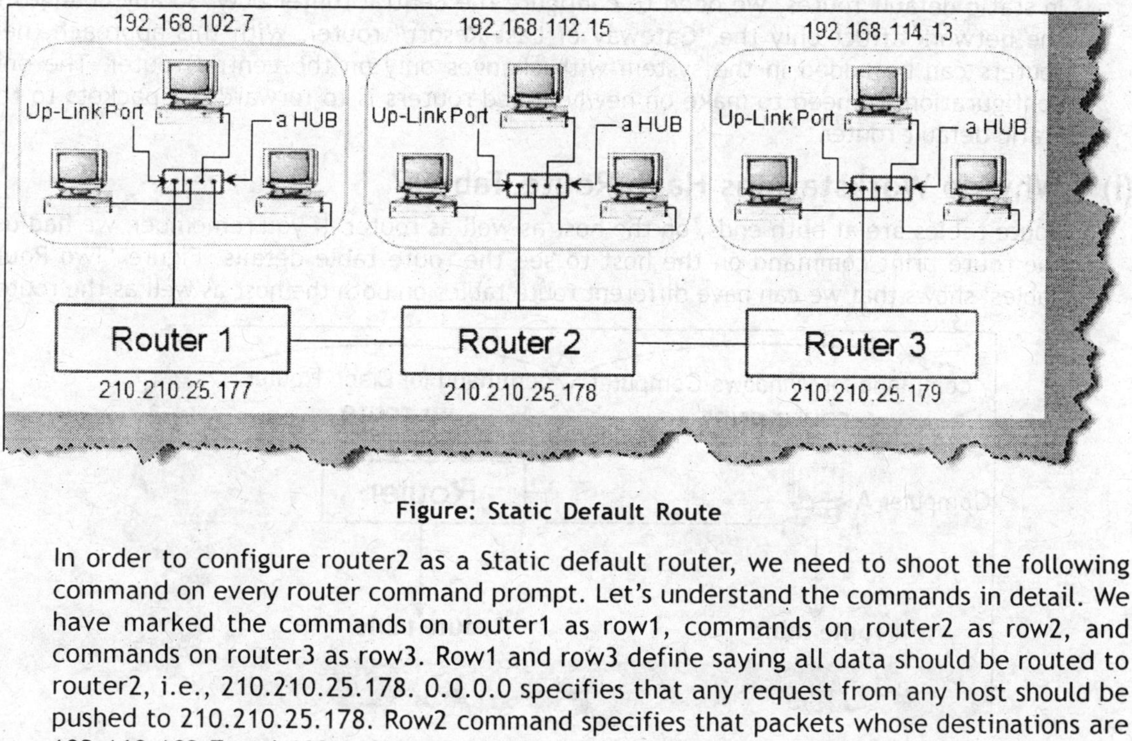

Figure: Static Default Route

In order to configure router2 as a Static default router, we need to shoot the following command on every router command prompt. Let's understand the commands in detail. We have marked the commands on router1 as row1, commands on router2 as row2, and commands on router3 as row3. Row1 and row3 define saying all data should be routed to router2, i.e., 210.210.25.178. 0.0.0.0 specifies that any request from any host should be pushed to 210.210.25.178. Row2 command specifies that packets whose destinations are 192.168.102.7 and 192.168.114.3 should be forwarded to router2. Router2 then takes a decision about where to forward the packets. So router2 becomes a central controller to forward data packets.

Router # config-term	Destination Host	Subnet Mask	Next HOP
Router - 1 (config)# IP route Router - 1 (config)# IP route	0.0.0.0	**0.0.0.0**	210.210.25.178
Router - 2 (config)# IP route	192.168.102.7	**255.255.255.0**	210.210.25.178
Router - 2 (config)# IP route	194.168.114.3	**255.255.255.0**	210.210.25.178
Router - 3 (config)# IP route Router - 3 (config)# IP route	0.0.0.0	**0.0.0.0**	210.210.25.178

Figure: Router Config for Static Default Route

(B) What is the Advantage of Using Static Default Routes?

In static default routes, we need to configure the central router only. So any changes in the network affect only the 'Gateway of Last Resort" router. With this approach, new routers can be added in the system with changes only on the central router. The only configuration we need to make on newly added routers is to forward the packets to the static default router.

(I) Why do Workstations Have Route Tables?

Route tables are at both ends, on the host as well as router. If you remember, we had use the route print command on the host to see the route table details. Figure 'Two Route Tables' shows that we can have different route tables on both the host as well as the router.

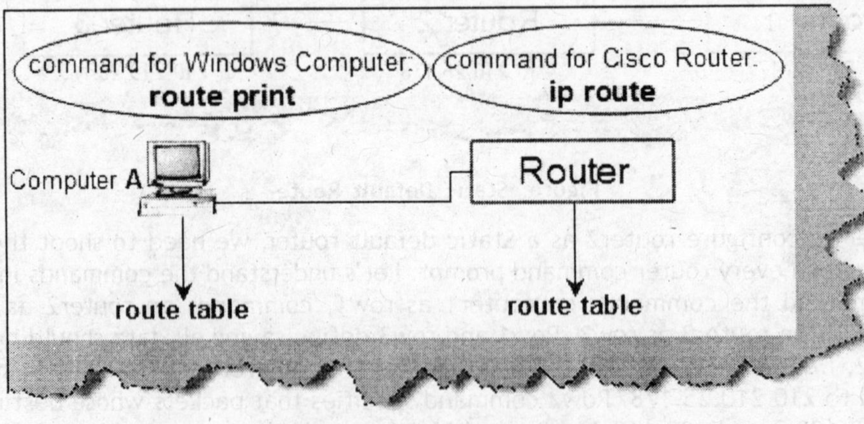

Figure: Two Route Tables

Now let's understand why we have a provision to change route tables from the host. Consider the scenario shown in the figure Hosts with Normal Settings.' We have one routerA which is connected by host1, host2, host3, and host4. All hosts send data to RouterA, which in turn decides where to send the data. Till here, everything is fine.

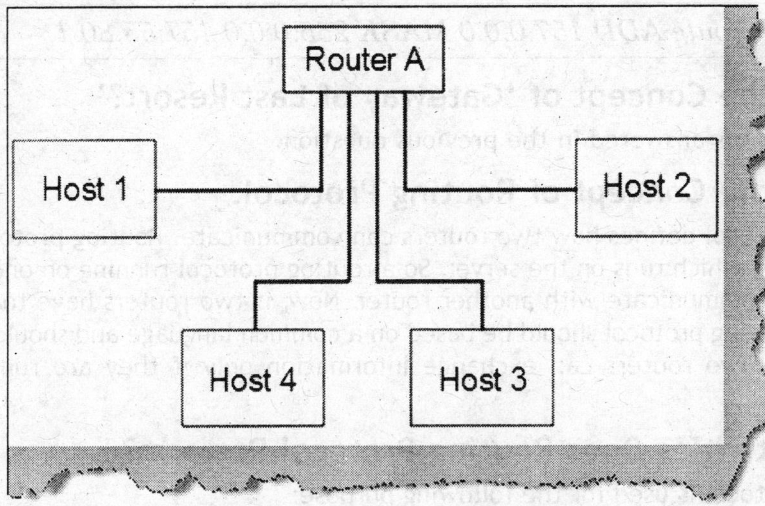

Figure: Hosts With Normal Settings

After some time, the network is modified as shown in the figure 'Host With Static Route on Workstation'. There is an extra external network added which can be accessed through Router B. As said before, all data is first sent to router A and from there the data is further forwarded to the host. But if you look at host1, it is directly connected to Router B. It will be an extra work for host1 to send packets to router A, and router A sends to router B. It would be really great if router B can directly send packets to the external network.

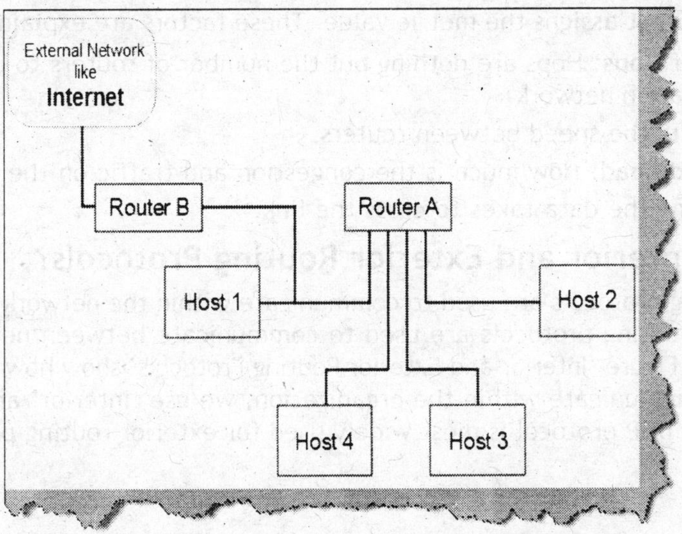

Figure: Host With Static Route on Workstation

So in order to add a new static route on the workstation we use the 'route add' command. Given below is the 'Route Add' command, which shows the command in action with sample values. After the 'route add' command, the data is sent directly to router B, where 157.0.0.0 is the destination, i.e., any internet IP address, and 157.55.80.1 is this router B IP address.

route ADD 157.0.0.0 MASK 255.0.0.0 157.55.80.1

(B) What is the Concept of 'Gateway of Last Resort?'

This question is answered in the previous question.

(B) Explain the Concept of Routing Protocol.

Routing protocol defines how two routers can communicate. Routing protocol is based on an algorithm which runs on the server. So a routing protocol running on one router should be able to communicate with another router. Now, if two routers have to communicate, then the routing protocol should be based on a common language and should have common vocabulary. Two routers can exchange information only if they are running the same protocol.

(I) What Activities Does Routing Protocol Perform?

Routing protocol is used for the following purpose:

- If there is a change in network, routing protocol helps us communicate these changes to all hosts, thus updating route tables.
- Routing protocol also helps us optimize the use of network bandwidth.

(I) What Metrics are Used by Routing Protocols to Determine the Best Path?

Routing metric is used to decide which route is best if we have more than one path available. This value is also called the cost of the route. There are many factors the route protocol considers before it assigns the metric value. These factors are explained in detail below:

- **Number of Hops**: Hops are nothing but the number of routers to be crossed to reach the destination network.
- **Bandwidth**: The speed between routers.
- **Traffic and Load**: How much is the congestion and traffic on the path?
- **Delay:** Time the data takes to cross the link.

(I) What are Interior and Exterior Routing Protocols?

Interior routing protocols are used to communicate within the network of an organization. And exterior routing protocols are used to communicate between networks of different organizations. Figure 'Interior and Exterior Routing Protocols' show how the protocols work. In order to communicate within the organization, we use 'Interior' and for external, we use 'Exterior.' BGP protocol is most widely used for exterior routing protocols.

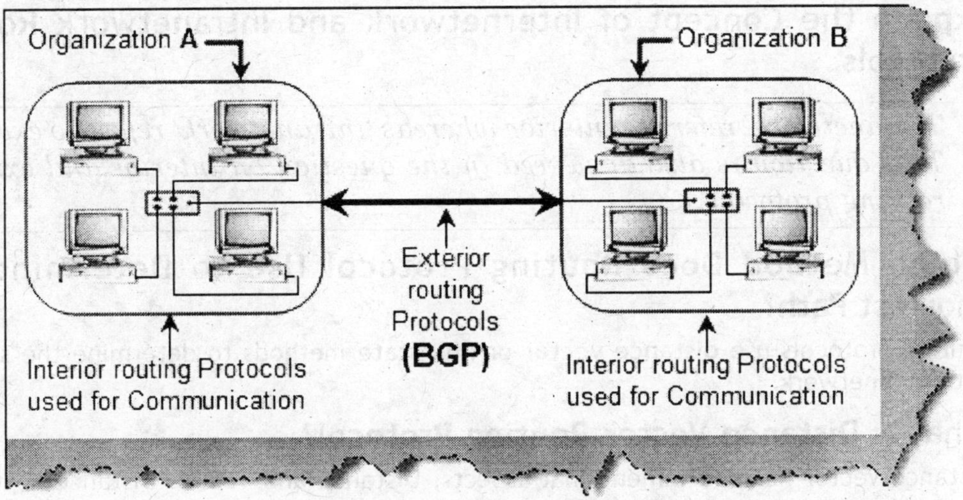

Figure: Classification of Routing Protocol

Figure 'Classifications of Routing Protocol' shows protocols used for interior and exterior protocols.

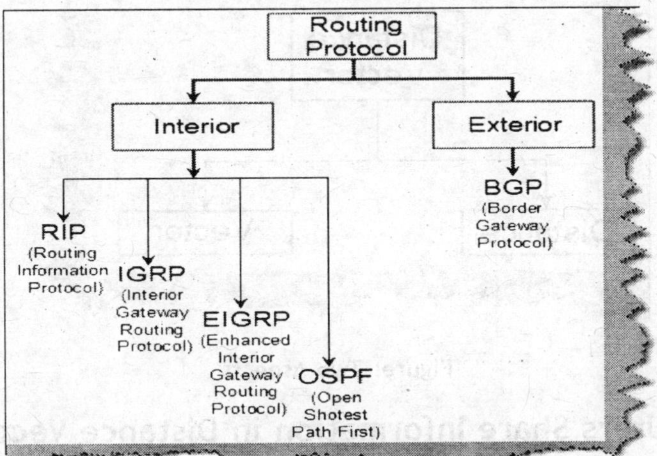

Figure: Interior and Exterior Routing Protocols

(l) Explain the Concept of Intradomain and Interdomain Routing Protocols.

Note: *'Intradomain' refers to interior routing protocol, whereas 'interdomain' to exterior routing protocol. Refer to the previous question for the answer to this one.*

(I) Explain the Concept of Internetwork and Intranetwork Routing Protocols.

> ***Note:*** *'Intranetwork' refers to interior whereas 'intranetwork' refers to exterior. This question is also answered in the question on interior and exterior routing protocols.*

(I) Which Method Does Routing Protocol Use to Determine the Shortest Path?

Routing protocols use **distance vector** or **link-state** methods to determine the shortest path in a network.

(B) What is Distance Vector Routing Protocol?

Distance vector has two dimensional aspects, Distance and Vector. Distance is the cost required to reach the destination host to which the packets are forwarded. Usually this distance is based on the number of hops. We will discuss the distance calculation in more detail in the coming questions. The second aspect Vector defines the next router where it should hop. Distance vector routing protocol works using these two aspects.

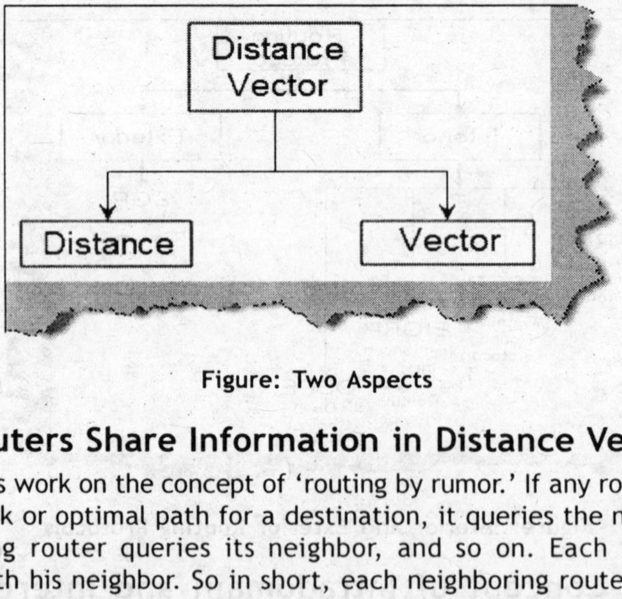

Figure: Two Aspects

(I) How do Routers Share Information in Distance Vector Routing?

Distance routers work on the concept of 'routing by rumor.' If any router wants information about a network or optimal path for a destination, it queries the neighboring router, and the neighboring router queries its neighbor, and so on. Each router shares routing information with his neighbor. So in short, each neighboring router receives information and then sends combined information to its neighboring router. As shown in the figure 'Distance Vector Protocol,' we can see how each router sends information to its adjacent router. In short, router A will take information from router B, and Router B from Router C.

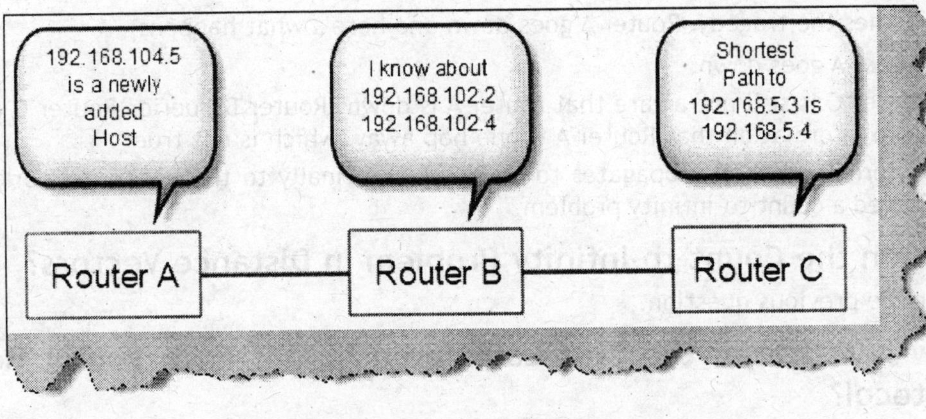

Figure: Distance Vector Protocol

(I) What is the Main Issue With Routing by Rumor?

Note: *In real life, we should never make conclusions on rumors. Any decision made on rumors is definitely harmful. Same hold for routing. Let's analyze the main issue with distance vector problem.*

Figure 'Distance Vector Problem' shows what the main issues with 'Distance Vector Problem' are. Consider a situation where we have four routers: Router A, Router B, Router C, and Router D. As said previously, 'Distance Vector' works on routing by rumor. So here's what happens:

- Router A communicates to B about itself.
- Router B gathers information based on what is said by Router A.
- Router C gathers information based on rumors sent by Router B. Router B communicates that Router A is two hops away from C. Router B updates his route table and updates the same information to router C.

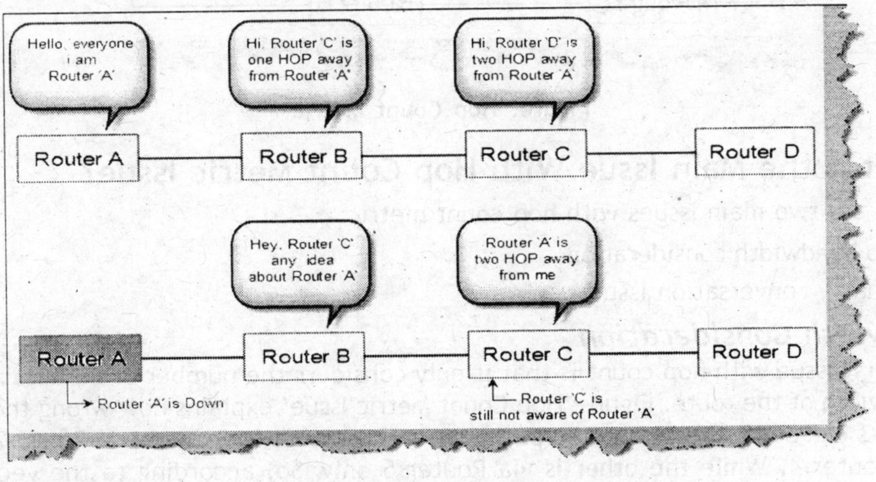

Figure: Distance Vector Problem

Now comes the tragedy, Router A goes down and here's what happens:

- Router A goes down.
- Router C is still not aware that router A is down. Router B queries Router C and gets stale information that Router A is one hop away, which is not true.

This information then propagates to Router D and finally to the entire network. This is also called a count-to-infinity problem.

(A) Explain the Count-to-Infinity Problem in Distance Vectors?

Refer the previous question.

(I) How is Metric or the Cost Calculated for Distance Vector Routing Protocol?

Distance vector uses hop count as the metric to decide the distance between the source and the destination. Hop count shows how many routers the packet needs to travel through to get to the destination. So, if there are three routers between the source and the destination, then the metric count will be 3. If we have two paths, then the routing protocol will pick up the shortest path depending on the hop count, i.e., the number of routers. In the figure 'Hop Count Metric,' we have three paths from Router A to Router I. Distance vector will use the path from Router B because it has only two hops, one is Router A itself and the second is Router B.

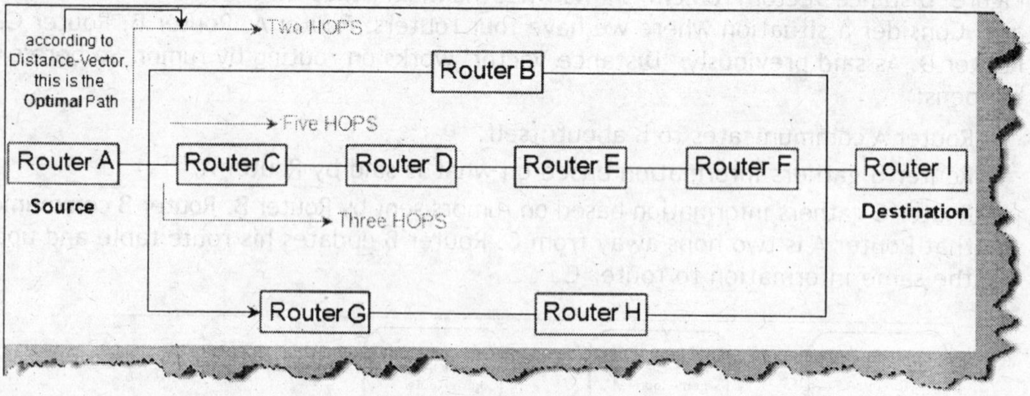

Figure: Hop Count Metric

(I) What is the Main Issue With Hop Count Metric Issue?

There are two main issues with hop count metric:

No bandwidth consideration.

Chatty conversation issue.

No Bandwidth Consideration

The first issue with hop count is that it only considers the number of metrics and not the bandwidth of the route. Figure 'Hop Count Metric Issue' explains how wrong the hop count metrics can be. Router 1 has two paths to reach destination, one is via Router2, Router 3, and Router 4, While the other is via Router 5 only. So, according to the vector routing protocol metric calculation, it will take the Router 5 router path because it has only two hop count while the first path has four hop counts. Till here everything is fine. But the path from Router2 to Router4 is the T1 line, and Router 5 is the 56 K line. The bandwidth of T1 is better (52 K.) So the number of hop metric will fail because the T1 line will have much better bandwidth than the 52 K line.

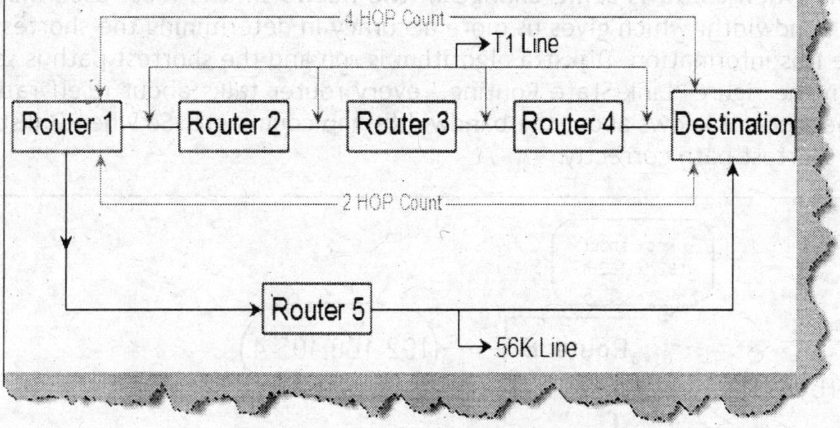

Figure: Hop Count Metric Issue

Chatty Conversation Issue

Even if we add factors like bandwidth in the metric, there are still problems. As we know, Distance Vector works on whispers and rumors, big networks becomes very chatty, which consumes a lot of network resources. Consider the figure 'Chatty Conversation Issue' where every router is broadcasting information. Consider a situation where we have a huge route table, this can be even more chaotic.

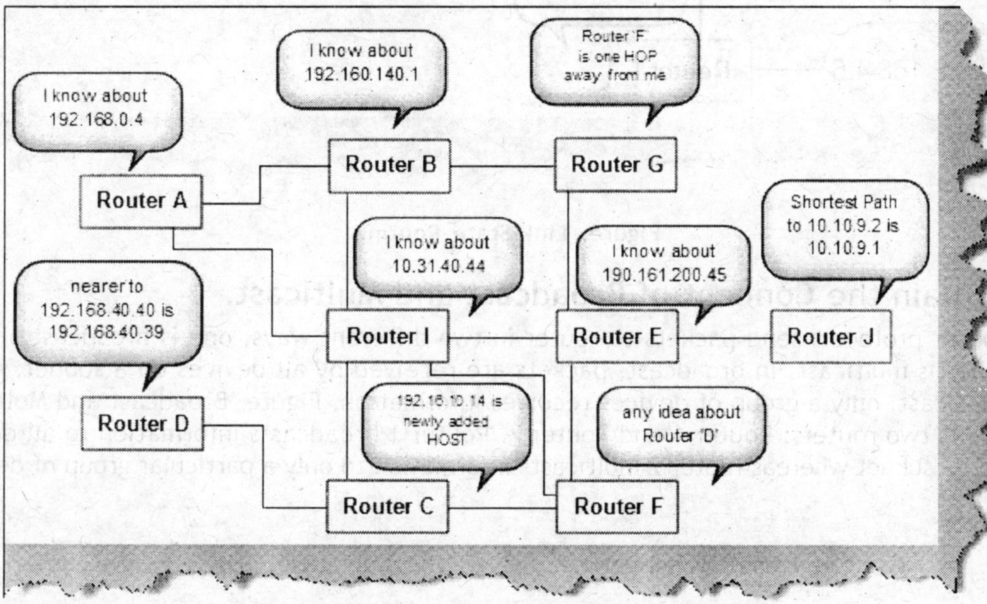

Figure: Chatty Conversation Issue

(I) Explain How Link-State Routing Protocols Work.

Link-state, unlike distance vector, does not rely on rumor information. It gets direct first-hand information from the router itself. This information is passed from router to router in form of LSA (Link-State Advertisements.) One more important point to note is **LSAs are sent only when there is some change in the network**. The most used metric for Link-State is bandwidth, which gives us more accuracy in determining the shortest path. Once we have this information, Dijkstra algorithm is run and the shortest path is sorted out. As shown in the figure 'Link-State Routing,' every router talks about itself rather than the entire network. It knows about the bandwidth, hop counts etc. So when Dijkstra is run, we get the shortest path correctly.

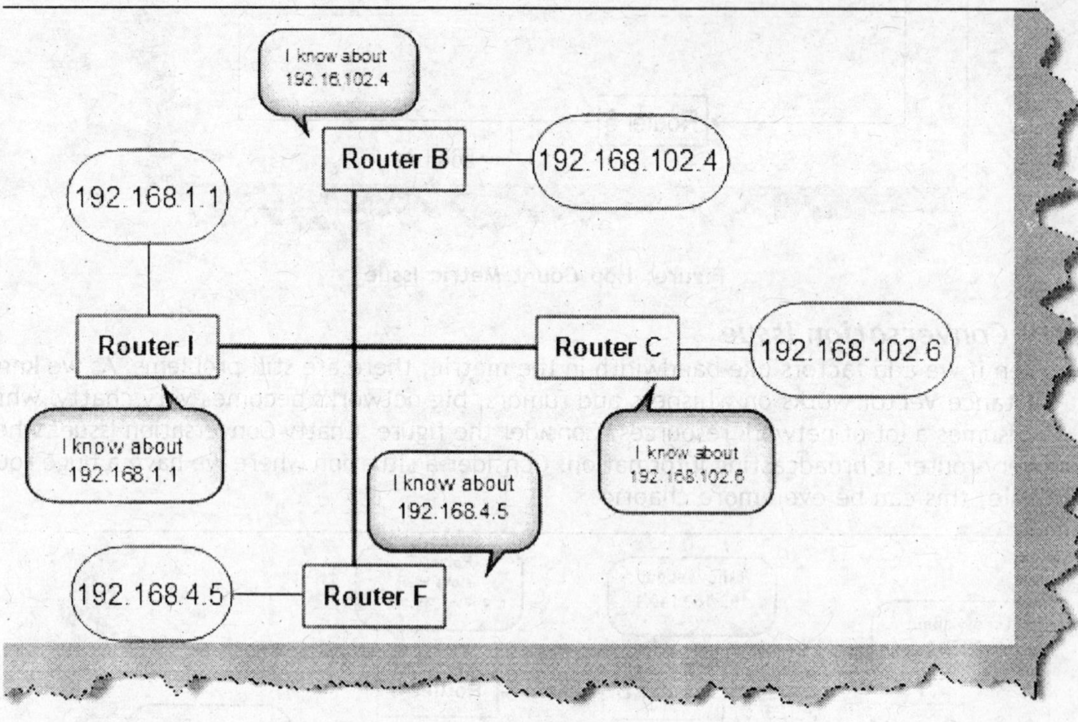

Figure: Link-State Routing

(B) Explain the Concept of Broadcast and Multicast.

Router protocols send packets to router in two different ways, one is broadcast and the other is multicast. In broadcast, packets are received by all devices on a subnet. And in multicast, only a group of devices receives information. Figure 'Broadcast and Multicast' shows two routers: Router 1 and Router 2. Router 1 broadcasts information to all devices in the subnet whereas router 2 multicasts information to only a particular group of devices.

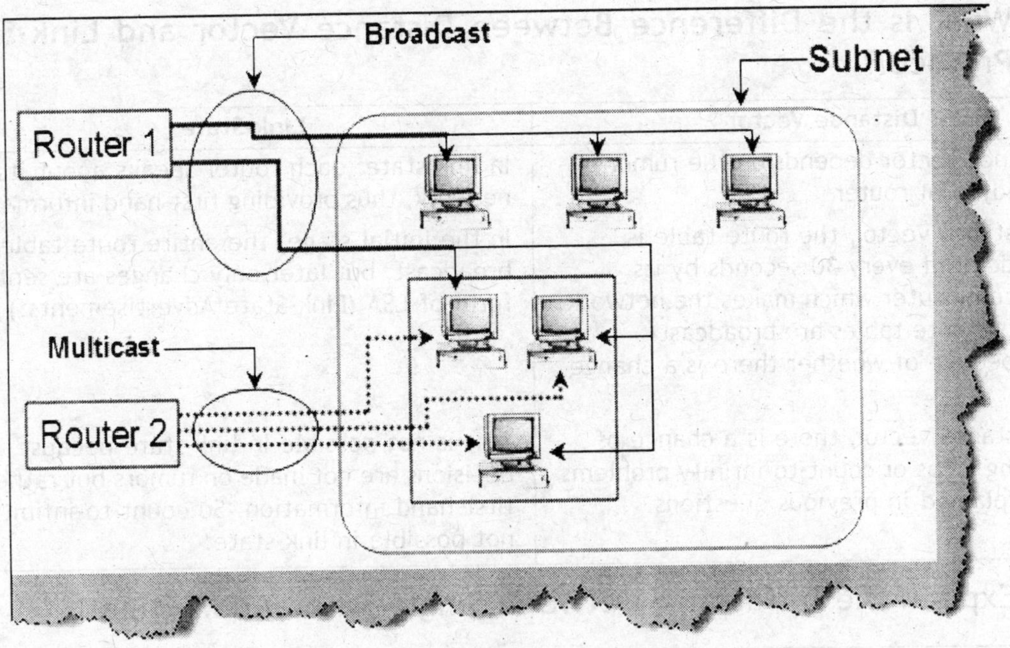

Figure: Broadcast and Multicast

(I) Which Protocol Falls in Distance vector and Which in Link-State?

Figure 'Protocol Classification' explains which protocol falls under Distance Vector and which falls under Link-State.

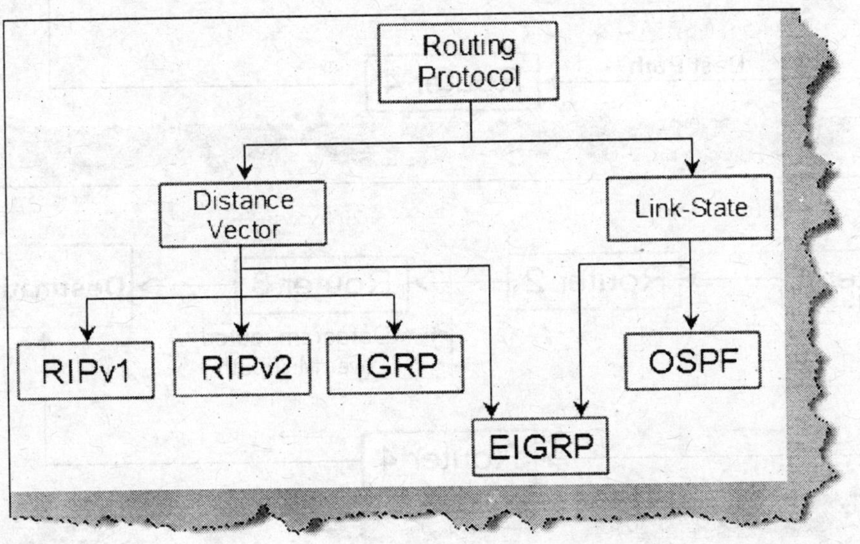

Figure: Protocol Classification

(I) What is the Difference Between Distance Vector and Link-State Protocol?

Distance Vector	Link-State
Distance vector depends on the rumor of the adjacent router.	In link state, each router speaks about its network, thus providing first-hand information.
In distance vector, the route table is broadcasted every 30 seconds by its adjacent router which makes the network chatty. Route tables are broadcast irrespective of whether there is a change or not.	In the initial stage, the entire route table is broadcast, but later only changes are sent in form of LSA (Link-State Advertisements.)
In distance vector, there is a chance of routing loops or count-to-infinity problems as explained in previous questions.	This is not possible in link-state because decisions are not made on rumors but rather on first-hand information. So count-to-infinity is not possible in link-state.

(I) Explain the Difference Between Single-Path and Multipath.

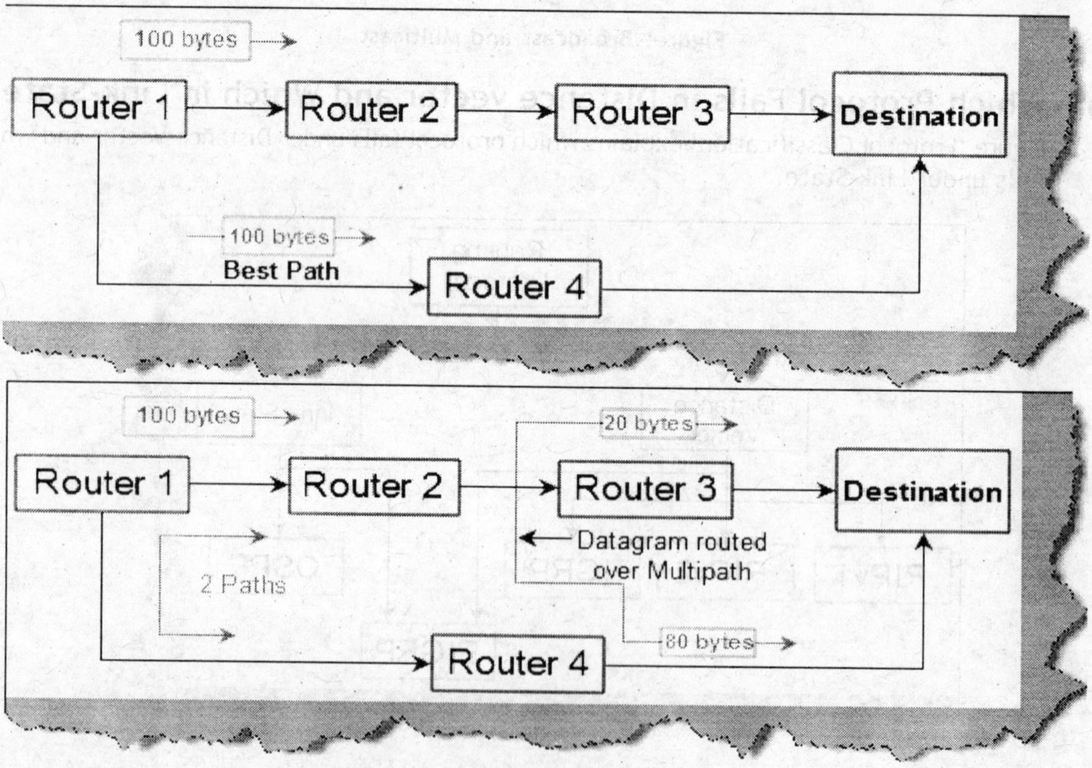

Figure: Single-Path and Multipath

When a router sends datagram packets to its destination, it can come across multiple paths.

Depending on the routing metric (which can be hop counts or bandwidth,) the router can make a choice of which path to use and transfer data on that path only. But in this situation, the complete data is passed only over the path which has less metric. This is called single-path. In multipath, also called multiplexing, the protocol does not choose one path but chooses to route datagrams over multiple paths, thus increasing network performance and reliability. This is called as multi-path or multiplexing. Figure 'Single-Path and Multipath' shows how they work. The first section of the figure shows that 100 bytes of data is divided over two paths with 20 bytes and 80 bytes each. The second section of the figure shows it used hop count metric and passed the data through one route over Router 4 path.

Figure 'Routing Methods' shows which protocol uses single-path and which multipath.

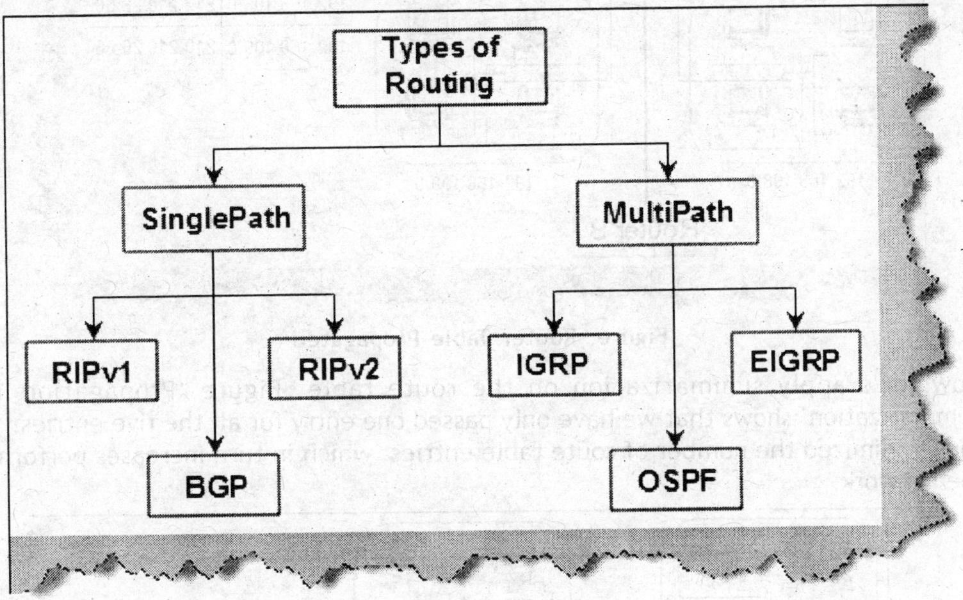

Figure: Routing Methods

(A) Explain Route Summarization.

Route summarization helps us reduce number of records in route tables. Even if the number of route table records is less, it still provides the path of all known networks. As the network becomes big, route table size also keeps on increasing. Imagine if big route tables have to be propagated across to different routers, how huge the task will be. Route summarization reduces the size to single route, which in turn refers to the path of multiple subnets. In short, summarization makes a summary of address tables for series of network addresses, thus reducing the size of route table. It is also called route aggregation because it summarizes group of routes into a single route.

(A) How are a Series of IPs Combined Into One Route Path in Route Summarization?

Let's take a sample network and try to understand how route summarization works. Consider the sample network in the figure 'Route table Propagated.' We have router A and Router B.

Router A is connected to 5 hosts. So router A propagates the following router table as shown in the figure with 5 hosts to router B.

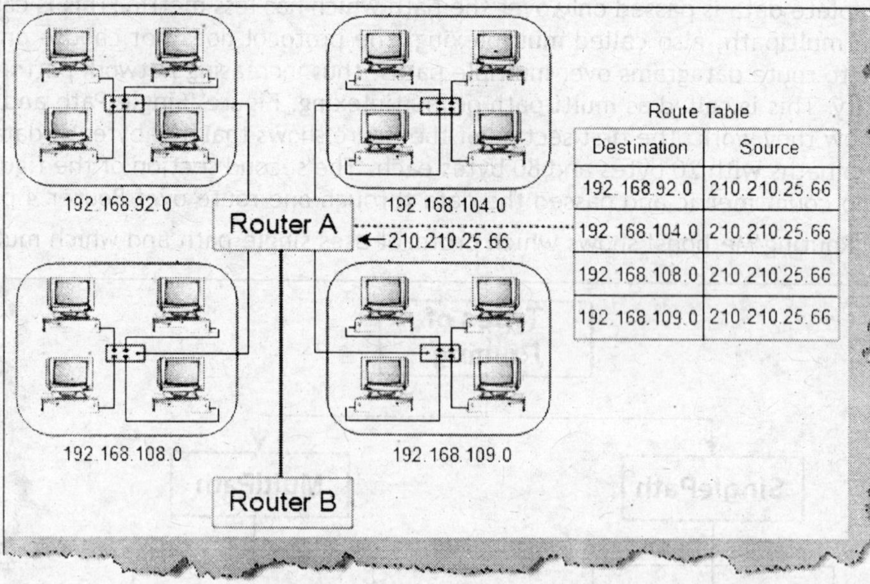

Figure: Router Table Propagated

Now let's apply summarization on the route table. Figure 'Propagation Through Summarization' shows that we have only passed one entry for all the five entries. We have thus minimized the number of route table entries, which in turn increases performance in the network.

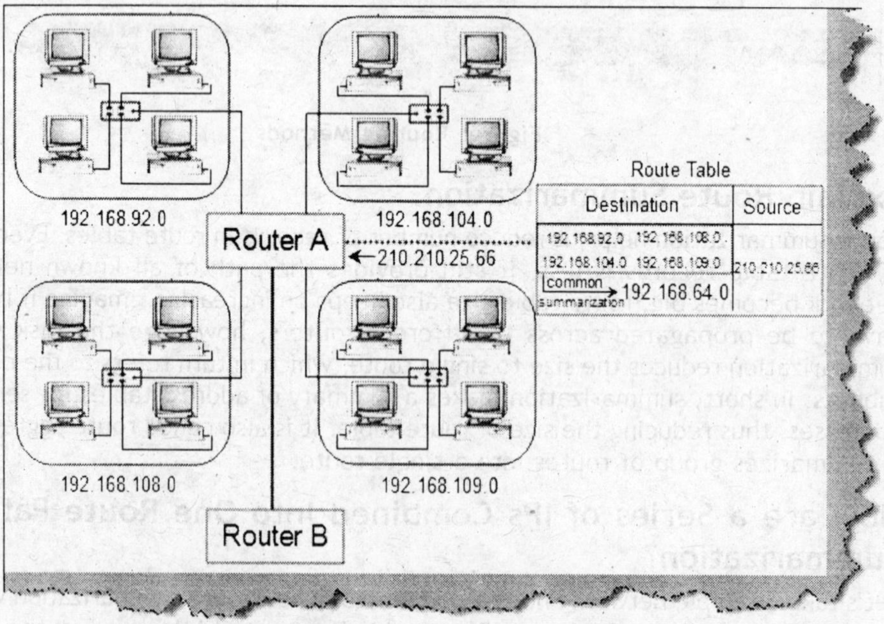

Figure: Propagation Through Summarization

Note: *Use the Calculator to convert from hexadecimal to binary, and vice versa.*

Now let's try to understand how route summarization actually works. We have tabularized the IPs in a table and converted the entire octet to binary as shown in the figure 'Route Summarization.' In order to summarize, we first need to take the common binary values from the octet. On the table, we have marked the common binary values with a rectangle. These common bits are taken, and the rest of the bits are marked zero. You can see in the figure that we have generated 192.168.64.0 from the common bits and the rest of the bits are marked zero. That means that this one IP summarizes all the IPs above.

common highest order bits

Address	1st Octet	2nd Octet	3rd Octet	4th Octet
192.168.92.0	11000000	10101000	1 011100	00000000
192.168.91.0	11000000	10101000	1 011011	00000000
192.168.101.0	11000000	10101000	1 100101	00000000
192.168.104.0	11000000	10101000	1 101000	00000000
192.168.108.0	11000000	10101000	1 101100	00000000
192.168.109.0	11000000	10101000	1 101101	00000000

summarized route

rest marked zero

192.168.64.0	11000000	10101000	1 000000	00000000

192.168.64.0 / 17

common bits

Figure: Route Summarization

(A) Explain RIP Protocol.

RIP stands for Routing Information Protocol. Below are some points you can revise for RIP from the interview point of view:

- It is a distance vector protocol and suited for small systems only. You can read about distance vector protocol in the previous questions.
- It uses hop count metrics for evaluating the network metrics. That means it evaluates how many routers are present on the current path and derives metrics accordingly. You can read more about hop count metric in the previous questions. RIP does not take into account bandwidth, reliability, load, and other factors.
- RIP has two versions RIP 1 and RIP 2. RIP 1 is a classful routing protocol and RIP 2 supports classless addressing network.
- In RIP 2, auto-summarization is set by default, but can be disabled manually. We can manually configure summarize subnet at any bit boundary.

- RIP 2 uses multicast to communicate with neighboring routers.
- CISCO implementation of RIP supports equal-cost multipath. But this support is only if the metric on both paths are the same. So on CISCO, if the metrics on two paths are the same, then equal packets are routed from both the paths.

Below is the command to set RIP on the router. You can also specify the version.

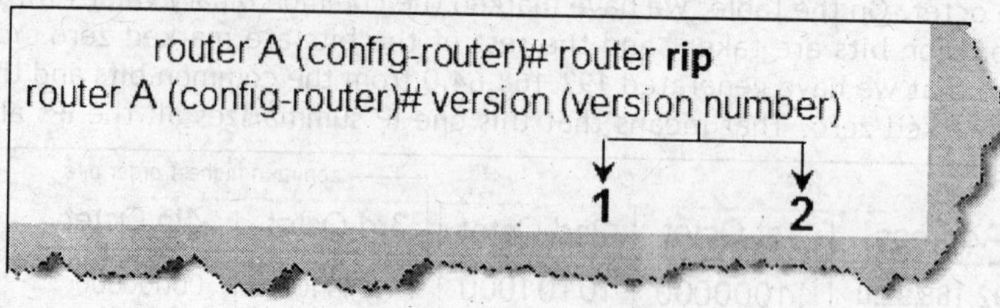

Figure: Set RIP Version

If you want to configure RIP using the network IP, then the command used is:

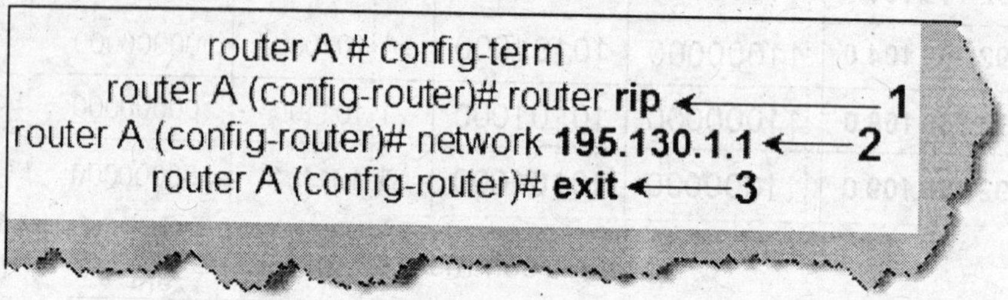

Figure: Configure RIP

Note:	*The points given above can be useful from the interview point of view. So just understand the concepts, these can be useful at any point of time.*

(A) How is Route Table Populated by RIP Protocol?

In RIP, when the first time router boots, it has knowledge only about the directly connected networks or static routes. So, in the first boot, only those networks are registered in their own route table entries. Figure 'First Boot' shows how the route tables are flourished. We have three routers in the network: Router A, Router B, and Router C. They are connected to 192.168.10.0, 192.168.20.0, and 192.168.30.0, respectively. In the same figure ,'First Boot,' we have also shown the route tables. You can see how only the networks directly connected are known to them.

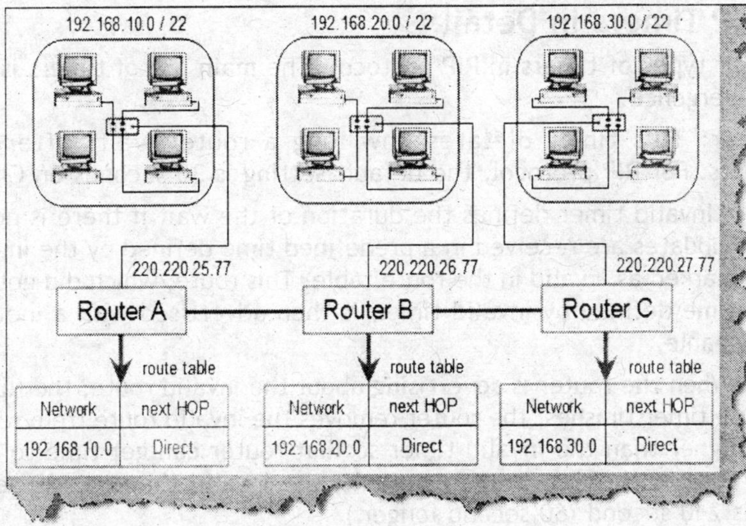

Figure: First Boot

After some time, Router A sends its route table entries to Router B. Figure 'Advertised Route' shows how the route table of Route B gets filled. Similarly all the route table entries are flourished and the network is updated about all the hosts in the network and their route.

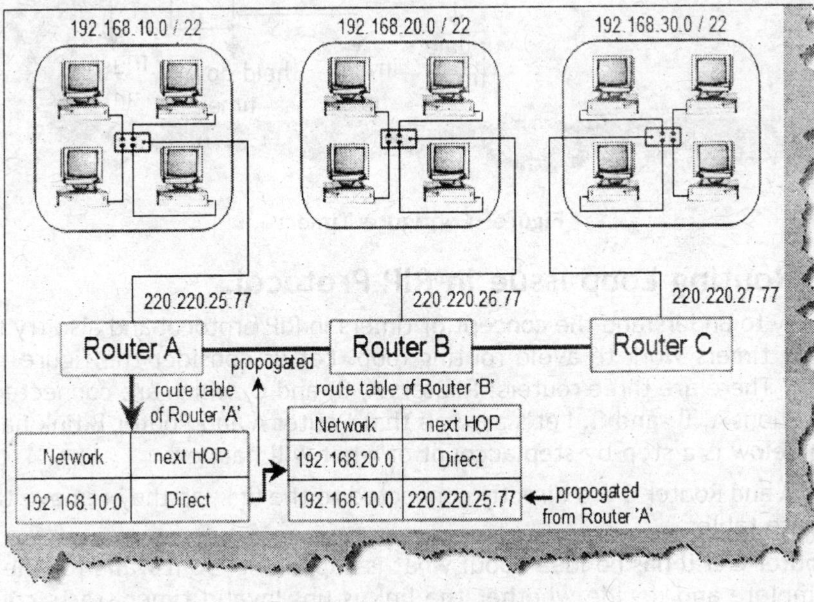

Figure: Advertised Route

(B) Explain Convergence in Networks.

Convergence is the time needed for all routers in a network to learn about all routes in the network. When all routers are updated with same route table information, then the network is called a converged, or a normalized, network.

(I) Explain RIP Timers in Detail.

There are four types of timers in RIP protocol. The main use of timers is to see how RIP manages convergence.

Update timer: This timer dictates how long a router waits after sending route advertisements. For RIP protocol, the default setting is 30 seconds on CISCO routers.

Invalid timer: Invalid timer defines the duration of the wait if there is no response from a route. If no updates are received in a predefined time defined by the invalid timer, then that route is marked as invalid in the route table. This route, which did not provide update in the given time defined by invalid timer, is then advertised with a metric of 16 which means unreachable.

Flush timer: When the router is advertising about the invalid route, the flush timer starts. When the flush timer finishes, the router removes the invalid route from route table. Flush timer is set higher than the invalid timer so that router can get time to advertise about the invalid route to the network. By default, the invalid timer is 180 seconds, and the flush timer is 240 second (60 second longer.)

Hold-Down timer: This timer is explained in the coming questions

The figure below shows the command to configure timer values on the router command prompt.

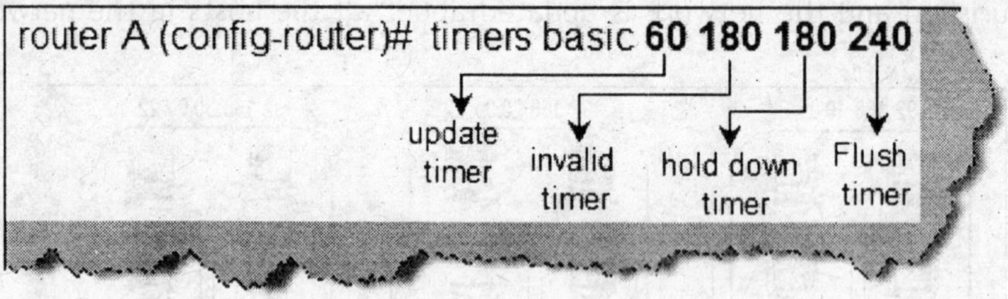

Figure: Configure Timers

(B) Explain Routing Loop Issue in RIP Protocol.

Let's first try to understand the concept of timers in RIP protocol and also try to understand how routing timers work to avoid routing loop. Let us consider the figure 'Routing Loop Issue in RIP.' There are three routers: Routers A, B, and C, which are connected to networks of organizations A, B, and C. Let's assume that Router A and Router B link has gone down. Explained below is a step-by-step account of what will happen:

- Router A and Router B are directly connected to the link, so they remove the entry from the route tables.
- But router C still has no idea about what is happening. So it waits for the invalid timer to complete and decide whether the link is up. Invalid timer starts counting, which means that if router C does not get any updates for 180 seconds it will mark this router as invalid and the route will be advertised as unreachable with a 16 metric.
- The routes will be advertised as unreachable until the flush timer expires. Once the flush timer expires, this route will be removed from the route table.

The same principle is explained in the figure below. We have published the route tables of individual router in this figure. You can see how with the direct link Routers A and B have removed the entries from the route table, but Router C is still not aware of the changes. Router C then uses the invalid and the flush timer fundamentals to know that the route link between A and B is down.

Ok, now where is the loop? Route B thinks that the way to Router A is through Router C. Router C still thinks that the way to Router A is through Router B. In short, the data keeps moving to and fro between Router B and Router C which leads to routing loop.

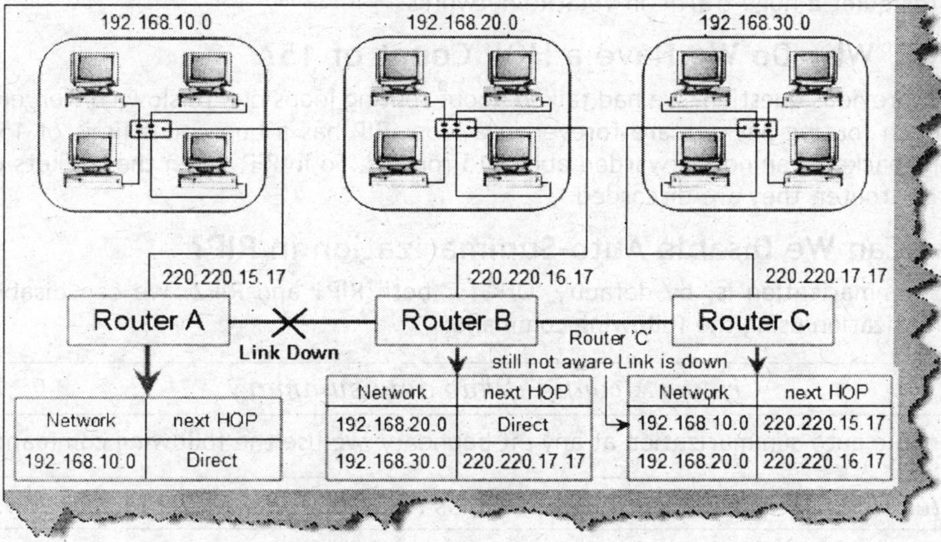

Figure: Routing Loop Issue in RIP

(A) How Can We Avoid Routing Loop Issue in RIP?

Given below are the different techniques that can be used to avoid routing loop:

Hold-Down timer: After a route is added, updated, or deleted in the route table, any updates regarding the route will be applied only after the hold-down timer expires. Until then, all updates are ignored. The default for hold-down timer is 180 seconds. So if the network is changing rapidly, this helps a lot. Let's take the network scenario given in the previous question. When the link came down, Router C propagated wrong or stale information to B. If Router B, after changing the status, did not take updates from Router C, things would have been different. This would have given enough time for Router B to propagate information back to Router C thus avoiding confusion and routing loops. Hold-down timer is not a foolproof solution, but we can avoid loops to a great extent.

Split horizon: In split horizon, we never advertise the route back to the source from where you learnt it. In short, in figure 'Routing Loop Issue in RIP' (please refer to the previous question) Router C should never advertise back to Router B. This would avoid the confusion that we had previously, and thus avoid loop back routing issue. Split horizon can be an issue because it can prevent propagation of routes on the network. If networks are attached to one single central router and if the routers do not update back to the logical network it can create issues.

If you do not want split horizon, use the command given below:

```
routerA(config-ip)#{no} ip split-horizon
```

Trigger updates: Trigger updates speed up convergence by propagating network changes instantly and not waiting for the update timer to notify. So as soon as there is a network change, such as, link down or new router added, trigger updates force the router to send the new route information to the other routers instantly. But the downside is that this creates quiet a huge traffic in volatile networks.

(A) In RIP, Why Do We Have a HOP Count of 15?

In the previous question, we had talked about routing loops due to slow convergence, due to which routing packets are forever in a loop. RIP has a hop count limit of 15, which means packets can not forwarded above 15 routers. So in RIP, when the packets come to the 16th router, they are discarded.

(I) How Can We Disable Auto-Summarization in RIP?

Auto-summarization is, by default, 'ON' for both RIP1 and RIP2. We can disable auto-summarization using the following command:

```
routerA(config-if)#no auto-summary
```

To enable auto-summarization at any bit boundary, we use the following command:

```
routerA(config-ip)#ip summary-address rip 192.168.101.0 255.255.255.0
```

(I) Explain IGRP.

IGRP stands for Interior Gateway Protocol. Below are some points to be noted during interview for IGRP:

- It was introduced to remove issues in RIP like hop count limitation and better metric system.
- It's a CiSCO proprietary protocol.
- IGRP uses bandwidth and delay to computer metric. This was one of the main reasons of introducing IGRP because RIP used hop count which can give misleading metrics.
- IGRP supports classful IP address. So it does not support subnet masking.
- It's a distance vector protocol.
- IGRP supports multipath facility.
- IGRP can transport data either by using broadcast or Unicast methodology. By default, IGRP uses broadcast to send packets but it can be configured for unicast as well.
- IGRP can also be configured for maximum HOP counts which can prevent routing loop issue.
- In CISCO, implementation of RIP multipath is done by using equal cost. So on CISCO implementation of RIP, if metrics on two paths are the same, then equal packets are routed from both the paths. But the multipath is implemented only if the metrics on both the paths are same. IGRP has an improvement over RIP in that it provided unequal-

cost multipath routing. That means even if we have unequal metrics, the packets are still routed on both paths.

Auto summarization is by default and can not be forcibly disabled or enabled.

(I) How Does IGRP Work?

IGRP works on the same fundamentals of RIP because it's a distance vector protocol. IGRP sends route table updates periodically to its neighboring route.

(I) How Many Timers Does IGRP Have?

IGRP timers are same as RIP, only that the values are different. So the fundamentals remain same, only the value changes. The table below shows these values:

Table: IGRP Timer Values

TIMER	RIP (Seconds)	IGRP(Seconds)
Update timer	30	90
Flush timer	240	630
Invalid timer	180	270
Hold-down timer	180	280

One of the important points to be noted is the value of the timers. The IGRP timer has more values than RIP, so IGRP is less chatty than RIP.

Note: *In IGRP, split horizon and poison reverse fundamentals remain the same. So, if the interviewer asks split horizon and poison reverse in context of IGRP, the answers remain same as those for RIP.*

(I) How Does IGRP Calculate Metric?

As mentioned in the previous question, IGRP uses bandwidth and delay to calculate metric. IGRP has cryptic formulae by which it calculates metric; we will try to understand how the formula is derived.

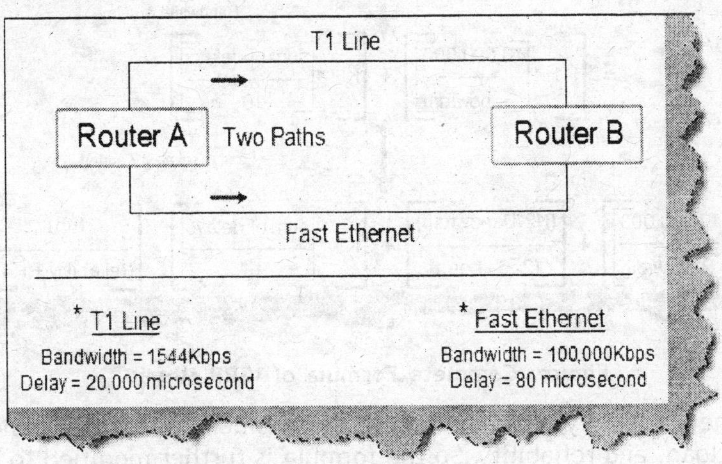

Figure: Two Paths For a Router

Let's consider the figure which has two paths, one path is the T1 line and other is on fast ethernet. T1 line has a bandwidth of 1544 kbps and delay of 20000 microseconds, and the other path is on fast ethernet with 100,000 kbps bandwidth and 80 microseconds delay.

So let's understand how IGRP will calculate metrics. We will go step by step to understand the IGRP metric formula. Once we understand the formula we will apply the same to the above network.

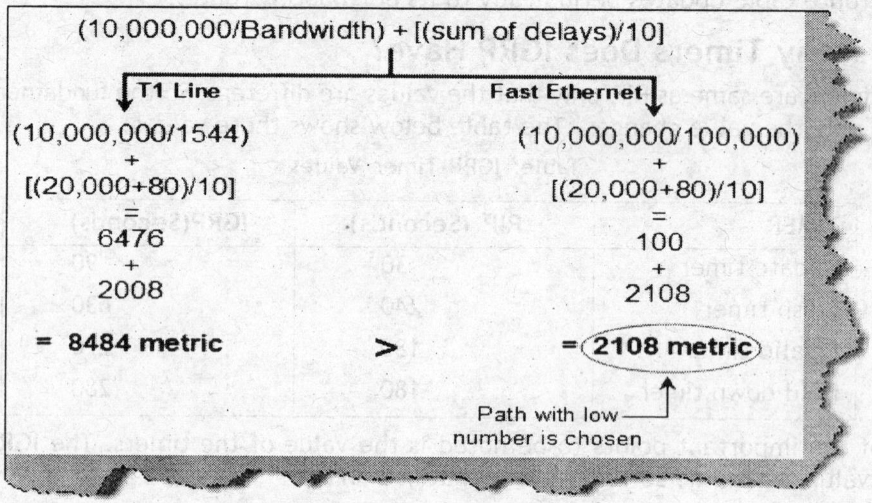

Figure: Calculating Metric

The basic formula is as shown below and we have substituted the values and calculated the same for both the paths. The lowest metric path is chosen, so for this scenario fast ethernet path is considered at the top priority.

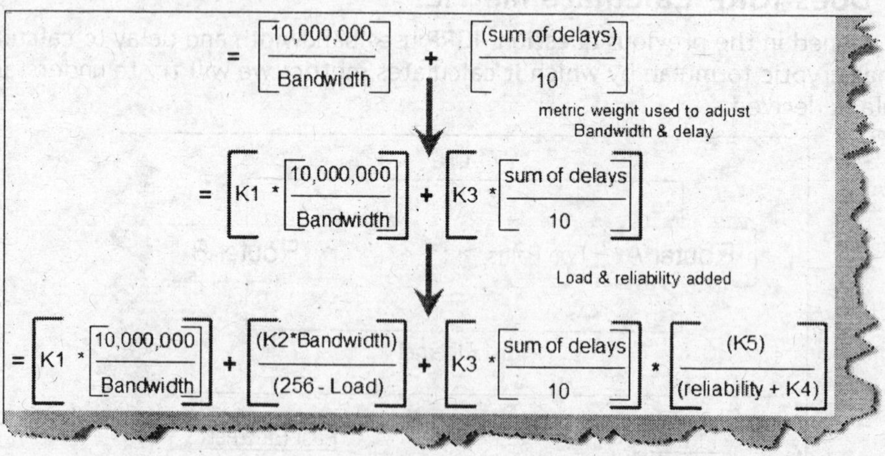

Figure: Complete Formula of IGRP Metric

The above metric is very basic and does not consider factors like bandwidth and delay adjustment, load, and reliability. So the formula is further modified to adjust bandwidth and delay. You can see from the figure 'Complete Formula of IGRP Metric' how the formula is further modified. To adjust bandwidth and delay, two variables are included: one is K1 and the other is K3. So by adjusting these variables we can change bandwidth and delay. K1 and K3 are equal to 1 if you do not want to do any adjustments. But again, we have still not considered load and reliability factors.

So the formula is further improvised using K2 and K5. If we do not want these factors to be considered, then values for K2 and K5 are zero. By using the metric command, we can configure k1, k2, k3, k4, and k5 values. Figure 'Configure IGRP Metric' shows how the command maps to the formula.

(I) Can Multiple Instances of IGRP Run On One Physical Router?

In IGRP, we can run multiple instances of routing process on a single router. In short, each routing process has different route tables. It is identified by autonomous numbers which uniquely identify instances. The figure shows how route tables are maintained in the same physical router for two different instances.

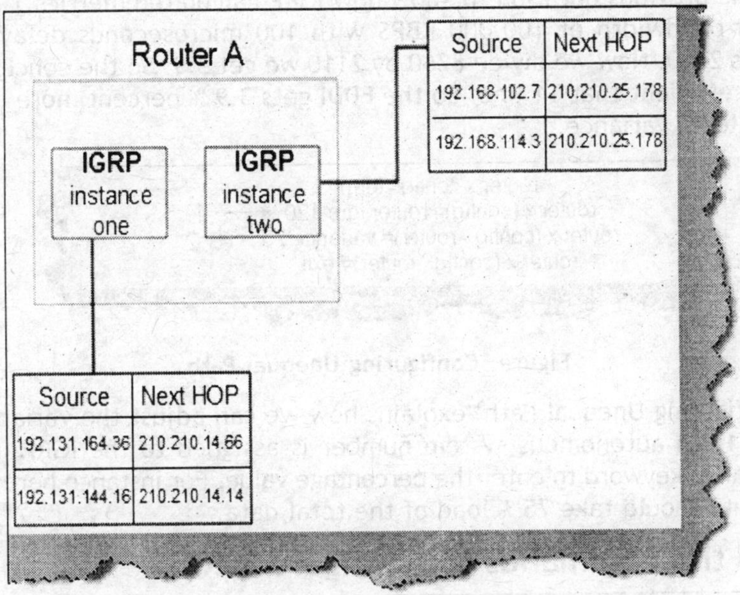

Figure: Multiple Instances

(I) How is Load Balancing Done in IGRP?

As mentioned in the previous question, IGRP supports multipath and unequal cost routing. This means that it can send packets over routes with unequal route cost. But there is a way by which the packets are distributed over the paths.

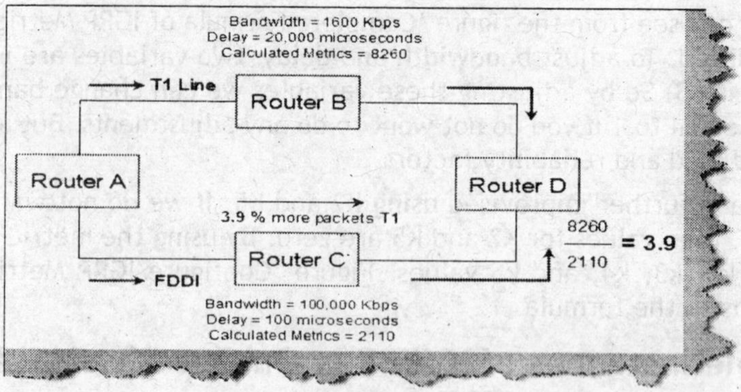

Figure: Variance

Consider the figure 'Variance,' it has two paths: one path has T1 line and the other FDDI. T1 has a bandwidth of 1600 bandwidth and delay of 20,000 microseconds, so the metric is 8260 (see the previous question to know how IGRP calculated metrics.) The second path, FDDI, has a bandwidth of 100,000 KBPS with 100 microseconds delay, so the metrics calculated is 2100. Now we divide 8260 by 2110 we get 3.9. So the conclusion is that FDDI is 3.9 times efficient that T1 line. So the FDDI gets 3.9 % percent more load than T1. 3.9 % is also called a variance.

```
router x config - term
router x (config)# router igrp 120 ←— 1
router x (config - router)# variance 75 ←— 2
router x (config - router)# exit
```

Figure: Configuring Unequal Path

Figure 'Configuring Unequal Path' explains how we can adjust the variance factor on the router.Step 1: An autonomous system number is assigned to the IGRP instance. Step 2: Use the variance keyword to enter the percentage value. For instance here we have entered that this route should take 75 % load of the total data.

(B) What are the Commands to Configure IGRP?

```
router x (config)# router igrp 150 ←—— 1
router x (config - router)# network 192.168.1.0 ←—2
router x (config - router)# passive - interface fast ethernet 0 ←—3
router x (config - router)# exit ←——— 4
```

Figure: Commands to Configure IGRP

Figure 'Commands to Configure IGRP' shows how IGRP is configured on a CISCO router. We will understand the commands step by step.

Step 1: This line enables IGRP with an autonomous system number of 150. If you look at the previous question, we had said that we can have multiple instances of IGRP on a single hardware router. This number helps us to identify the instance uniquely.

Step 2: Here we add the network which needs IGRP advertisements.

Step 3: In this step, we suppress the advertisements on the fast ethernet interface.

Step 4: We are done with the configuration and exit the command prompt.

> **Note:** *One of the differences in command as compared to RIP is that in IGRP we assign autonomous system numbers. This helps IGRP isolate instances and maintain different route tables for every instance.*

> **Note:** *Adjusting timer values , split horizon commands, and concepts remain same as for RIP.*

(I) Explain EIGRP.

EIGRP stands for 'Enhanced Interior Gateway Routing Protocol.' Given below are some points for EIGRP:

- It's a Cisco proprietary protocol and only available on Cisco routers. It's the most widely used protocol.
- Support classless networks.
- It's an interior protocol as the name suggests.
- It is hybrid of distance and link state.
- Bandwidth and delay is used to calculate metric.
- Supports multipath routing. EIGRP has the ability to use equal and unequal cost for multipath routing.
- Summarization can be done on bit boundary which allows more flexibility.
- There is not hop count limitation as we had for RIP protocol.

(I) What Does Neighbor Terminology Mean in EIGRP?

A Router which is sharing a network link with other routers is called a neighbor.

(I) What are the Different Types of Packets in EIGRP?

There are five types of packets in EIGRP; we will try to understand these packets one by one.

Hello Packets: This is used to discover and maintain neighbors. Hello packets are multicast which help discover neighbors. Hello packets contain IP addresses of the sending router. Hello packets are sent every 5 second on high speed bandwidth, whereas on low speed bandwidths, they are sent every 30 seconds. If a router does not get a hello packet update, it considers the neighbor as invalid.

Update Packets: These packets are used to update routing information. Topology tables are passed in the update packets. Update packets are sent in two scenarios, first when the neighbor establishes information, and second when there is a change in the network.

Query and Reply Packets: If a route is lost, then query packets are sent to neighbors to ask whether they know about the lost route. Neighbors reply back for query packets with reply packets.

ACK Packets: These packets do not have data. They are used to acknowledge packets that are sent by RTP (Reliable Transport Protocol.)

(I) How Does EIGRP Protocol Update Route Information to its Neighbors?

EIGRP does not periodically transmit the entire route table to its neighbor like RIP does. EIGRP transports information only two times, first when the routers exchange information and second when there is an update in the network. This is one of the marked improvements in link-state over distance vector. EIGRP has incorporated this good quality, thus making marked improvements over RIP and IGRP.

(B) What is the Concept of Successor in EIGRP?

The route with lowest metric from the source to the destination is called a successor. We can have more than one successor if the multipath is enabled on EIGRP.

(B) What is DUAL in EIGRP?

DUAL, which stands for Diffusing Update Algorithm, performs route calculations and assured route free from routing loops by performing feasibility test.

(I) Explain Reported Distance (RD,) Feasibility Distance (FD,) and Feasibility Condition (FC).

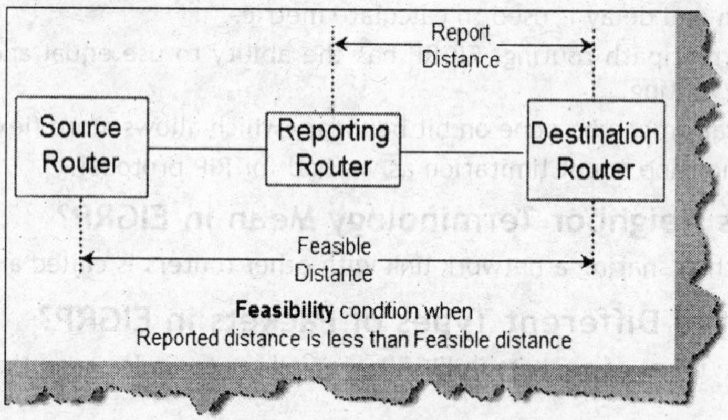

Figure: RD, FD, and FC

In EIGRP, a router gets information about route metrics from his neighboring router. The metric of the route from the reporting neighbor to the destination router is called **Reported Distance** or **Advertised Distance.**

In order to get a clear picture, the figure 'RD, FD, and FC' shows three routers. Source router learns from the reporting router. Reporting router sends metric values from it to the destination router. The metric between reporting router and destination router is the reported distance.

Feasible Distance is the overall metric from the current router to the destination router. In short, it includes reported distance metric plus metrics from source router to reporting router.

When metrics of a route's reported distance is less than feasible distance, we say that the route has met the **feasibility condition**. The route which meets the feasibility condition is either installed or kept as a stand-by route.

(I) Explain the Concept of Successor and Feasible Successor?

The route which has the lowest metric is called successor. Routers can have multiple successors if multipath is enabled. Routes which meets feasibility condition but are kept as backup are called feasible successors. Routes with a lower metric are installed as backup. Feasible successors are installed on the topology table (we will be covering this fundamental soon,) when the successor fails, the feasible successor takes over.

(I) Explain Passive and Active Route States.

When a route is operating normally, it is in a **passive state**. Now, when the route becomes invalid, DUAL comes in to action and goes through the topology table to get a feasible successor. If no feasible successor is found, the route goes into an **active state** and DUAL starts computing by sending query packets to other routers to find a replacement path.

(I) What is SIA or 'Stuck-in-Active?'

If no replies are received regarding an active route, the route is considered to be in the SIA mode.

(I) How do Packets and Timers Work in EIGRP?

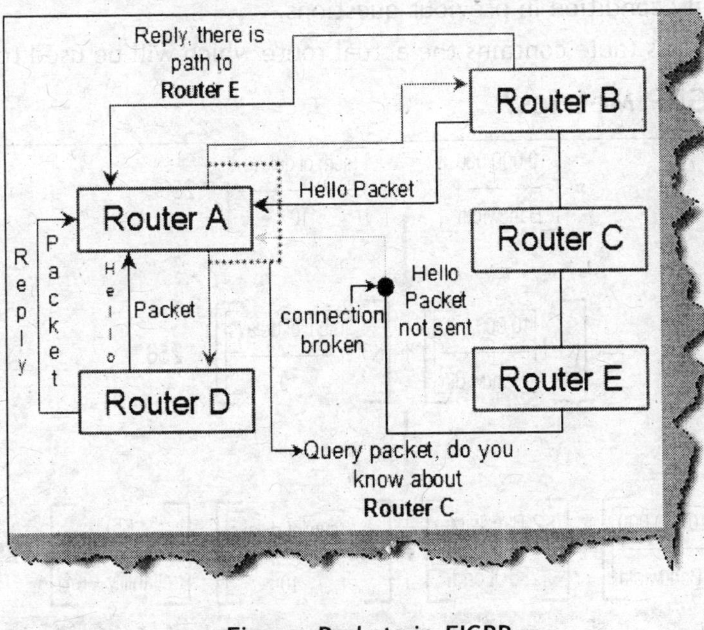

Figure: Packets in EIGRP

Neighbors are discovered by multicasting of HELLO packets. HELLO packets contain IP addresses of the sending router. If it is a high speed T1 line, then HELLO packets are sent in every 5 seconds and if it is a low speed line, then it's sent every 60 seconds. As said, HELLO packets are multicast, which reduces network resource wastage.

Figure 'Packets in EIGRP' shows how the HELLO packets communicate. You can see Router B, Router C, and Router D are sending continuous HELLO packets to Router A. Now for some reason, the link between Router C and Router A goes off. That means Router C is not able to send HELLO packets to Router A. So now, the hold-timer starts counting. Every time a router sends a HELLO packet the hold timer is reset, thus ensuring that it is a valid route.

In this scenario, because the link is broken, Router C is not able to send packets. So after the hold timer expires, neighbor router C is invalidated. Router A now sends reply query packets to other neighbors asking if they know any other way in which it can contact router C. Neighbors responds with a reply packet either suggesting a route or saying that 'they have no idea about any other route to Router C.' Router B responds with a reply packet stating it knows about that there is a route through Router E. DUAL algorithm is then run to see if it meets the feasibility condition. We have already defined feasibility condition in previous questions. If its meets the feasibility condition, it uses the route.

(I) What are the Different Tables Used in EIGRP?

We have three tables in EIGRP:

Neighbor tables: This is the first table that is flourished. It contains all the neighbors that the router is aware of.

Topology tables: This contains only routes which meet feasibility conditions. Please read about feasibility condition in previous questions.

Route tables: This table contains the actual route which will be used to forward traffic.

(I) Explain EIGRP Metrics?

$$= \left[\frac{10{,}000{,}000}{\text{Bandwidth}}\right] + \left[\frac{(\text{sum of delays})}{10}\right] * 256$$

$$= \left[K1 * \left[\frac{10{,}000{,}000}{\text{Bandwidth}}\right] + K3 * \left[\frac{\text{sum of delays}}{10}\right]\right] * 256$$

$$= \left[K1 * \left[\frac{10{,}000{,}000}{\text{Bandwidth}}\right] + \left[\frac{(K2 * \text{Bandwidth})}{(256 - \text{Load})}\right] + K3 * \left[\frac{\text{sum of delays}}{10}\right]\right] * \left[\frac{(K5)}{(\text{reliability} + K4)}\right] * 256$$

Figure: EIGRP Metric

EIGRP metric is same as IGRP. The only difference is that it's scaled up by multiplying with 256. This is done to add granularity to the metric.

(I) Explain How EIGRP Finds its Successor and Feasible Successor.

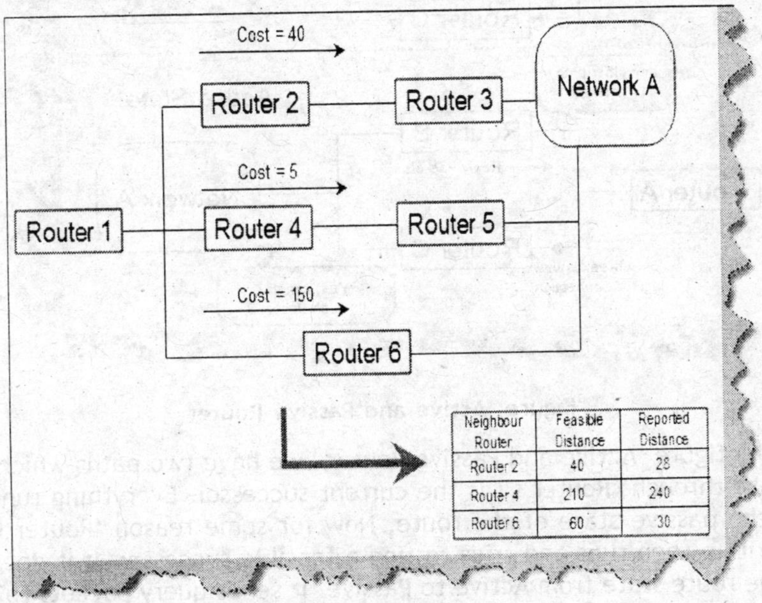

Figure: EIGRP in Action

Let's understand how EIGRP figures out its successor and feasible successor by a sample example. Consider the figure 'EIGRP in Action" where router 1 has to send connect to 'Network A.' It has three paths, one through 'Router 2,' second 'Router four,' and third 'Router 6.' We have also given the cost of all the router paths. EIGRP checks for the low-cost path which is through router 4.

So EIGRP registers router 4 as the successor path to 'Network A.' But there are other paths also from which we can choose feasible successor for backup. In order that the path needs to be registered in the topology table as feasible successor, the reported distance of the path should be less than the current successor's feasible distance. Current successor is 'Router 2' with a feasible distance of 40. Reported distance of router 6 is less than the feasible distance of 'Router 2,' which makes it a feasible successor. Reported distance of 'Router 4' is greater than the feasible distance of Router 2, which means it does not meet the feasible condition and is not considered as a feasible successor. So now, when route path of Router 2 comes down, Router 6 will be used as a back-up route path. If Router 4 path goes down, then DUAL will come in to action. It evaluates both the paths using feasibility condition and considers Router 6 as the back-up router and makes it a successor.

(I) Explain Active and Passive Routes.

Active and Passive are state of a route. When DUAL algorithm in EIGRP does not find any feasible successor, it changes the state of the route from passive to active. A route becomes active when the algorithm is not able to find any replacement, so it turns up to the neighbor routers for any other path.

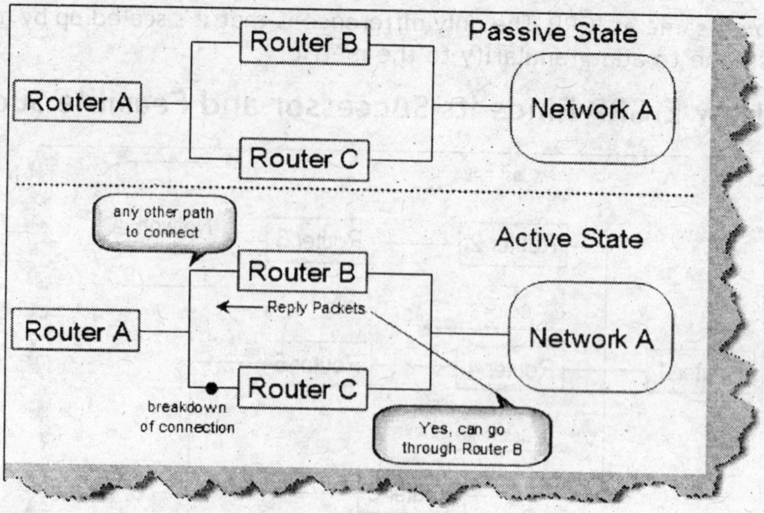

Figure: Active and Passive Router

Consider the figure 'Active and Passive Router,' we have two paths which go to 'Network A.' The path through 'Router C' is the current successor. Everything running normally is called as the passive state of the route. Now for some reason 'Router C' comes down. DUAL algorithm then runs and tries to find a feasible successor. If it does not get any, it changes the route state from Active to Passive. It sends query packets to the neighboring routers, i.e., Router 'B,' if it knows about any path. Router 'B' then sends reply packets saying that there is a path from Router 'B.' DUAL then considers this path and makes it a current successor.

> ***Note:*** *We are not covering EIGRP commands as they are very much the same as the previous IGRP. Please refer to CISCO documentation for the same.*

(I) Explain OSPF

OSPF, which stands for 'Open Shortest Path First,' is used for large networks. Below are some points which you should note for OSPF during interviews:

- OSPF was introduced to overcome the shortcomings of RIP, such as, 15 hop count limitation, CIDR support , routing loop issues, and sluggish convergence
- It's an open standard and widely used. As it is an open standard runs mostly on all platforms.
- It scalable protocol and can be used on very large networks.
- It as interior protocol and uses link state for building up routing protocol.
- OSPF sends data over multipaths.
- Uses multicast for sending data.
- OSPF supports classless IP addressing scheme.
- OSPF supports hierarchical routing.

(I) How Does OSPF Populate Route Tables?

OSPF is a link-state routing protocol. Som one of the biggest differences is that it does not share information about it neighbors. It only says about its own route and not about others. So it only tells about its own network which it is aware about and not of others. Every router maintains its own link-state database. As said earlier, every router advertises its own route information to his neighbors. These advertisements are called link-state advertisements. Every router maintains its own link-state database. When the network is converged (in the previous section you can see what convergence means,) LSA database of all routers are same.

Once the router is fully loaded, SPF (Shortest Path First) is run on the individual LSA database. Once the SPF algorithm is run, the router gets an area view of the network from its perspective. To determine the shortest path, cost is considered as the factor.

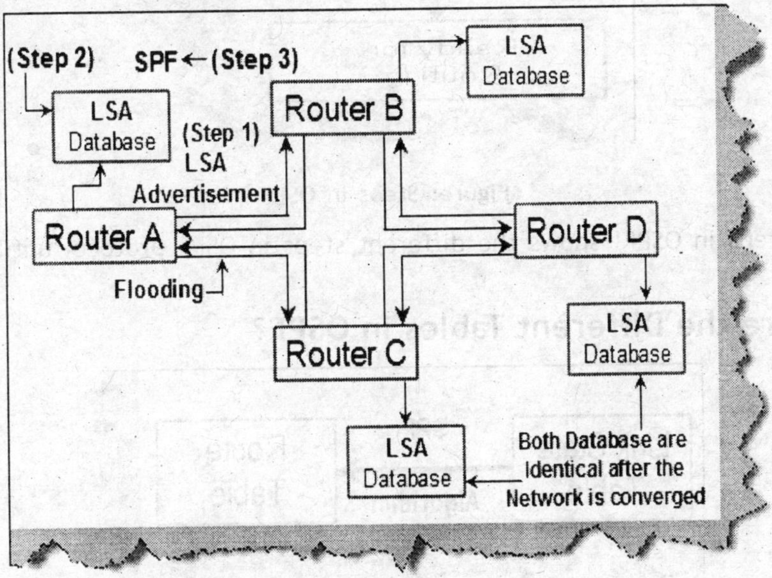

Figure: OSPF in Action

Figure 'OSPF in Action' shows four routers which are interconnected. So in the first step, router send advertisements. In the second step, using the LSA individual, an LSA database is built. In the final step, an SPF algorithm is run and the route table is populated.

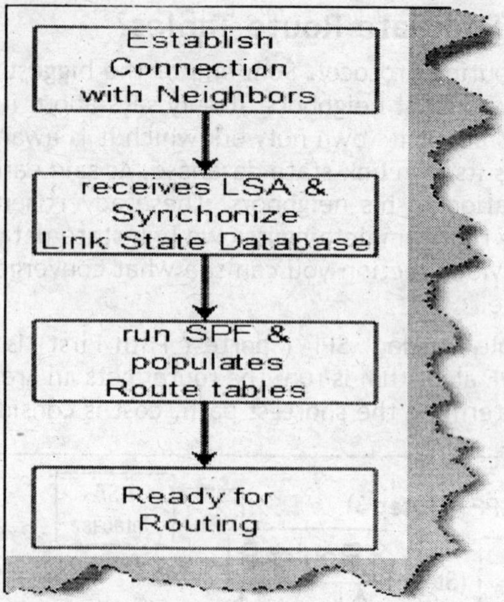

Figure: Steps in OSPF

Figure 'Steps in OSPF' shows the different steps in OSPF protocol until it is ready for routing.

(I) What are the Different Tables in OSPF?

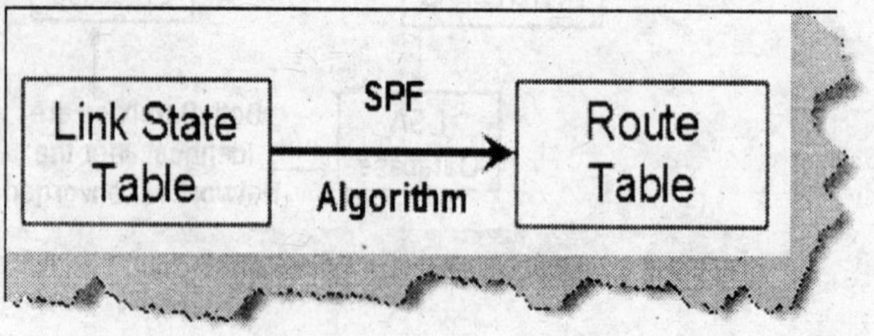

Figure: SPF Algorithm

OSPF uses three main tables:

- **Neighbor Table**: Contains a list of all known routing neighbors.
- **Link State/Topology Table**: Contains a list of networks with their states. Link state table grows, exposing topology of the network.
- **Route Table**: This is populated after the SPF algorithm is run on the link state table. It contains routes to forward traffic.

(I) Explain Different Areas in OSPF.

Areas: It is a logical grouping of routers that share the same link-state database. OSPF was introduced to form a hierarchical structure for flow of data. Areas are used to group routers to exchange information locally. You can see in the figure 'OSPF Areas' how Area 2 is a logical group of IR. IR stands for 'Internal Router.'

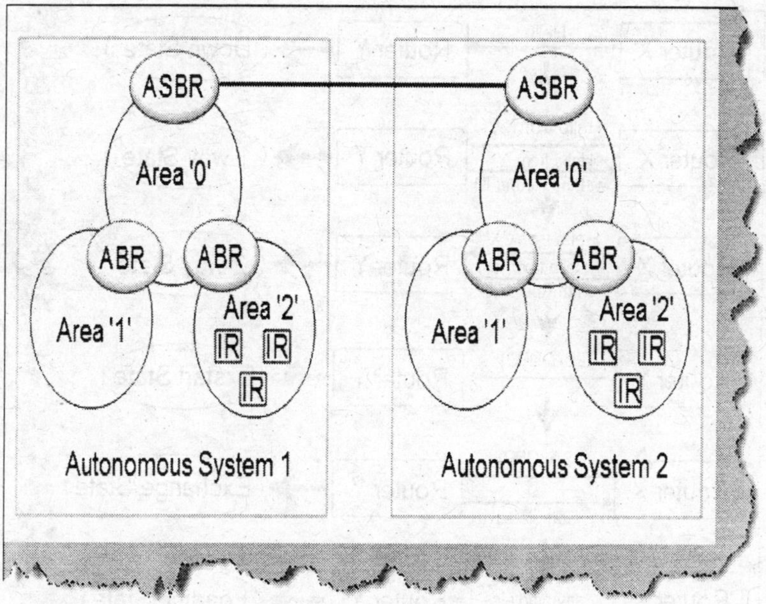

Figure: OSPF Areas

Backbone Area: This is a mandatory area in an OSPF network. Backbone area is always Area 0. All areas are connected to Area 0. All routing traffic is passed through Area 0. You can see in the figure we how Area 0 (i.e. Backbone area) connects Area 1 and Area 2.

IR (Internal Router): An internal router only connects with in internal area and does not communicate with external areas.

ABR (Area Border Router): This acts as a communication channel between two areas. You can see from the figure how ABR connects two areas.

Autonomous System Boundary Router (ASBR): ASBR connects autonomous system. Autonomous systems are those whose communicating protocols that are different or they belong to different organizations. In the figure 'OSPF areas,' we have two autonomous system areas 1 and 2. Both these areas are connected by ASBR.

(I) Explain Different Router Types in OSPF.

Please refer to the previous question for the answer.

(B) Explain Designated Router and Backup Designated Router?

LSA packets are not transmitted by every router to every router. OSPF chooses a designated router that sends the routing updates to all routers. DR also shares its link database with a back-up router that is called BDR (Backup Designated Router.) When DR comes down, BDR comes into action. Routers on the network elect a DR and BDR.

(I) Explain Different Router States in OSPF.

Given below are the different router states in OSPF:

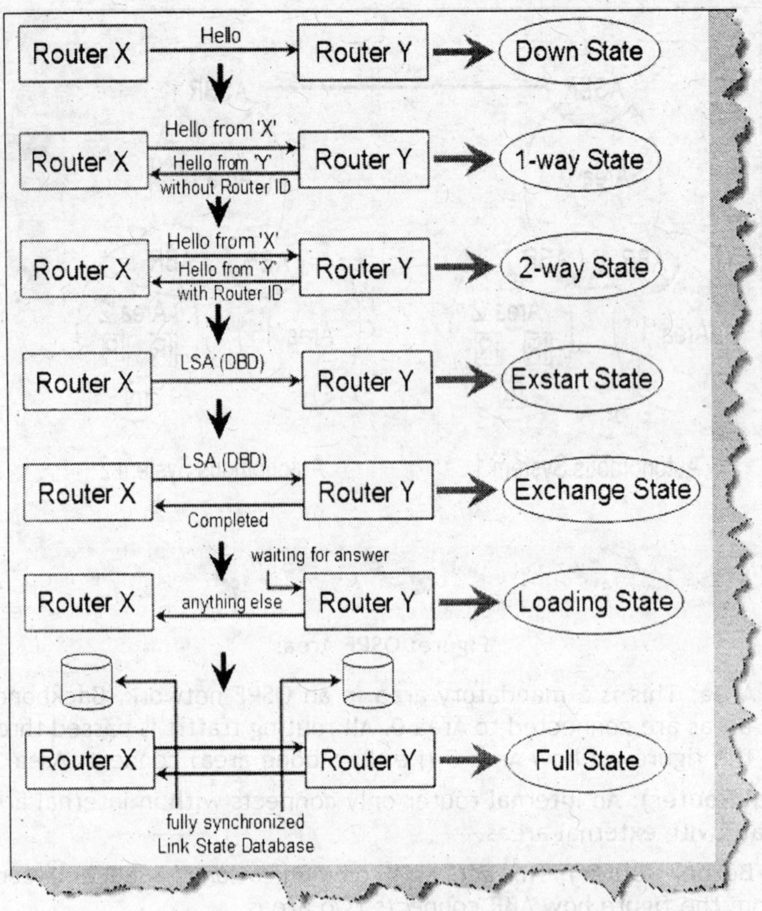

Figure: Router States

Down State: It is the initial state of the router, which mean a router receives packets from another router but has not yet received any reply from the other router. For exmple, you can see in the figure 'Router State' how the router communication moves through different states. So, in the first state you can see Router X has sent a hello packet but Router Y has not sent back any acknowledgement yet. This is the down state of the router communication.**Init state or 1-way state:** In this state, Router Y has sent back a reply but has not sent the router ID in it. This is termed as Init or 1-way state.**2 way state**: In this state, Router Y has received a hello packet with the router ID also. This is called 2-way state of router communication.

Exstart State: In this state, link-state database are exchanged between routers. So, one of the routers becomes master and the other slave. For example, in the figure 'Router State,' we have shown the Exstrat state where Router X sends LSA information to Router Y, where Router X is the master and Router Y a slave.

Exchange state: When the master router sends Database Description (DBD) packets, after completion slave responds with acknowledgement. This is termed as exchange state.

Loading state: When a router is waiting for some information after the initial exchange of DBD packets, it is called the loading state.

Full State: After the exchange of LSA packets, link-state database of every router is fully synchronized. In the figure 'Router State,' the final state is the full state where Router X and Router Y are fully synchronized, which indirectly means that both link-state databases are identical.

(l) Explain Different OSPF Packet Types.

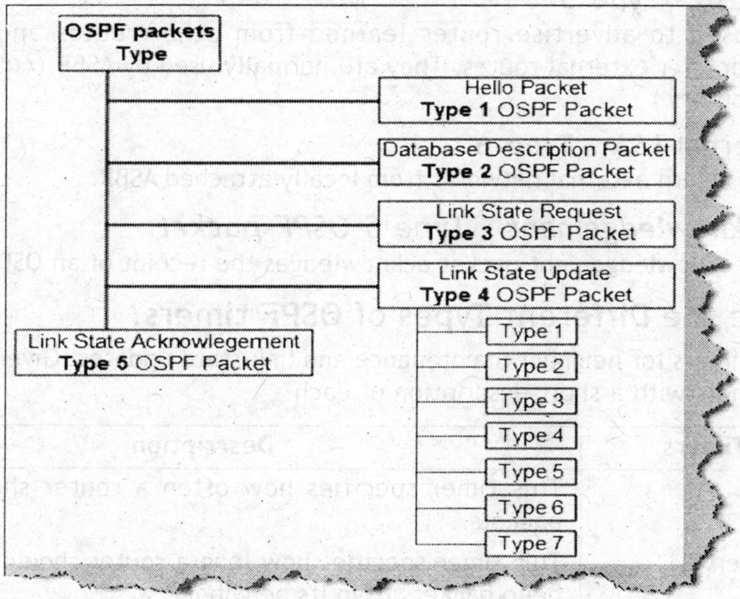

Figure: OSPF Packet Type

There are five types of packets which are commonly used, as shown in figure 'OSPF Packet Types.'

Hello Packet - Type 1 OSPF Packet

This packet builds and maintains neighbor relationships.

Database Description Packet - Type 2 OSPF Packet

These packets are initially exchanged when routers are initially exchanging their link-state databases.

Link State Request (LSR) - Type 3 OSPF Packet

This packet type is used to request information about a link learned from another router.

Link State Update (LSU's) - Type 4 OSPF Packet

There are eleven types of Link-state advertisements that are used to transmit pieces of its link databases. We will only discuss six which are most commonly used.

- **Router LSA - Type 1**

  This packet describes routers links and their states, and is the most commonly used type of packets.

- **Network LSA - Type 2**
  This LSA describes the number of router connected to the subnet and are generated only by DRs.
- **Summary LSA - Type 3**
  These are summarization packets and contain only subset information of LSA type 1 packets. These packets travel from non-zero areas to area 0. As said earler, they are summarization packets they are used by Area Border Routers (ABR).
- **External LSA - Type 5**
  They are used to advertise routes learned from other routes and perform route summarization for external routes. They are normally used by ASBR (Autonomous System Boundary Routers.)
- **NSSA External LSA - Type 6**
  They help us learn external networks from locally attached ASBR.

Link-State Acknowledgement - Type 5 OSPF packet:

Link-State acknowledgement packet acknowledges the receipt of an OSPF packet.

(I) What are the Different Types of OSPF timers?

OSPF uses timers for neighbor maintenance and link-state updates. Given below is the list of OSPF timers with a short description of each.

Type of Timers	Description
Hello Timer	This timer specifies how often a router should send hello packets.
Router Dead Interval	This timer specifies how long a router should wait to receive hello packets from its neighbor.
SPF Hold-Time	This timer specifies how long a router should wait after calculating the route table and before calculating the route table again.
LsAge and MaxAge timers	Every LSA packet is associated with an Age in minutes. So, if an LSA packet reaches an age of 30 minutes it is refreshed. This age is called LsAge. If the LSA packet reaches an Age of 1 hour, it is deleted from the database. This Age is termed as MaxAge.
Poll-Interval	This interval specifies how much a router should poll a neighbor that has been transitioned from a status of 2-way to a status of Attempt.
LSA Retransmit-Interval	For every LSA sent, a response is given back about the acknowledgement that the packet is delivered. If the LSA is not delivered then LSA is transmitted again. This interval specifies the frequency of the Retransmit packet.
Wait timer	This is the time a router should wait to see a DR or BDR in the network.

Transmit Delay	The age of LSA is tracked. In case if we receive multiple LSAs for the same route, then newer information can be chosen. Transmit delay timer helps by incrementing the age of an LSA packet as it exits every interface.
RxmInterval	This is the wait period of a router before retransmitting the database description packet.

(I) How Does SPF Algorithm do Route Determination?

To do a route determination, routers transform LSDB information into an SPF tree. So it will have nodes which have branches that are further divided into more branches. A router tree is constructed from the LSA database. If the LSA database changes, then a new router tree is calculated again and new best router determination done. In order to understand how the tree is constructed, let's consider the network and router with costs associated given below. Consider the figure 'SPF Algorithm,' which has four routers that are connected to four networks.

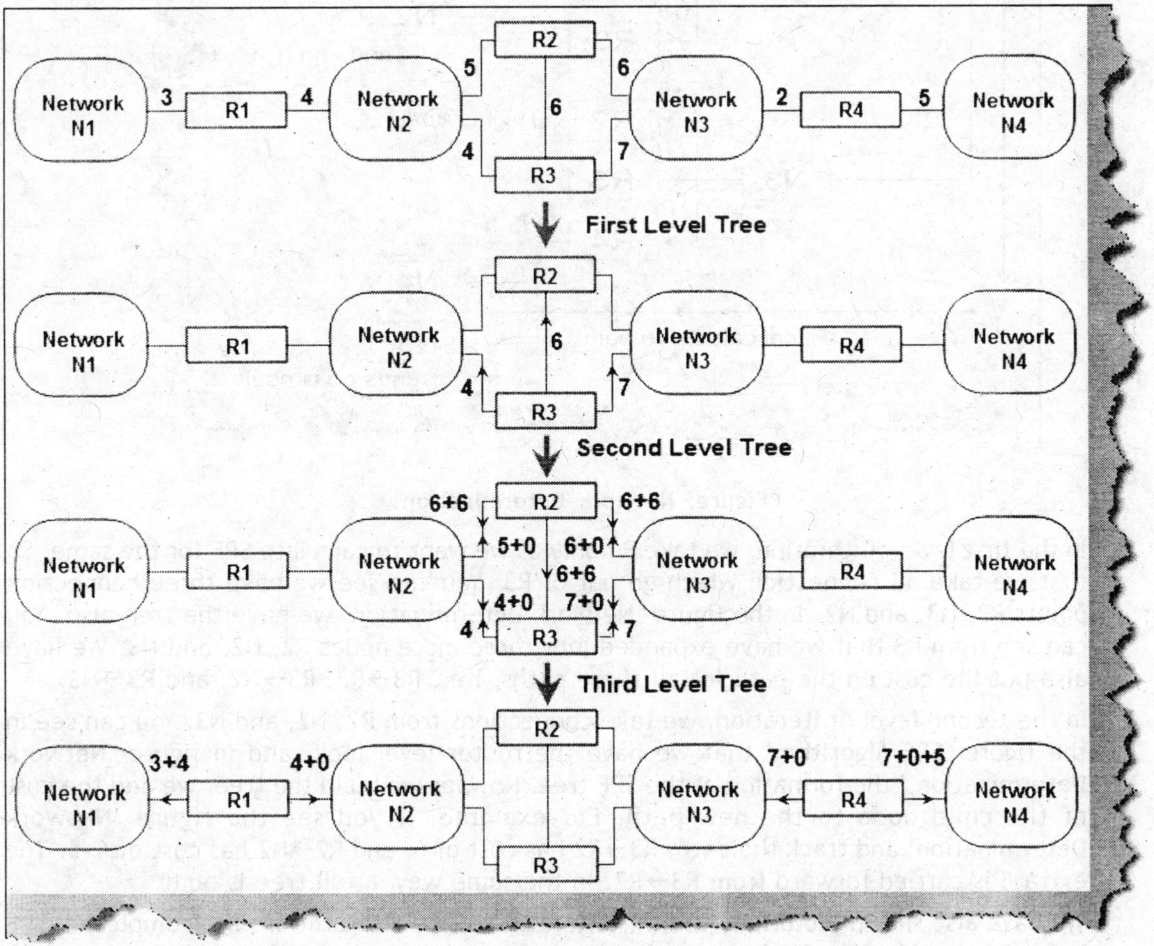

Figure: SPF Algorithm

SPF algorithm runs on the network and it passes to various levels depending on how deep the network is. So the first network is a complete network with sample cost attached to it. An SPF tree is constructed from a router perspective, which means that the SPF is different for different routers. For this scenario, we will consider SPF from the perspective of Router R3.

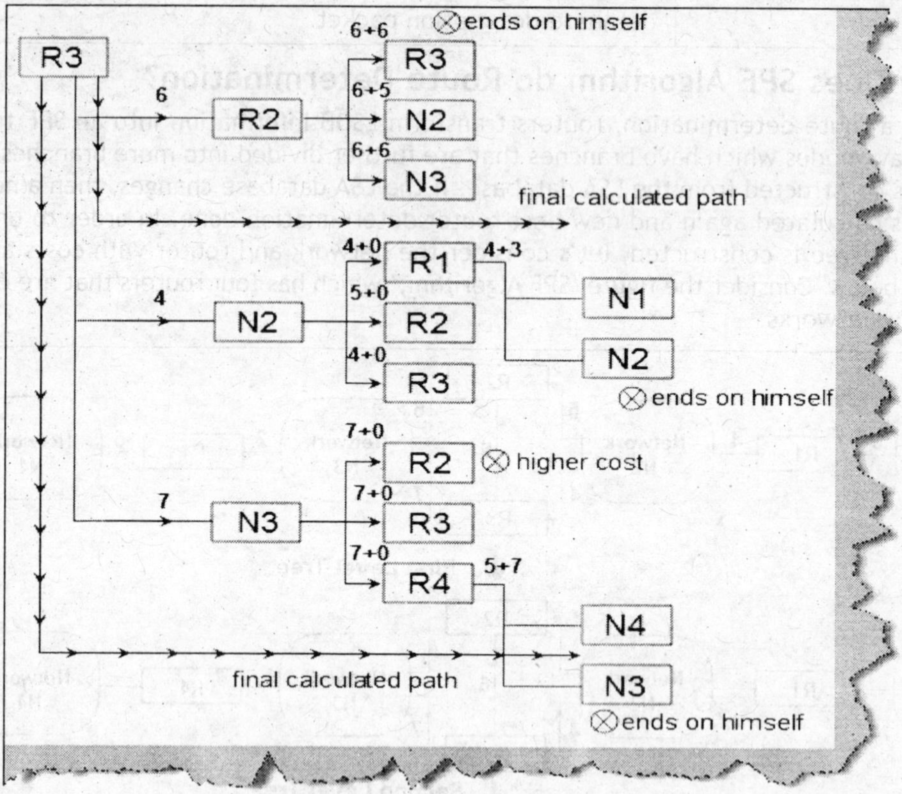

Figure: Network Determination

In the first level of iteration, we take R3 only as we want to calculate SPF for the same. So first we take all connection which go out of R3. You can see we have three connection points R2, N3, and N2. In the figure 'Network Determination' we have the tree also. You can see from R3 that we have expanded into three more nodes R2, N2, and N3. We have also put the cost on the path for all three paths, i.e., R3→R2, R3→N2, and R3→N3.

In the second level of iteration, we take connections from R2, N2, and N3. You can see in the figure 'SPF Algorithm' that we have the router level look, and in figure 'Network Determination,' the formation of the SPF tree. Now, as we build the tree, we add the cost of the child node to the new path. For example, if you see the figure 'Network Determination' and track the path, R3→R2 has cost of 6, and R2→N2 has cost of 6+5. The extra 6 is carried forward from R3→R2. In the same way, a full tree is built.

We have also shown pictorially the third iteration. Once all iterations are completed, SPF checks for two things in the tree, first how many destination ends on it. For example, R3→R2→R3 ends on itself. So these kinds of self-pointing routes are removed. The second check it does is for less cost path. R3→N3→R2 has a cost of 7, while R3→N2→R2 has a cost of 5. The N2 route is of less cost, so the SPF does not validate the R3→N3→R2 path.

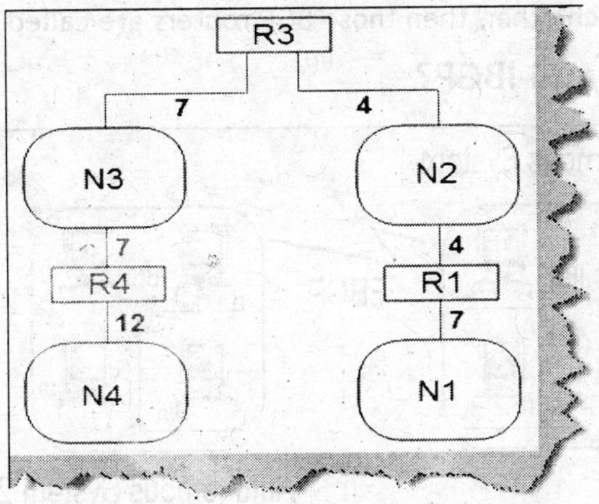

Figure: Calculated SPF Tree

In figure 'Network Determination,' we have shown arrow paths for the final route. Figure 'Calculated SPF Tree' shows the final output of the SPF algorithm. This tree is from the perspective of R3.

(B) Explain Autonomous Systems.

Autonomous systems are a collection of networks under common administrative control and share common routing strategy.

(B) What are the Different Types of Dynamic Protocols?

There are two types of dynamic protocol: IGP (Interior Gateway protocol) and EGP (Exterior Gateway Protocol.) IGP routing protocols are used to exchange routing information in routers within the same autonomous system. And EGP is used to communicate router information between different autonomous systems.

(I) Explain Autonomous Numbers in EGP.

Autonomous numbers is a unique number assigned to an autonomous system. Autonomous system numbers also called AS numbers. AS numbers are assigned by an American body authority ARIN. This is the same body which assigns IP addresses. AS numbers are 16 bit numbers which range from 1 to 65535. Numbers from 1 to 64511 are public, and ASN and from 64512 to 65535 are private ASNs.

(I) What is BGP?

BGP is the king of external routing protocols. Following are some points to remember for this protocol:

- BGP comes under the category of exterior gateway protocol and used to connect autonomous systems.
- It uses path vector and supports multicasting of datagram packets.
- Its uses classless IP addressing scheme.

(I) Explain the Concept of BGP Speakers and Peers.

Any router configured for BGP will take the role of BGP speaker. When BGP speakers forms a connection with each other, then those BGP routers are called BGP peers.

(I) What are EBGP and IBGP?

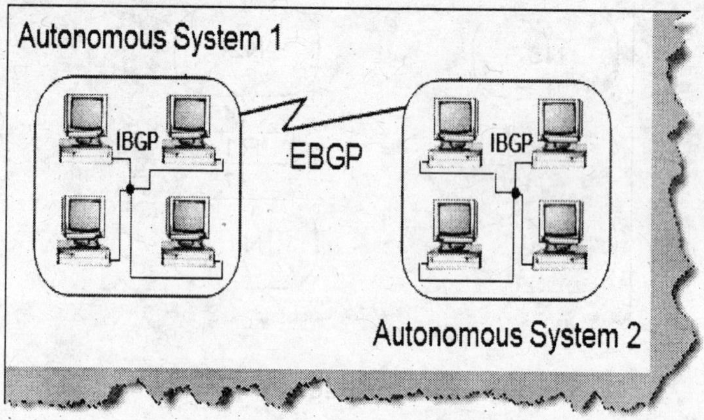

Figure: EBGP and IBGP

EBGP stands for External BGP while IBGP stands for Internal BGP. BGP operates in one of these modes. Figure 'EBGP and IBGP' explains both the concepts pictorially. EBGP is used to communicate between autonomous systems while IBGP is used to communicate within an autonomous system.

(I) What is RIB?

RIB stand for 'Routing Information Base.' RIB is basically a database for routing information. There are three types of RIBs. These three kinds of RIB's can be stored in one database or in multiple databases depending on how the vendor has implemented the same. Below is the detail information about the three RIBs:

Adj-RIBs-In (Adjacent Routing Information Base In): This is also called feasible routes. This database has raw routing information which is got from the BGP speaker. It has all the routes that BGP speaker is aware of.

Loc-RIB (Local RIB): Loc-RIB is the result of applying routing policies to data or routes on Adj-RIB's data.

Adj-RIBs-Out (Adjacent RIB Out): Routes which are advertised to BGP peers are stored in Adj-RIBs-Out table. This is the place where summarization of route happens.

(A) Explain the Concept of BGP Confederations.

BGP confederations help us reduce size and complexity of IBGP mesh. It allows a single AS to be broken in to smaller ASs. Figure 'BGP Confederations' shows how AS 64010 is broken in to smaller AS, i.e., 64011, 64012, and 64013. For external Ass, any inside AS system, i.e., 64011, 64012, and 64013 is requested by 64010. In the same figure, we have listed the commands for doing BGP confederations.

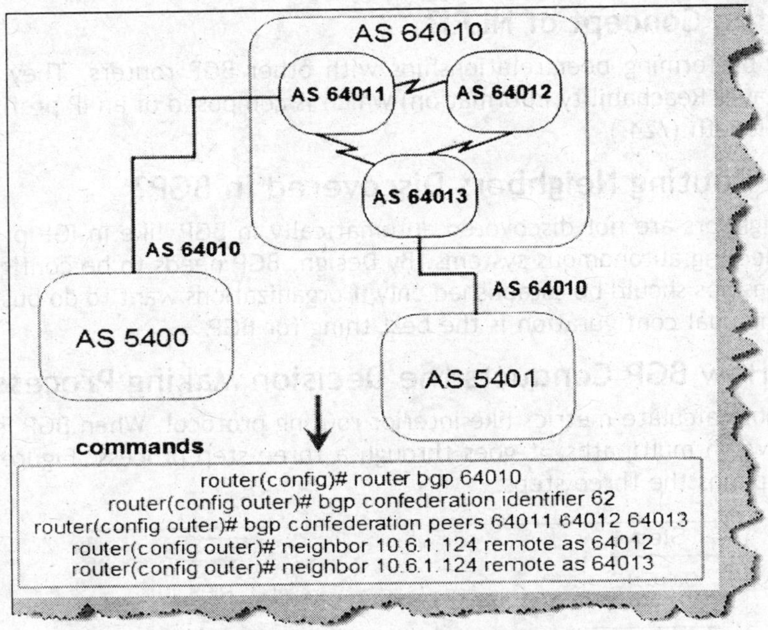

Figure: BGP Confederations

(A) What are BGP Path Attributes?

Every BGP route has a set of attributes that convey routing information and policies. Let's understand these attributes in detail.

AS_PATH: This attribute contains full path to the destination network. It is actually a list of system autonomous IDs. One of the significances of AS_PATH is to prevent routing loops. So if its own autonomous system is found in AS_PATH, it rejects the route as this would cause routing loops.

NEXT_HOP: This attribute specifies the IP address that packets should be forwarded to.

ORIGIN: This is an attribute that can be used to evaluate which route to use for forwarding traffic. ORIGIN has three possible values IGP, EGP, and Incomplete. In BGP, routes learnt from interior is given more priority than those learnt from external systems. So ORIGIN with value IGP gets more preference than EGP or incomplete.

MULTI_EXIT_DISC: Multiple Exit Discriminator (MED) is an attribute that can be used by External BGP enabled routers in case there are multiple paths. In short, it's like a metric that can be used to make a choice when we have multiple routes to the same destination.

LOCAL_REF: This attribute is like MED. It can be set to prefer one path over another in case of multiple paths. But LOCAL_REF is used only internally, i.e., by IBGP.

ATOMIC_AGGREGATOR: This attribute is active when a route is summarized. In the same context, there is one more attribute called AGGREGATOR which gives us information about which router summarized this route.

(I) Explain the Concept of NLRI?

BGP works by forming peer relationships with other BGP routers. They exchange NLRI (Network Layer Reachability Information) which is composed of an IP prefix (.210.25.177) and prefix length (/24.)

(A) How are Routing Neighbors Discovered in BGP?

Routing neighbors are not discovered automatically in BGP, like in IGP protocols. BGP is about connecting autonomous systems. By Design, BGP needs to be configured manually. BGP relationships should be established only if organizations want to do business with each other. So, manual configuration is the best thing for BGP.

(A) Explain How BGP Conducts the Decision Making Process.

BGP does not calculate metrics like interior routing protocol. When BGP is challenged to choose between multipaths, it goes through a three-step process. Figure 'BGP Decision Process' explains the three steps.

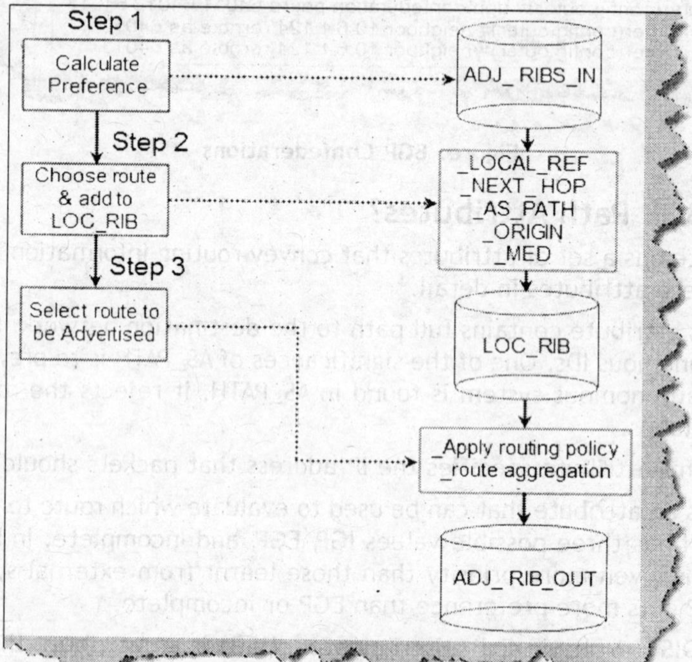

Figure: BGP Decision Making Process

ADJ_RIBs_IN stores all raw and unprocessed routing data. ADJ_RIBs_IN has all the routes which the BGP router knows about. In the figure 'BGP Decision Making Process' we have numbered all the three steps. In the first step, preferences are applied on the data of ADJ_RIBs_IN. For that it uses the LOCAL_REF as the policy to define preference.

In the second step, it applies NEXT_HOP, AS_PATH, ORIGIN, and MED attributes to see if it is a qualified route. Following are the things checked for each attribute:

AS_PATH: Routes having smallest value of AS_PATH is selected. It also checks if the route is looped or not. This is done by checking if it is in the path. If the AS itself is in the path, then it will form a routing loop, so these kind of routes are dropped.

- MUD: Select the route which has the smallest MED.
- ORIGIN: Select the route which has the smallest value of ORIGIN.
- NEXT_HOP: Checks if the NEXT_HOP is reachable. If the destination is not reachable then it drops the route.

In the third step, routing policy and aggregation is done and new set of data termed as ADJ_RIB_OUT is generated. ADJ_RIB_OUT is the data which will be finally propagated to other BGP peers.

(B) Explain the Concept of Redistribution.

Redistribution is the process of sharing routing information between two different routing protocols. We need redistribution in the following scenarios:

- When two organizations have different routing protocols.
- When organizations are geographically dispersed, organizations might run IRP and ERP protocols, i.e., different kind of protocols.

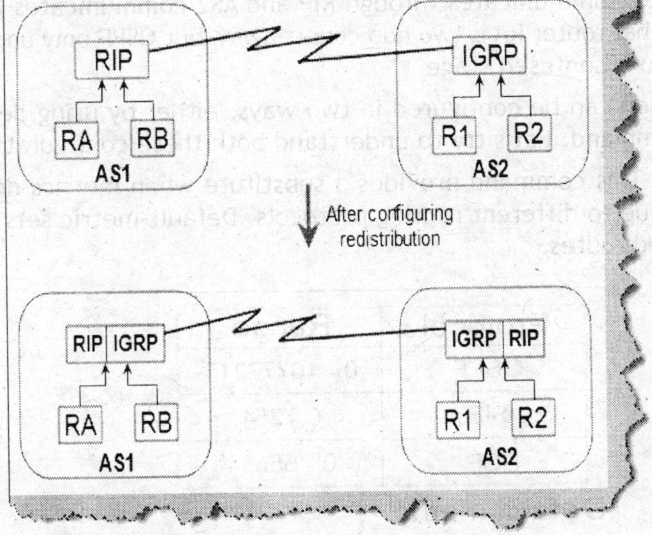

Figure: Configuring Redistribution

Figure 'Configuring Redistribution' shows how we wanted to connect two autonomous systems AS1 and AS2. In order to communicate, we need to configure redistribution so that both the autonomous systems can communicate.

(I) Explain the Concept of One-Way Redistribution and Mutual Distribution.

One-way redistribution happens when routing information of a routing protocol is shared with another routing protocol. The other routing protocol does not share its routing information with the sharing routing protocol. Mutual redistribution is the opposite of the same, here, both the routing protocols share their routing information with each other.

(I) How Does Metric Translation Take Place in Redistributing Routes?

Every routing protocol has own way of calculating metrics. For instance RIP uses hop count and OSPF uses bandwidth for metric calculation.

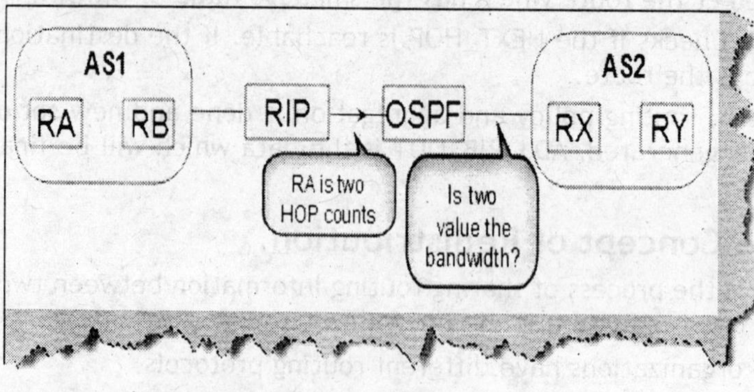

Figure: Metric Issue of Redistribution

Consider the figure 'Metric Issue of Redistribution.' We have two autonomous systems: AS1 and AS2. AS1 communicates through RIP and AS2 communicates through OSPF. So RIP communicates that router RA is two hop counts away, but OSPF only understands bandwidth. This can lead to a confused stage.

Metric translation can be configured in two ways, either by using default-metric or with redistribute command. Let's try to understand both these configurations in detail.

Default-Metric: This command provides a substitute when metrics do not convert during redistribution due to different routing protocols. Default-metric sets a default metric for the redistributed routes.

Protocol	Range
OSPF	0 - 16777215
ISIS	0 - 254
BGP	0 - 65534

Default metric command

```
router(config)# router bgp 106
router(config router)# default metric 6
router(config router)# end
```

Figure: Default-Metric Command

The figure 'Default-Metric Command' shows a range of values for routing protocols. In the same figure, we also have the command which sets the default-metric value to 6 for BGP routing protocol.

```
R1(config)# router rip
R1(config router)# redistribute IGRP 100 metric 1
```

Figure: Redistribute with Optional Keyword

Redistribute with optional keyword: When the keyword metric is used in the redistribution statement, it means that we are setting the metrics of external route. Figure 'Redistribute with Optional Keyword' shows the commands. Here we have configured one-way redistribution from IGRP routing protocol to RIP with 100 metric. It means that IGRP will be overridden with 100.

3

Firewall

(B) Define a Firewall.

Firewall is a system which enforces access control policy between two networks. Many firewalls emphasize on blocking traffic while some emphasize on permitting traffic. Figure 'Firewall Definition' shows how a firewall stands between external and internal networks, and controls traffic. It can be said that a firewall stands between trusted and non-trusted networks.

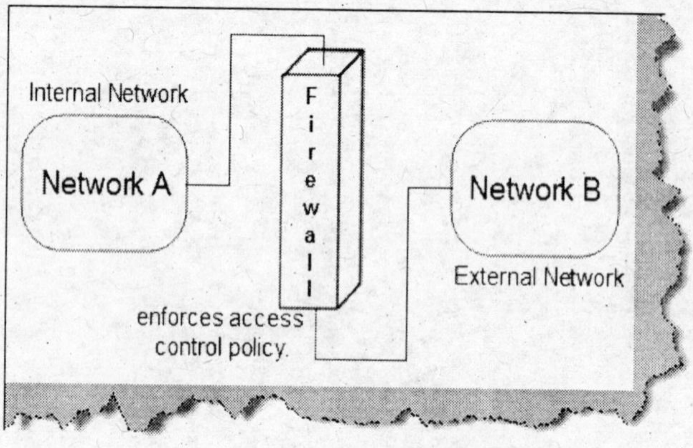

Figure: Firewall Definition

Firewall is not about only technical implementation of tool, but it's also about a strategy to be implemented for internet-reachable resources.

(B) What Are The Different Types of Firewalls?

Firewalls are classified depending on which OSI layer data they use for applying rules. There are four types of firewalls: Packet filter, Circuit level gateway, Application gateway, and Stateful inspection. Figure 'OSI and Firewalls' shows how different firewalls operate on OSI layer. In the coming questions, we will be looking into individual details of all the firewalls soon.

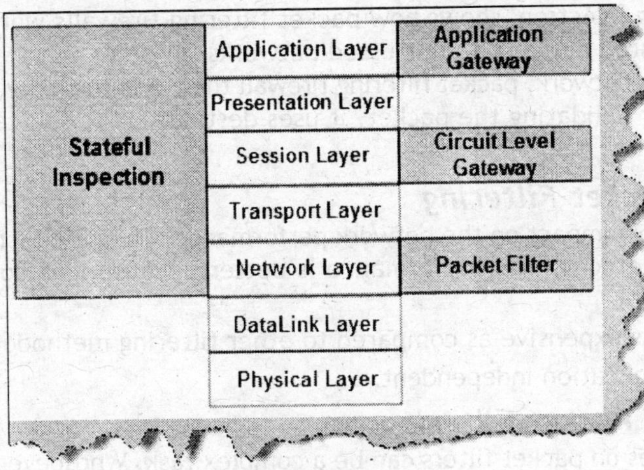

Figure: OSI and Firewalls

Packet filtering: It's the simplest packet screening method. As the name implies, it filters packets only. Packet filtering firewalls operate on the network layer of OSI. In packet filter, each packet header information is examined and compared with the rules and filters. All packets are examined individually irrespective if they belong to the same connection or not (we will come to this later on.) Packet filtering uses the following factors to see if traffic has to be allowed or denied:

- Source IP and Destination IP addresses
- Protocol type (TCP/UDP)
- Source port and destination port

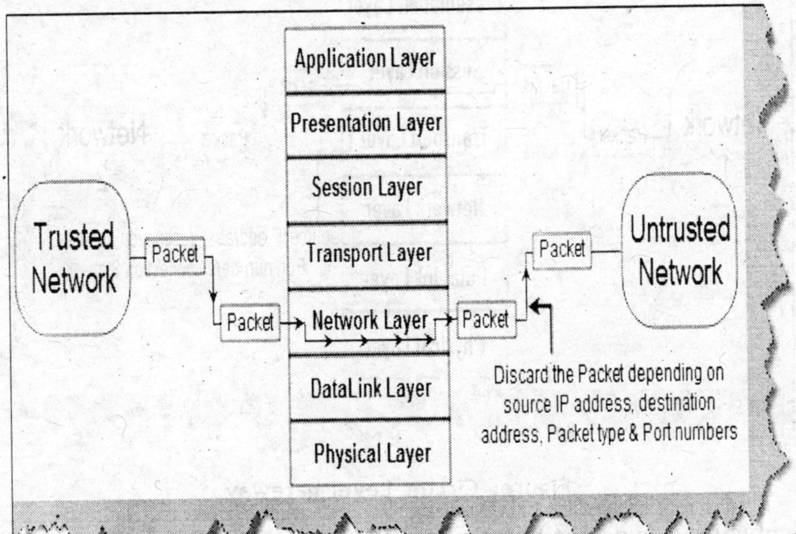

Figure: Packet Filtering in Action

As said previously, packet filtering works on the network part of the OSI model. Figure

'Packet Filtering in Action' shows how packet filtering firewalls works. When packets are sent from a trusted network to untrusted networks, in other words you can say from one network to other network, packet filtering firewall then uses the network layer for validating the packet. For validating the packet, it uses destination IP, Source IP, Packet type, and the port number.

Advantages of Packet Filtering

- They have low impact on the network performance. They are faster compared to other screening methods. The performance is better because it is done at lower levels of the OSI model.
- They are less expensive as compared to other filtering methodology.
- They are application independent.

Disadvantages of Packet Filtering

- Defining rules on packet filters can be a complex task. Whosoever is configuring packet filters should know about services and protocols in detail.
- Packet filtering is prone to attacks like IP spoofing, buffer overflow, and ICMP tunneling.
- Packet filtering only looks at the packet information and takes decisions accordingly. It does not perform user authentication.
- Packet filtering makes direct connection between two end points which can prove dangerous at times.

Circuit Level Gateway Filtering

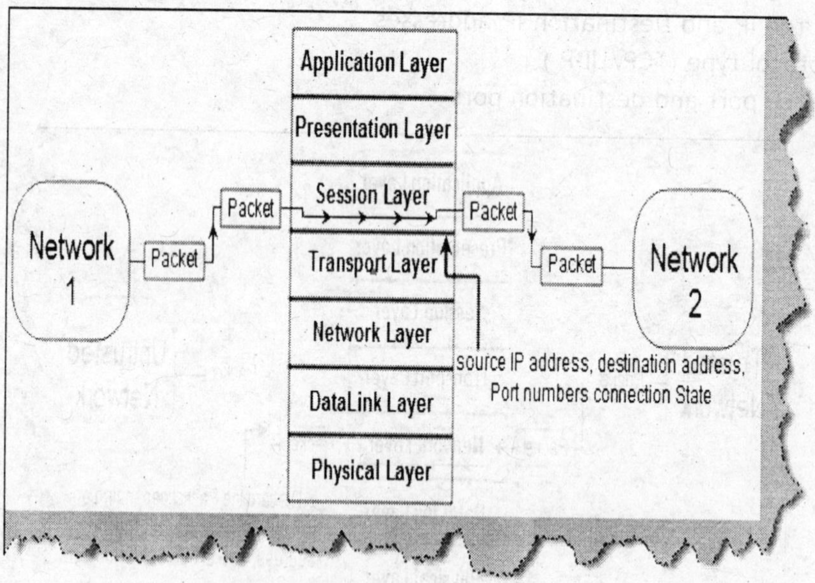

Figure: Circuit Level gateway

Circuit level gateways do not examine individual packets. They monitor just TCP and UDP sessions. They monitor handshaking between the packets and judge whether the request session is legitimate. When packets are passed through the circuit level gateway, it looks as if it's coming from a gateway, this helps us hide information about the private network.

The most important thing is to check if the request is legitimate. A request is legitimate if the response is coming from request sent by the internal network. In short, it should be a proper session initiated by the internal network host.

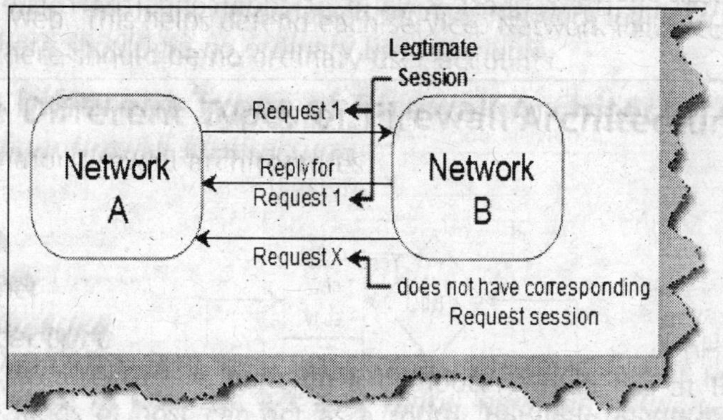

Figure: Legitimate sessions

Figure 'Legitimate Session' explains the clear concept of legitimate sessions. We have two networks 'Network A' and 'Network B.' Network A sends a request 'request 1' which is replied by Network B. This reply is legitimate because it was initiated by the internal network. Now see Request X coming in which has no internal request sent from Network A. This is not a legitimate session. These kinds of packets are dropped by Circuit Level Gateway.

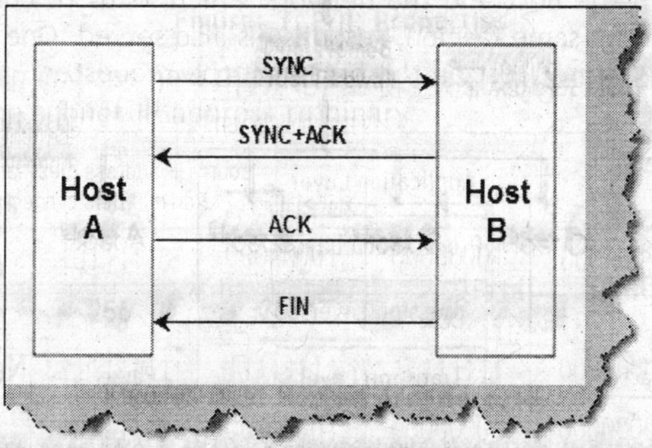

Figure: Handshake Session

Circuit level gateway uses the handshake methodology to detect if the session is a legitimate session. Figure 'Handshake Session' shows how the SYNC and ACK flags are used to track for legitimate sessions. So when Host A sends packet, it sends the SYNC value with it, when Host B replies it replies with SYNC + ACK value. So Host A can understand from these flags that this was a legitimate session. Once every thing is done, the FIN flag is sent to close the session.

Application Gateways and Proxies

These types of firewall operate at the application level of OSI model. Figure 'Application

Gateway Firewall' shows how the application gateway firewall functions. A client issues a request for a network and connection is established with the application gateway. The proxy or the application gateway firewall determines if the request is valid by comparing with rules and filters. If the request is valid, it then sends the request on its behalf to the network.

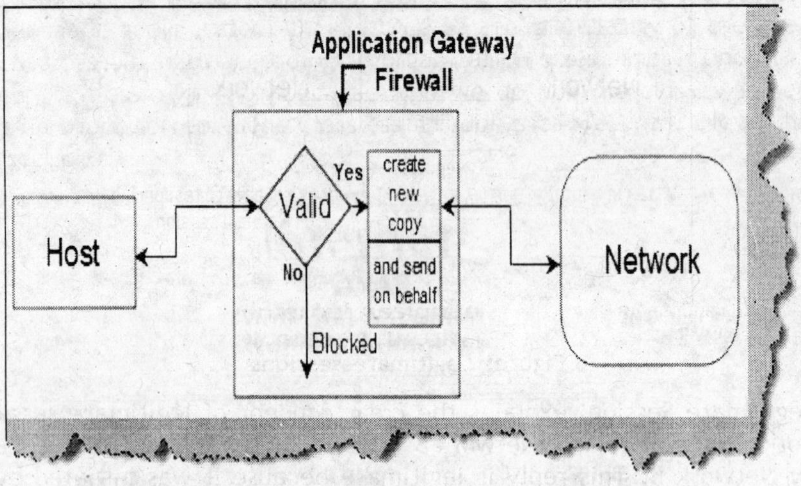

Figure: Application Gateway Firewall

As the request is sent on behalf of the application gateway firewall, there is no direct connection between the host and the network which leads to complete isolation of the internal network. In the same fashion, response is also served. One of the important points is that it creates a new request on the behalf of the requester.

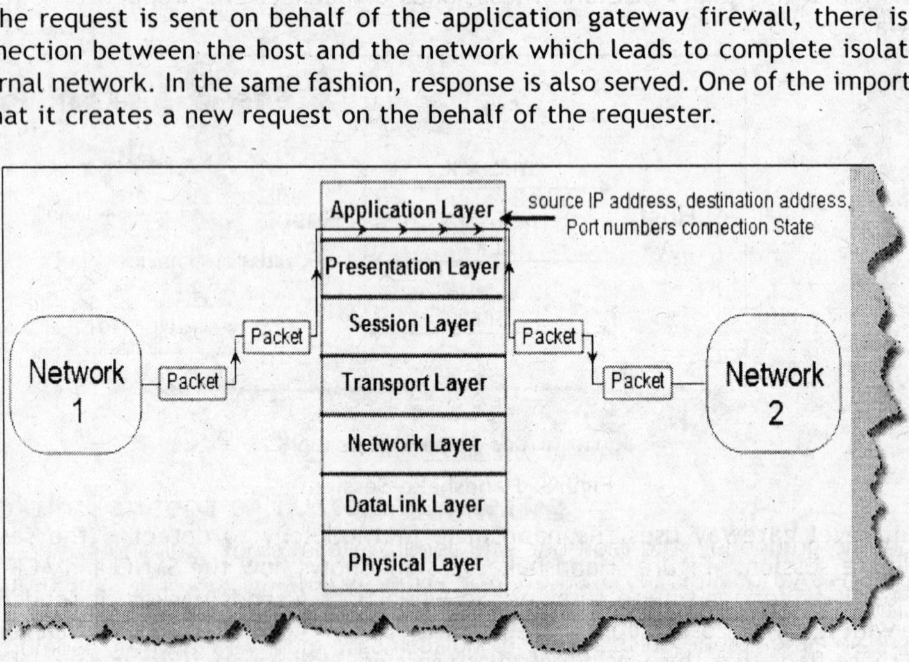

Figure: Application Gateway Acts on the Application Layer

Advantages of Application Gateways and Proxies

- They do not allow direct connections, so it truly keeps the internal and external networks isolated.
- As they work on application level of OSI, you can have more control on the traffic. They can permit or deny application-specific features.
- They have the best filtering mechanism because they can validate the actual packet content.
- They also offer good user authentication.
- They provide logging mechanism for user activity and different types of traffic.

Disadvantages of Application Gateways and Proxies

- One of the significant weaknesses is performance. As this gateway inspects at the application level, they are slower.
- They require additional client configuration for implementation.
- Large-scale client scalability can be a big issue.

Stateful Inspection

Stateful inspection is combination of all the above types of firewalls. It uses all the five layers in the OSI model. In short, they filter packets at the network layer, check if the session is legitimate using the session layer and evaluate the contents of the packets at the application layer. Figure 'Stateful Inspection' shows the levels at which the packets are inspected. So, right from application to the network layer, the packets are inspected.

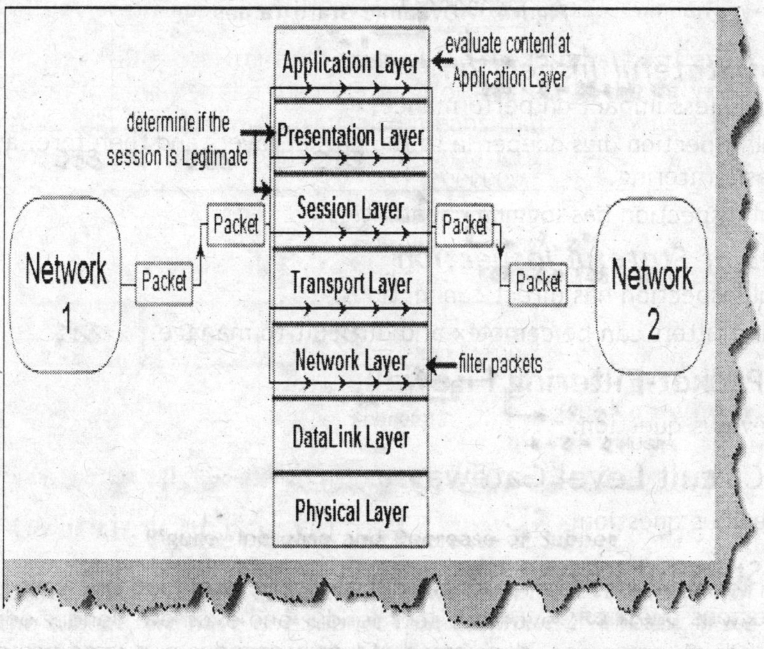

Figure: Stateful Inspection

As packets pass through the firewall, it's examined and stored in dynamic state tables. These packets are compared with rules and filters, and then decisions are made on the results of the comparison. Once it passes the filters, this state table is then scanned to see are the packets from the same legitimate connection. Figure 'Dynamic State Tables' shows how they work.

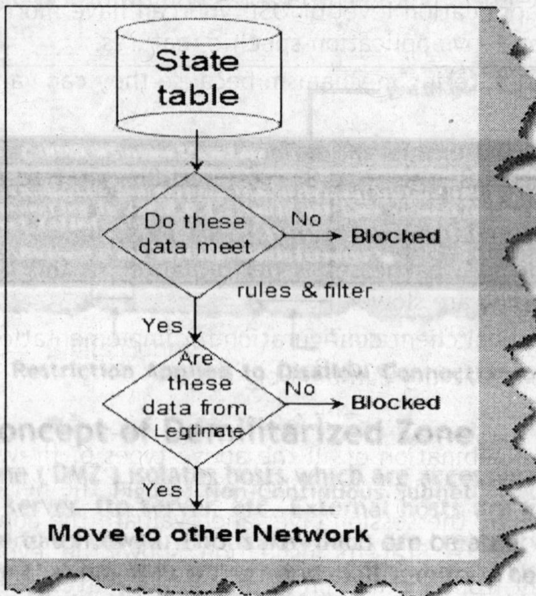

Figure :- Dynamic State tables

Advantages of Stateful Inspection

- They have less impact on performance.
- Stateful inspection digs deeper in to the packet layers and therefore, are more secured than basic filtering.
- Stateful inspection has logging capabilities.

Disadvantages of Stateful Inspection

- Stateful inspection has direct connections.
- Rules and filters can be complex and difficult to manage.

(B) Explain Packet-Filtering Firewall.

See the previous question.

(B) Explain Circuit Level Gateway.

See the previous question.

(B) Explain Stateful Inspection.

See the previous question.

(B) What is an Application Gateway?

See the previous question.

(I) Is NAT a firewall?

NAT is commonly thought of as a firewall, but our answer will be 'No.' But make sure you have logical reasons to convince the interviewer. Here is ours, but many may differ. NAT represents one IP address for all internal hosts to the external network. In short, it hides the network from outside users. By definition, a firewall should have rules and filters while NAT only hides.

> ***Note:*** *In the 'Routers' section, you can take an indepth look at why NAT came into the picture.*

(B) Are Personal Firewall Actually Firewalls?

Personal firewalls protect individual hosts from an untrusted network like the Internet. They do not meet the actual definition of a firewall because they control access to one specific device and not between networks.

> ***Note:*** *In the CD, we have provided a Zone Alarm setup. Feel free to experiment with the same. For example, in the figure we have shown two snaps. In the first snap, we have given access to policies to connect to local HTTP 80 port. You can see that after we telnet on 80 it connect to the web server. The blank screen after telnet is an indication of the same. In the second figure, we have removed the access policy due to which telnet to 80 port has failed. The example is on very granular level to show how firewalls actually work. In actual corporate scenarios, we have complex policies that need to be applied.*

Figure: No Restriction to Connect to Local 80 Port

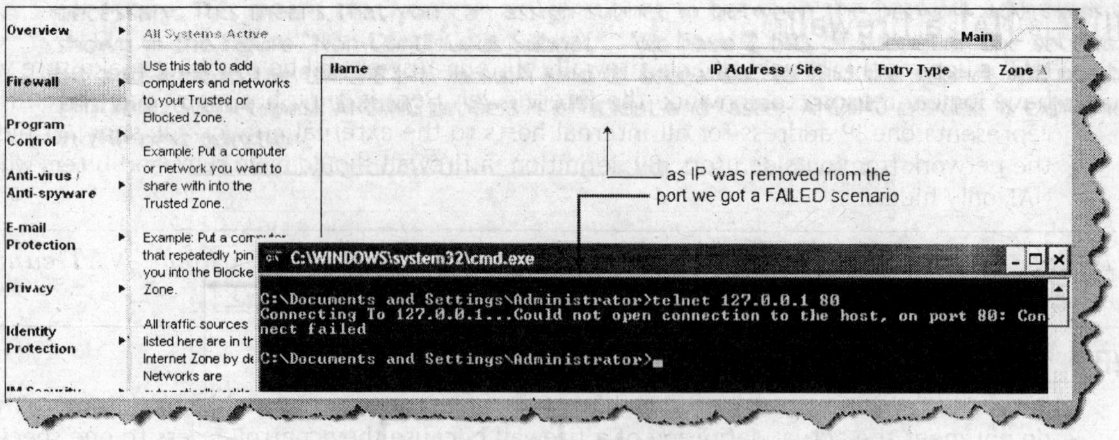

Figure: Restriction Applied to Disallow Connection on 80 Port

(B) Explain the Concept of Demilitarized Zone.

A Demilitarized Zone (DMZ) isolates hosts which are accessible from an outside network, for example, web server, ftp server, etc. External hosts are kept in a separate network zone and connected to a firewall. This is how DMZs are created. Figure 'Demilitarized Zone' shows the DMZ area that has web servers and mail servers. The sales network and finance network is separated from the DMZ. One of the important things to be noted is that the DMZ connects through the firewall. So if you want to connect to the DMZ internally or externally it's only through the firewall.

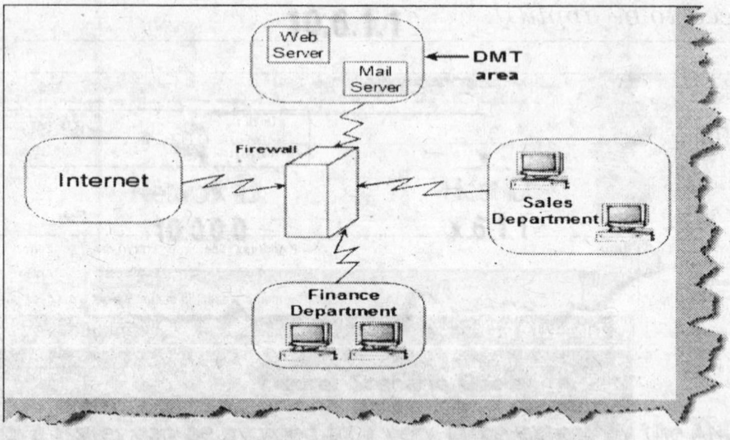

Figure: Demilitarized Zone

(I) What Does a Bastion Host Mean?

A bastion host is a special secured computer which is publicly accessible and designed to withstand external attacks. It may process incoming mail and news requests, or it may provide access to resources through the Web or FTP. A bastion host is obviously the centre of any attack on your network and should therefore be secure. A bastion host should only run the services specified by the site security policy, everything else should be disabled. It may even be a good idea to run multiple bastion hosts, perhaps one hosting mail and news, and the other the Web. This helps defend each service. Network logins to the bastion should be disabled and there should be no ordinary user accounts.

(A) What Are the Different Types of Firewall Architectures?

There are three major firewall architectures:

- Dual-Homed
- Screened-Host
- Screened-Subnet

Dual-Homed Architecture

Dual-homed host architecture is built on a computer which has at least two network interfaces. These kinds of host can act as a router between networks, but in order to implement this architecture we need to disable the routing feature. In short, there is no direct connection from one network another. Dual-homed hosts sit between the internal network and the Internet as shown in the figure 'Dual-Homed Architecture.'

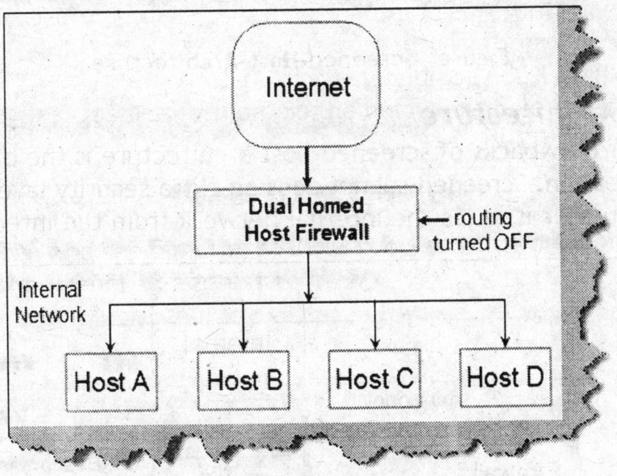

Figure: Dual-Homed Architecture

The dual-homed host acts like a proxy between the external network and the internal hosts.

Screened-Host Architecture

Dual-homed architecture provides services from host to network with routing turned off. Screened-host architecture provides services from host to network with a separate router. In this, the primary security is provided by packet filtering.

Figure 'Screened-Host Architecture' shows how the bastion host sits inside the internal network. Any host through the internal network can only connect through the bastion host. Even *vice-versa*, if any external host from the network wants to avail the services of internal network it has to go through the bastion host.

One of the disadvantages of screened-host architecture is that if the attacker breaks the bastion host there can be major security issues.

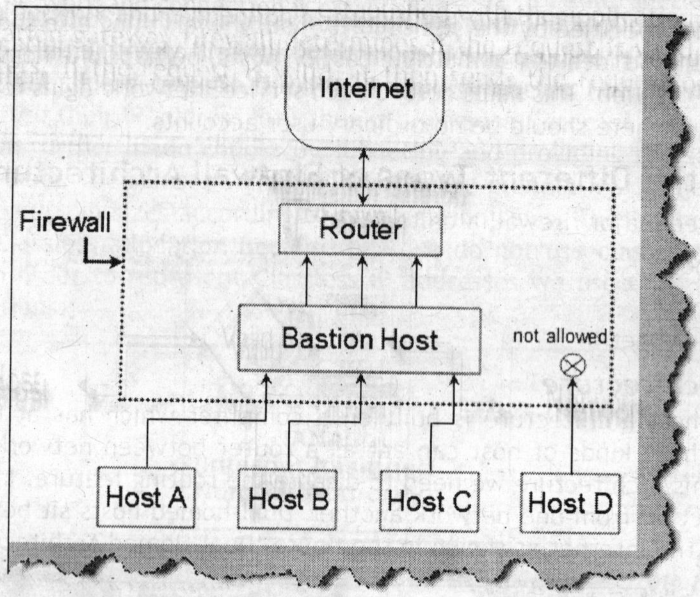

Figure: Screened-Host Architecture

Screened-Subnet Architecture

One of the major drawbacks of screened-host architecture is the bastion host as discussed in the previous section. Screened-subnet adds an extra security layer by adding a perimeter network which further isolates the internal network from the Internet.

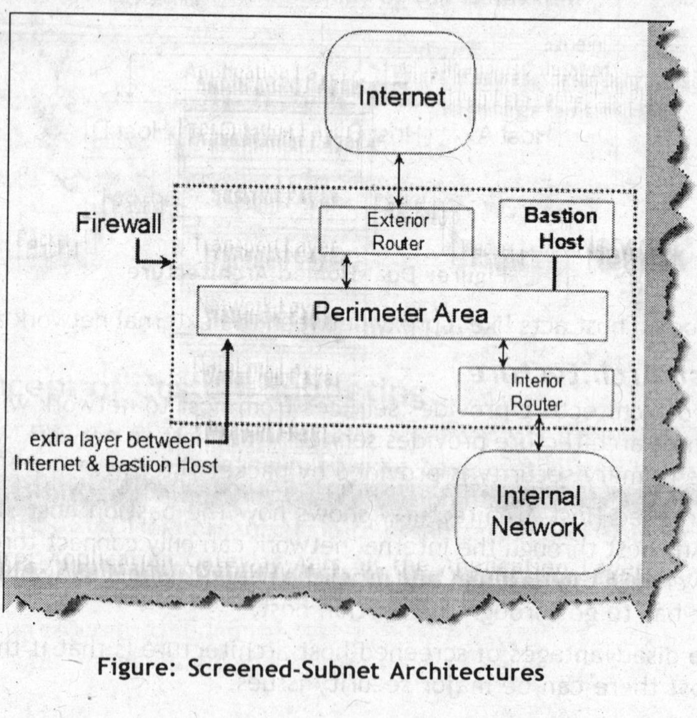

Figure: Screened-Subnet Architectures

Figure 'Screened-Subnet Architectures' shows how the perimeter area adds an extra security layer between the bastion host and the Internet. So the perimeter serves as one more layer of security. Interior network protects the internal network from the Internet and the perimeter network. Exterior router protects both the perimeter area and the internal network from the Internet. The exterior router is normally provided by an external group like ISP.

(A) Explain Dual-Home Architecture

See the previous question.

(A) Explain Screened-Host Architecture.

See the previous question.

(A) Explain Screened-Subnet Architecture.

See the previous question.

(B) What is the Use of Perimeter Area?

See the previous question.

(B) What is IP Spoofing and How Can It Be Prevented?

IP Spoofing is a technique using which an attacker gets unauthorized access to computers and sends messages to another computer with a forged IP address indicating that the message is coming from a trusted host. There are a few variations on the types of attacks of using IP spoofing.

IP spoofing can be prevented in two ways:

- Check if the request is legitimate.
- Or use IPSec and VPN.

(I) Which Firewall Have You Worked With ?

This question has to be answered according to an individual's experience.

> ***Note:*** *We have dedicated a complete chapter to VPNs. We will cover the firewall-based approaches of VPN in the section, 'VPN.'*

4

VPN

(B) Explain the Difference Between Trusted and Untrusted Networks?

Trusted networks are defined as networks which share the same security policy and procedures. Untrusted networks are the opposite of trusted networks, they do not follow the same security policy. Untrusted networks' security policies are unknown and unpredictable. The most secure policy is to allow connections to trusted networks only.

(B) Briefly Define VPN.

VPN is an encrypted, encapsulated, authorized, and authenticated communication process between nodes through an open, unsecured routed network.

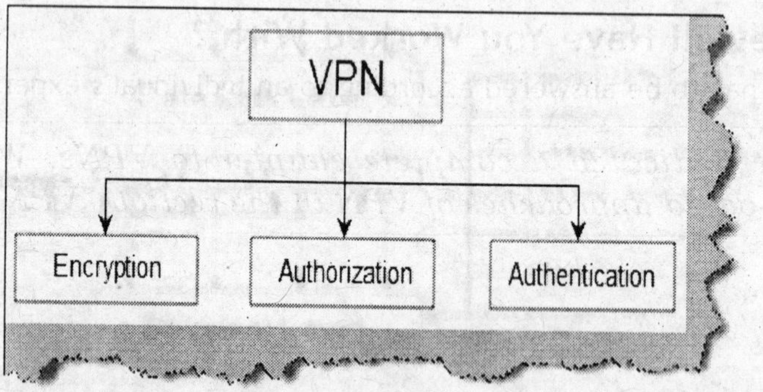

Figure: VPN Definition

Figure 'VPN in Action' shows how different networks are connected by tunnels formed by VPN. This tunnel is encrypted, encapsulated, authorized, and authenticated. So when data is transmitted over the Internet, it's secured.

Let's understand the four capabilities of VPN, i.e., encrypted, encapsulated, authenticated, and authorized.

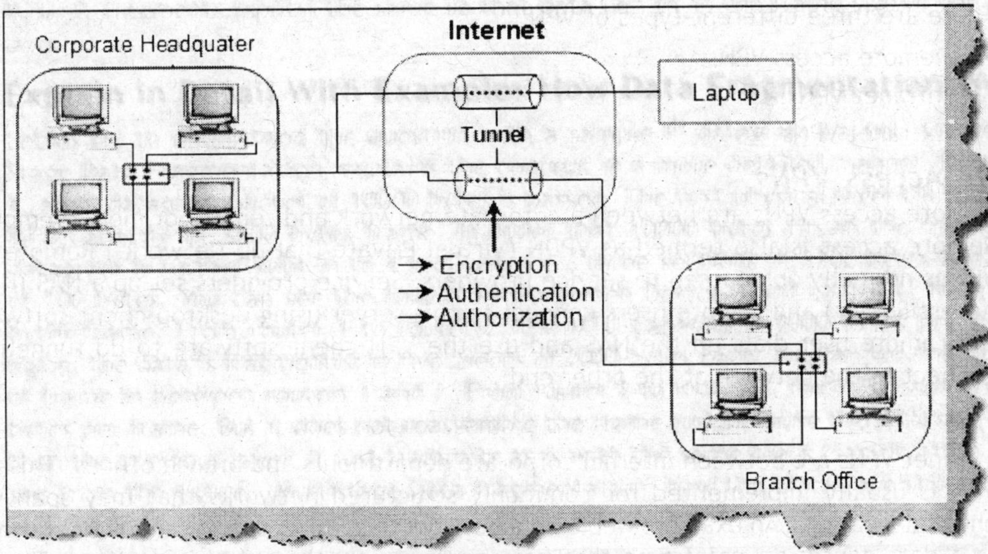

Figure: VPN in Action

Encryption guarantees that the data is read by the intended recipient only. Authentication ensures that data is delivered and read by the intended recipient only. Authorization is a process of granting or denying access to a resource.

(B) What are the Different Types of VPN?

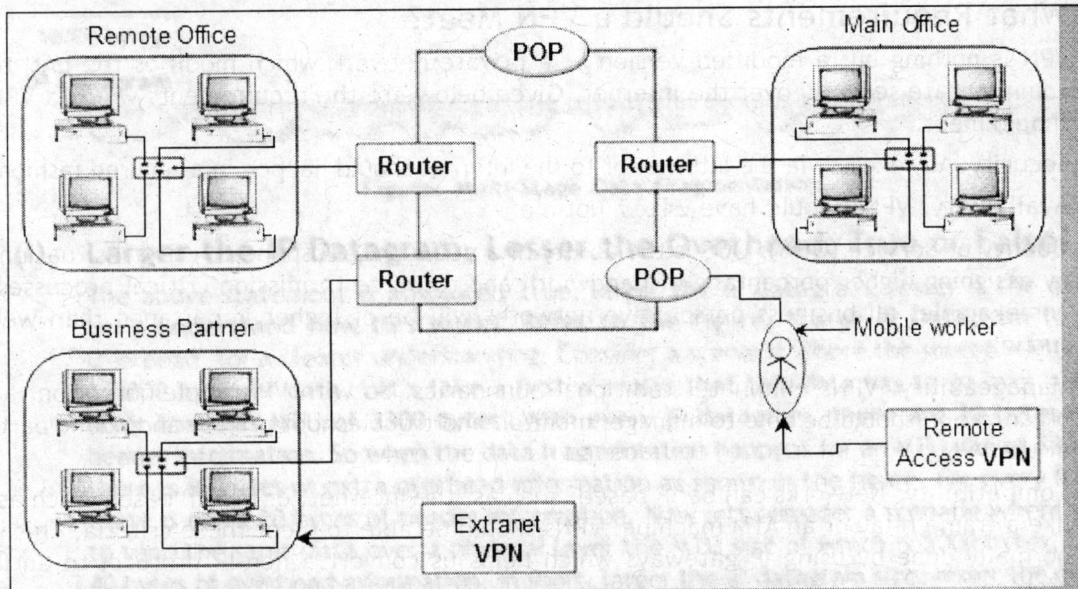

Figure: Three Types of VPNs

There are three different types of VPN:

- Remote access VPNs.
- Intranet VPNs.
- Extranet VPNs

Remote Access VPNs

Remote access VPNs are between a corporate network and remote or mobile employees. Remote access is also termed as VPDN (Virtual Private Dial-up Network.) Remote access VPN is normally outsourced to service providers. Service providers set up a NAS (Network Access Server) and remote users connect to this server using desktop client software. So the remote user dials up the NAS and use the VPN client software to do tunneling and connect to the network at the other end.

Intranet VPNs

Intranet VPNs are between internal corporate departments and branch offices. This type of VPN is usually implemented for commonly structured networks that may span various physical locations. An example would be a network that exists in several buildings connected to a data-center or mainframe that has secure access through private lines. These may need strong encryption and strict performance and bandwidth requirements.

Extranet VPNs

Extranet VPN's between are a corporation and its strategic partners or customers. This type of VPN uses the Internet as its base and deals with a wider scale of users and locations to allow customers and branch offices to access corporate resources across various network types.

(B) What Requirements Should a VPN Meet?

VPN is nothing but a modified version of a private network which modifies the LAN to communicate securely over the internet. Given below are the requirements which a VPN should meet:

Security: Any access via the Internet or to the Internet should happen in a secured fashion.

Availability: VPNs should have 24 x 7 uptime.

Quality of Service (QOS): QOS is the ability of a network to respond to critical situations by assigning higher percentage of bandwidth and resource to mission critical processes. For example, all business perspective networks will be of higher importance than web surfing.

Manageability: VPNs eliminate traditional boundaries. So with VPN implementation, an organization should be able to manage, monitor, and troubleshoot private and public parts of the VPN.

Compatibility: Networks can be IP based, such as, the Internet, or non-IP based, such as, like a frame relay or an ATM machine. VPNs should be able to meet these criteria. This is normally done by using IP gateways which helps us convert a non-IP protocol to an IP protocol.

(I) In How Many Ways Can VPN Architecture Be Implemented?

VPN can be implemented in many different ways. But there are four major ways of looking at VPN architecture, figure 'VPN Architecture View' shows these ways in a more detailed fashion. We will understand every section step by step.

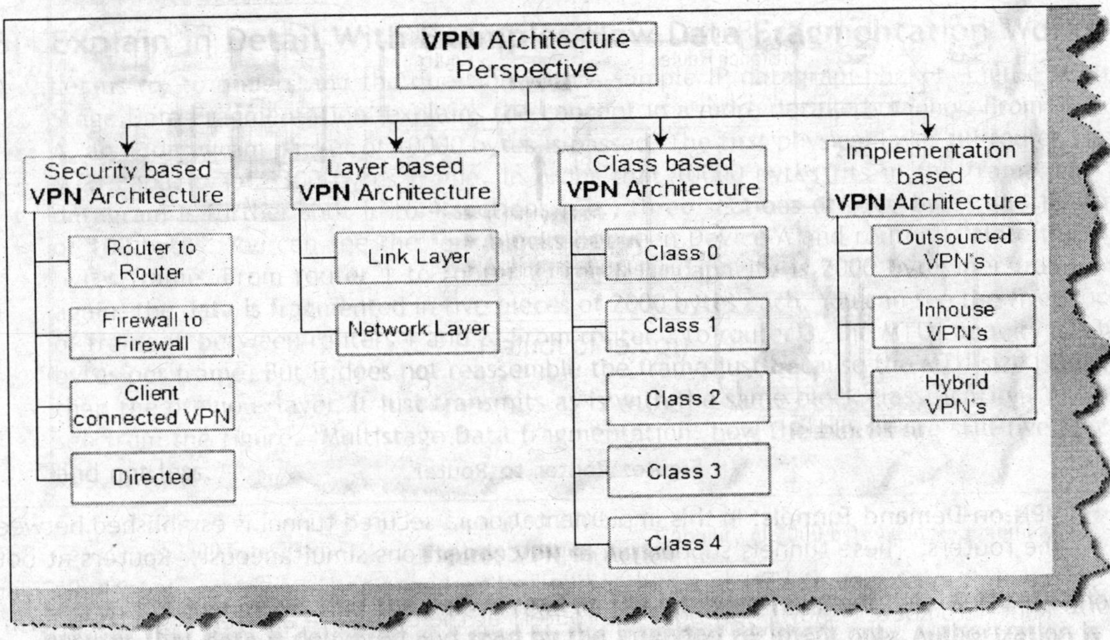

Figure: VPN Architecture View

Implementation-Based Architecture

In this, the architecture is decided depending on which end is implementing the VPN. So depending on which end is responsible for implementing the VPN, the architecture is decided. There are three main categories for implementation-based architecture:

Outsourced VPNs: In this architecture, the service provider is responsible for giving the VPN solution. So it is the responsibility of the service provider to implement tunneling. In this architecture, the organization does not need to change its existing infrastructure. When a user tries to access a remote resource, the user is authenticated with the NAS located at the ISP. Once the authentication is done, the user sends and receives data through a secured established tunnel.

In-House VPNs: In this architecture, the entire responsibility of establishing the VPN is handled by the organization itself. The role of the service provider is very small in the VPN activity. As the VPN is controlled by the organization, it has full control over the VPN.

Hybrid VPNs: This architecture offers the benefits of both outsourced and in-house VPNs. It is used when the organization does not outsource the complete VPN to one provider. So you have multiple providers controlling the VPN. This helps us eliminate the monopoly of one service provider, thus ensuring availability if one ISP goes down.

Security-Based VPN Architecture

From the security aspect, we can classify security-based VPNs into the following three categories:

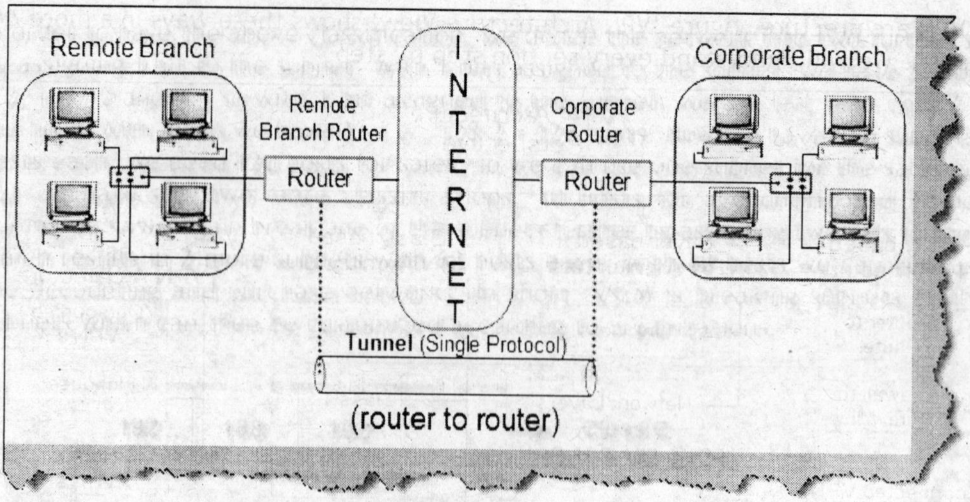

Figure: Router to Router

VPN-on-Demand Tunnels: In this implementation, a secured tunnel is established between the routers. These tunnels support multiple connections simultaneously. Routers at both the ends must support VPN capabilities like key exchange and encryption algorithm. Figure 'Router to Router' shows how both the routers at the corporate and remote branch form a tunnel for communication on the Internet.

VPN-on-Demand Multiprotocol Tunnel: This architecture is an extension of 'VPN-on-Demand Tunnel.' It supports multiple tunneling protocols within the Internet. This tunneling protocol is not specific to any protocol. Non-IP data can be tunneled across the Internet using this architecture.

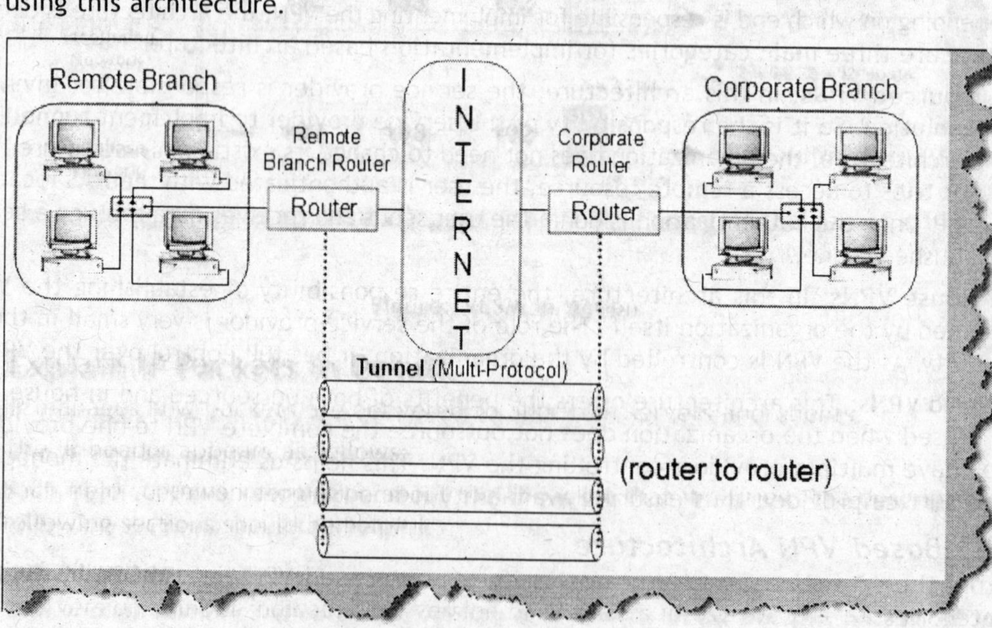

Figure: Multi-Protocol Tunneling

Figure 'Multi-Protocol Tunneling' is a modification of VPN-on-Demand tunneling, only that the tunnel can now do multi-protocol tunneling.

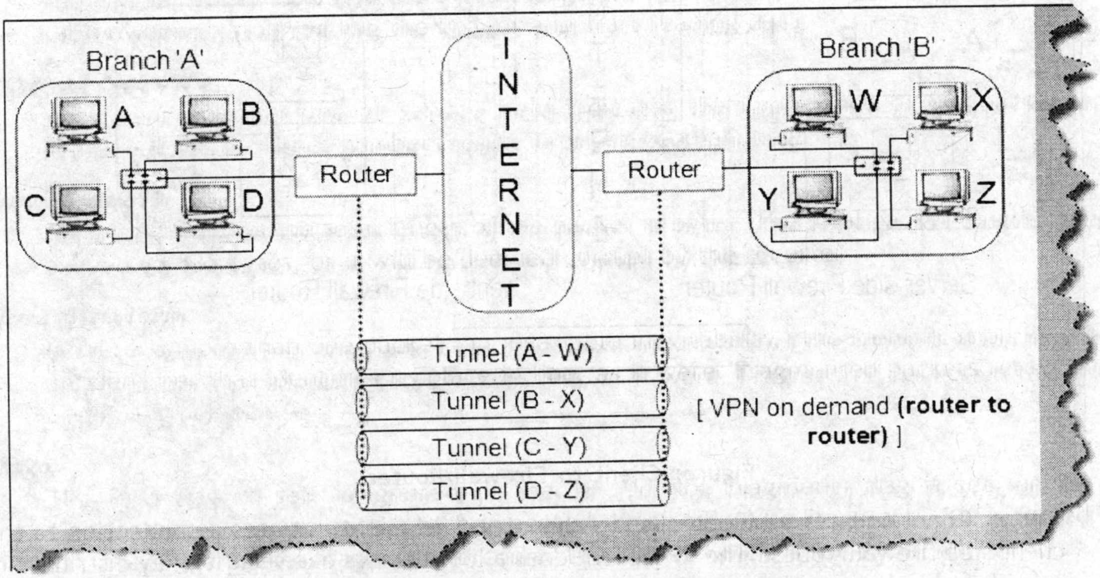

Figure: VPN-on-Demand Router to Router

VPN-on-Demand Encrypted Session: In this implementation, separate tunnels for each request is established between two routers. So even if we have requests for the same network, multiple connections will be opened. Figure 'VPN-on-Demand Router to Router' shows how for every communication a new tunnel is opened. For example, if computer A wants to communicate with Computer X, a separate tunnel is spawned. A major disadvantage of this architecture is overheads.

Firewall-to-Firewall VPNs

This is same like the router, only that the VPN is established between two firewalls.

VPN-on-Demand Tunnels: This is very much similar to router to router, the only difference we have firewalls now.

VPN-on-Demand Multiprotocol Tunnel: Again, this is same as the router to router multiprotocol tunneling, only that it's replaced with a firewall.

Client-Connected VPNs

In client connected VPNs, an encryption and tunnel mechanism is installed on the client itself. Due to this, the VPN client plays an important role for tunnel establishment. In this, the VPN session is negotiated between the client and the firewall/router. The VPN client has huge process burdens like key distribution, complex processing, management, and security. VPN clients should also be compatible with a large variety of operating systems.

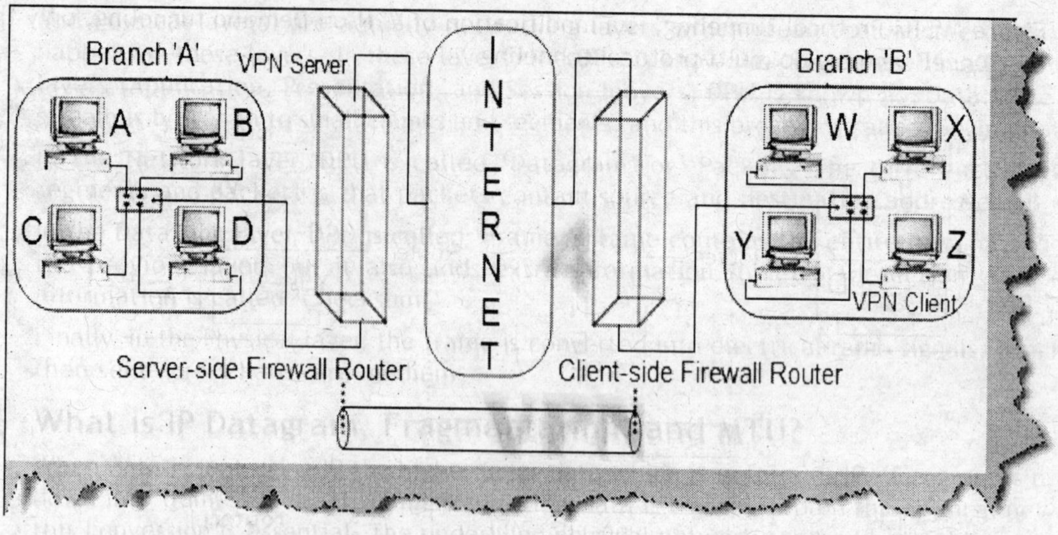

Figure: Client to Firewall/Router

Figure 'Client to Firewall/Router' shows how the VPN client initiates a connection to the client side firewall/router. The VPN client does a lot of things like security, key distribution, etc. The tunnel is established right from the VPN client to the server side router or firewall.

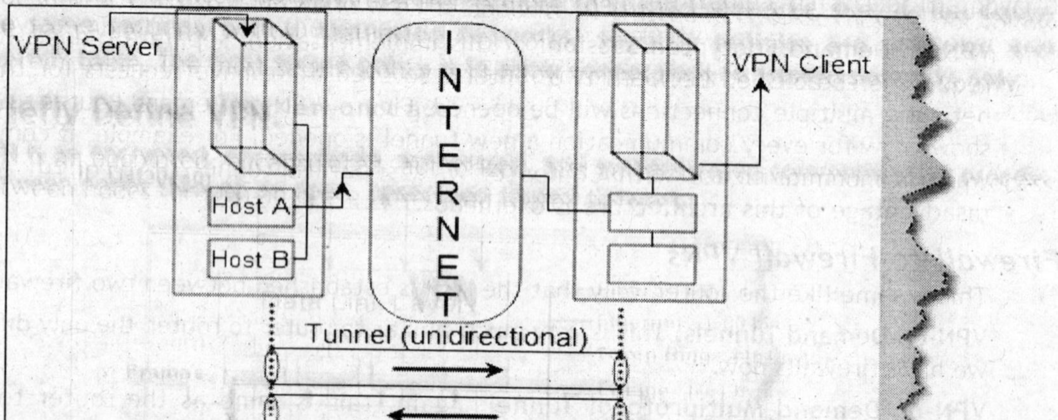

Figure: Directed VPNs

Directed VPN: In directed VPNs, we do not have bidirectional communication tunnels. Only unidirectional tunnels are established between the communicating ends as shown in the figure 'Directed VPNs.' Security is more stringent in directed VPNs. In bidirectional tunnels, if a hacker gains access to a network he gets access to all networks connected to that network.

Layer-Based VPN Architecture

VPN architecture can also be viewed depending which OSI layer the VPN setup functions on. Depending on the same, they are classified into the following two categories:

Link-layer VPNs: As the name suggests, link-layer VPNs use the link-layer of the OSI model. They are limited to local networks as they use MAC addresses.

Network-Layer VPNs: Network-layer VPNs use Layer 3, i.e., the network-layer for VPN connections.

Class-Based VPN Architecture

Depending on purpose, size, scope, and complexity, VPN architectures are divided into the following five classes:

Class 0 VPNs: These are meant for small organizations with an intranet limited to a single site. Minimum requirements for Class 0 VPN are as follows:

- VPN server with at least Windows 2000.
- VPN client with at least Windows 98 or 95.
- Tunneling protocol, such as, PPTP.
- Internet access options, such as, a DSL or a T1 line.

Class 1 VPNs: It is suited for small to medium organization with 2 to 20 remote networks. Class 1 is more secure than Class 0 because of encryption, IPSEC, and strong remote user authentication mechanism. Given below are the requirements for Class 1 VPNs:

- DES Encryption.
- User authentication mechanism.
- Remote dial and access client software.
- Good and fast Internet line like T1 or T3.
- One or more VPN gateway.

Class 2 VPN's: These are mainly suited for medium-scale organizations with 10 to 100 remote networks. This class offers stronger security than Class 1 and hence is a bit costly. Main requirements for Class 2 VPNs are as follows:

- IPsec and 3DES-based data encryption.
- User authentication mechanism.
- Two to Six VPN gateways that can support 500 simultaneous sessions.
- Extra security mechanism like AAA, RADIUS, NAT, etc.
- Remote dial access and remote access client software.
- Fast access options, such as, T1 or T3.

Class 3 VPNs: These are suited for medium to large organization with hundreds of remote sites. Class 3 supports extranets in addition to site-to-site and remote connectivity. Given below are the requirements for Class 3 VPNs:

- ISP connectivity with 24x7 uptime.
- IPSEC and 3DES data encryption
- User authentication mechanism, such as, soft tokens.
- In-house certificate service.
- Good Internet options, such as, ISDN and XSDL with T1 or T3.
- Extra security mechanism, such as, AAA, RADIUS, NAT, etc.

Class 4 VPN's: These are suited for large organizations with intranet spread across server thousand remote sites. The security offered is maximum. This class is the most scalable and adaptable in future. Given below are the minimum requirements of Class 4 VPNs:

- ISP connectivity with 24x7 uptime.
- IPSEC and 3DES encryption.
- User authentication mechanism, such as, soft tokens.
- In-house certificate service.
- Good internet options, such as, ISDN and XSDL with T1 or T3.
- Extra security mechanism, such as, AAA, RADIUS, NAT, etc.
- Properly defined remote policy.

(I) What are the Different Authentication Mechanisms Used in VPNs?

Following are the common authentication mechanisms used in VPNs:

Login ID and Password: In this, we use the operating system's login id and password to verify the user's identity.

S/Key Password: It's a one-time password system where one does not want a long-term password. Let's try to understand how S/Key authentication actually works. It's a two-fold process, one is the password generation and the other is authentication.

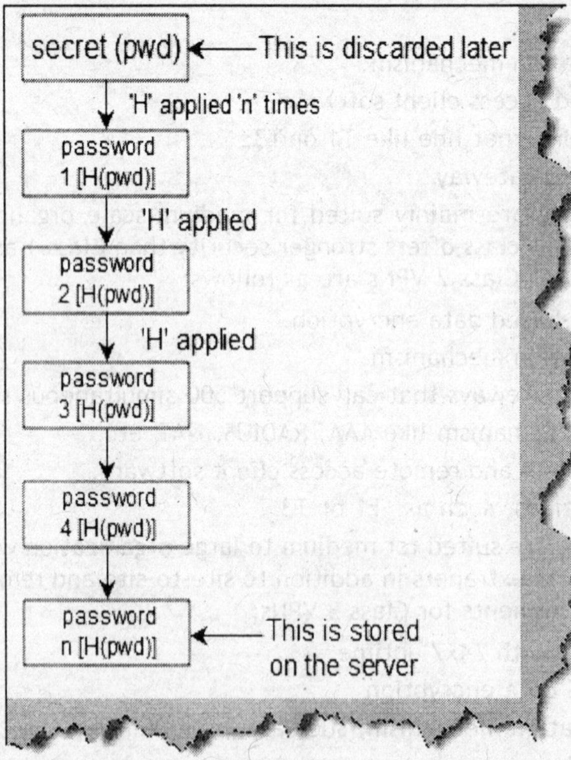

Figure: S/Key Password Generation

The password is generated on the server. Let's understand, step-by-step, the password generation process.**Step 1**: A secret 'pwd' key is either provided by the user or generated by the computer.**Step 2**: 'H,' i.e., the cryptographic function is applied 'N' times and 'N' passwords are generated.**Step 3**: The secret key, i.e., 'pwd' is then discarded.**Step 4**: The end user is provided with those 'N' passwords in reverse order.**Step 5**: The first (n-1) passwords are discarded and only the last password is stored for user authentication. Figure 'S/Key Password Generation' shows howthe password is generated 'n' times using 'h' the cryptographic function.

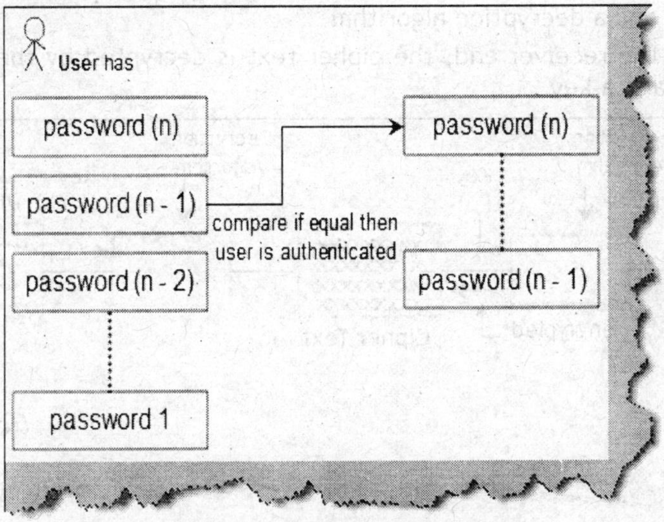

Figure: S/Key Authentication

As mentioned in the previous section, after the passwords are generated, they are sent to the end user. The first one is not used, so it's scratched off. Step 1: User Provides the second password from the password list.Step 2: Server checks this with its current password. If valid, it authenticates the user. Figure 'S/Key Authentication' depicts how the password is validated.

RADIUS(Remote Access Dial-In User Service): It's an internet security protocol which run with a client-server model. RADIUS authenticates the client with its own internal username/ password list which it maintains. RADIUS transactions between client and RADIUS server can be encrypted.

Two-Factor Token-Based Mechanism: As the name suggests, it uses DUAL authentication to validate a user's credentials. It uses two things, token and password to authenticate a user. So during the authentication process, we have a hardware-based electronic device which generates a token and a password like the PIN number. ATMs (Automated Teller Machine) are an excellent example of this kind of authentication mechanism. Your ATM card gives you a hardware-based identification token and you also need a PIN number for the password. Any one of these two factors fails and you are not able to access your account.

(B) Explain the Basics of Encryption in VPN.

Authentication and encryption are two very important aspects of VPN. Authentication, we discussed in the previous question. Encryption, also called 'cryptography,' is the mechanism of converting data into an unreadable format called 'Cipher Text.' So when data is transmitted over an unsecured mechanism, it cannot be read by hackers.

Figure 'Basic Encryption Fundamentals' shows how basic encryption works. So we have basically a sender and a receiver, and data passes through the follwing process:

- Sender wants to send a plain text.
- Plain text is encrypted using an encryption algorithm with a key which will encrypt the same.
- The output of the previous step leads to unreadable cipher text. It can only be encrypted by the key and a decryption algorithm
- Finally, at the receiver end, the cipher text is decrypted by the help of decryption algorithm and a key.

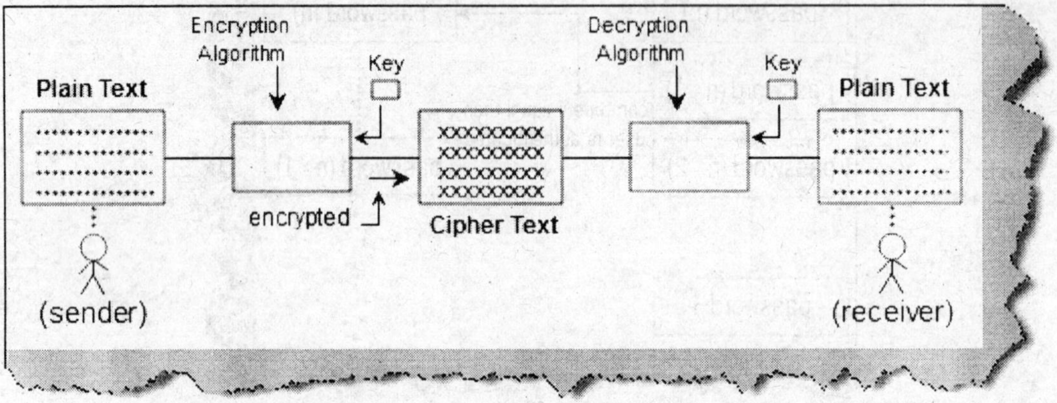

Figure: Basic Encryption Fundamentals

(I) What is the Difference Between Symmetric and Asymmetric Cryptosystems?

Symmetric cryptography is based on a fixed key. It is also called the 'single-key algorithm.' The fixed key is also called 'Private' or 'Secret' key. The private key must be shared between both parties before the cryptography process. In short, if the key is known to a third party, there is a possibility of the message getting hacked, that's why the name private key. Figure 'Symmetric Cryptosystem' shows how it works.

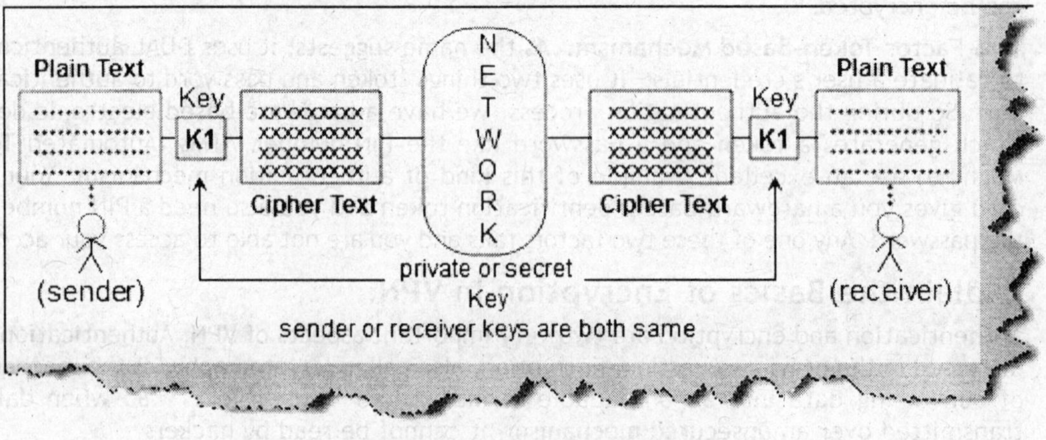

Figure: Symmetric Cryptography

Asymmetric cryptography is not based on fixed key. It uses two keys, one is the private and the other is the public key. The public key is distributed freely while private key is known only to the owner. The public key is used for encrypting purposes while the private key is use for decrypting purposes. Figure 'Asymmetric Cryptography' shows how we need the two keys, one is the public key for encrypting messages and is shared between both the ends, whereas the private key is different at both the ends.

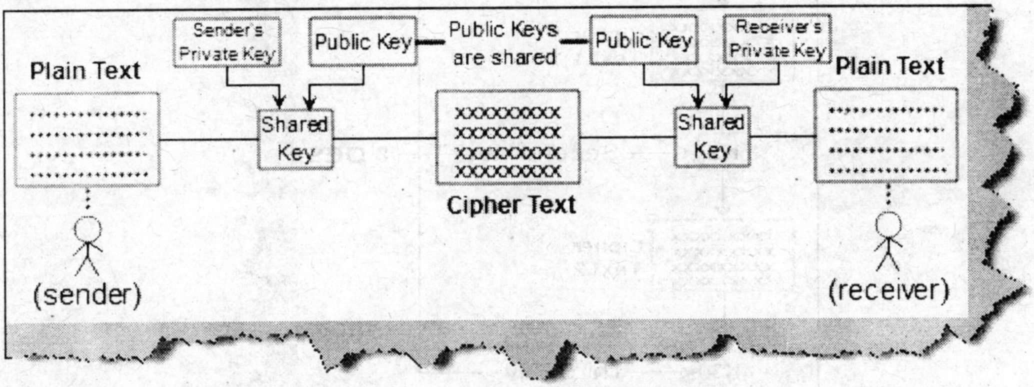

Figure: Asymmetric Cryptography

(I) what are the Different Symmetric Algorithms?

Depending on the length of the key, many symmetric algorithms have been developed. Some of the symmetric algorithms in VPN are explained below:

Data Encryption Standard (DES): DES has a key length of 56 bits. Earlier, the proposed key length was 128 bits, but to increase processing speed it was made to 56 bits. Due to short key length, it is vulnerable to brute-force attacks.

Triple Data Encryption Standard (3DES): 3DES also uses a 56-bit key. But it is more secured than DES because it has three keys. Figure 'Triple DES' shows how the encryption process operates. The first key encrypts the plain text data. The cipher output of the first encryption is encrypted again by a second key. This way the encryption process is repeated thrice, therefore the name 3DES.

RC4 (Ron's Code 4): This algorithm's key length can go up to 256 bytes. Because the key length is bigger than DES, it's a stronger encryption mechanism as compared to DES. RC4 uses XOR mechanism for encryption, which is quiet fast as compared to DES. RC4 generates a stream of random bytes and XOR's them with the original text. Because of the XOR, RC4 requires a new key every time.

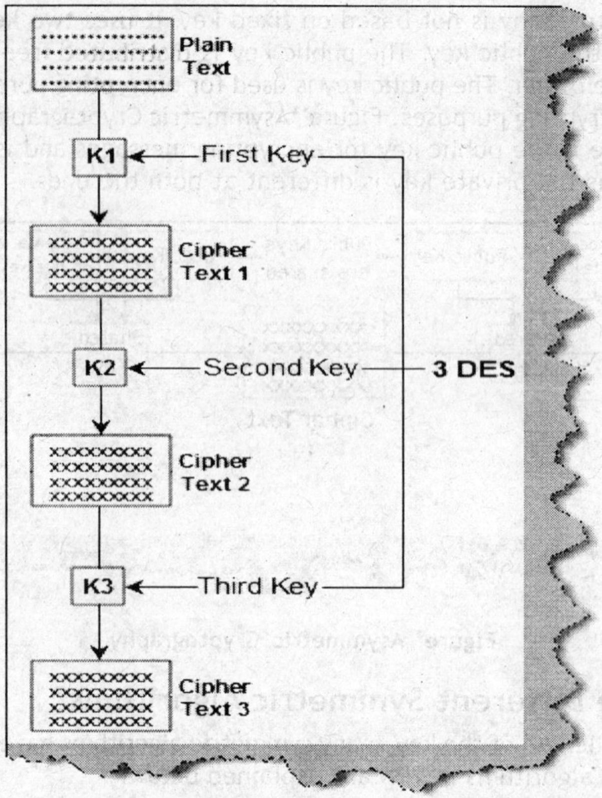

Figure: Triple DES

(B) What are the Disadvantages of Symmetric Algorithms?

There are two major problems with symmetric algorithms:

- There is just one key and if that's known to an intruder everything is gone.
- Key management can become problem for large number of communications. When we say key management, we mean by setup, distribution, and key replacement. This can be expensive and time consuming.

(I) What are the Different Asymmetric Algorithms?

In VPN solutions, there are two major asymmetric algorithms DH (Diffie-Hellman,) and RSA (Rivet Shamir Adleman).

DH Algorithm: In this algorithm, every communicating entity gets a pair of keys. The algorithm works in the following manner:

- Sender gets the recipient's public key. The public key is shared between all parties.
- Sender then uses his private key and recipient's public key, which results in a new key called the shared key.
- The message is then encrypted using the shared key and this encrypted message is then forwarded to the recipient.
- Recipient then generates a shared secret key which involves his own private key, and decrypts the message.

The biggest disadvantage of the DH algorithm is that a hacker can intercept the request for public key and send its own public key to both communicating ends.

RSA Algorithm: Due its strong authentication mechanism, RSA is now the defacto standard for asymmetric cryptography. Given below are the steps for how RSA implements encryption:

- Sender's public key is sent to the recipient.
- Sender uses a hash function and compresses the size of the original message. This compressed message is termed as Message Digest (MD.)
- Sender uses the private key and makes a unique digital signature from the same.
- Both the message and the signature are then sent to the end recipient.
- Recipient then decrypts the signature using the sender's public key.
- Recipient then compares the message-digest send previously and the one generated from the digital signature to see if it matches. This ensures that the data was not fabricated.

Figure 'RSA Algorithm' shows how the RSA algorithm actually works. You can compare the steps defined with the figure below for better clarity.

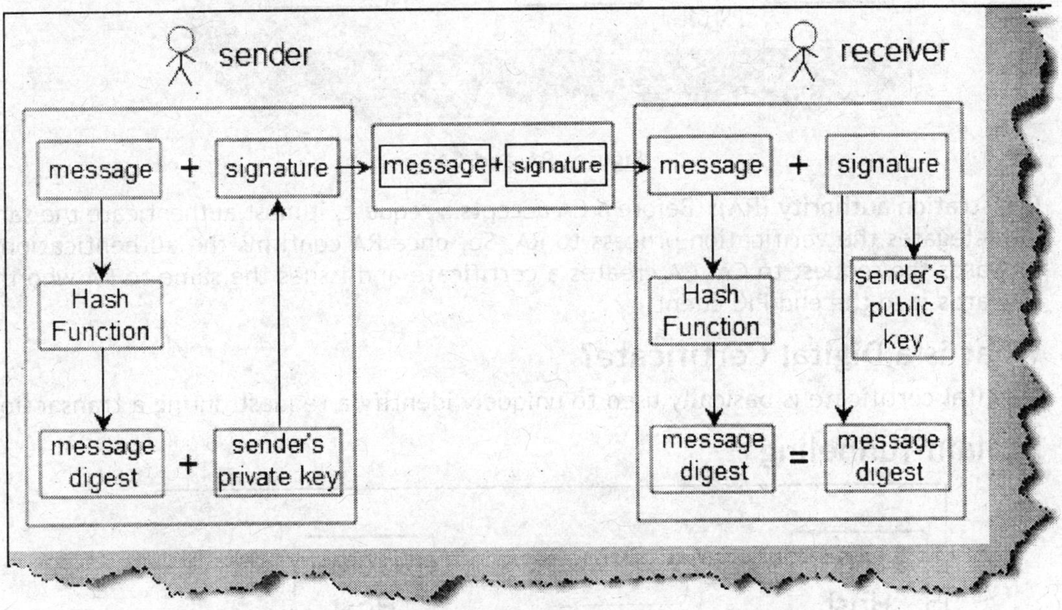

Figure: RSA Algorithm

(I) Explain the Different Components in PKI?

PKI (Public Key Infrastructure) is a system by which we can manage keys and secure data for exchange. PKI has the following components:

- PKI client
- Certification authority (CA)
- Registration authority (RA)
- Certificates
- Certificate distribution system

PKI client: PKI client requests a digital certificate from CA or RA. In order that PKI client can participate in any transaction, PKI client should get a certificate. Once the client gets the certificate it uses the certificate to identify itself. The end client needs to safeguard the certificate. PKI client should protect the certificate from intruders. So it's the responsibility of the PKI client to keep the certificate secure.

Certification Authority (CA): CA is a trusted third party which issues digital certificates to PKI clients. Before it issues digital certificates, it verifies if the PKI client is genuine. A well-known CA is Verisign.

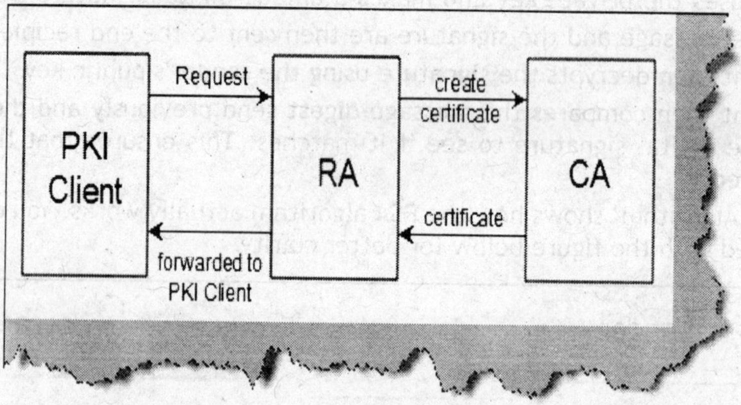

Figure: RA and CA

Registration authority (RA): Before a CA accepts a request, it must authenticate the same. CA delegates the verification process to RA. So, once RA confirms the authentication, it forwards the request to CA. CA creates a certificate and issues the same to RA who then forwards it to the end PKI client.

(B) What is a Digital Certificate?

A digital certificate is basically used to uniquely identify a request during a transaction.

(B) Explain Tunneling

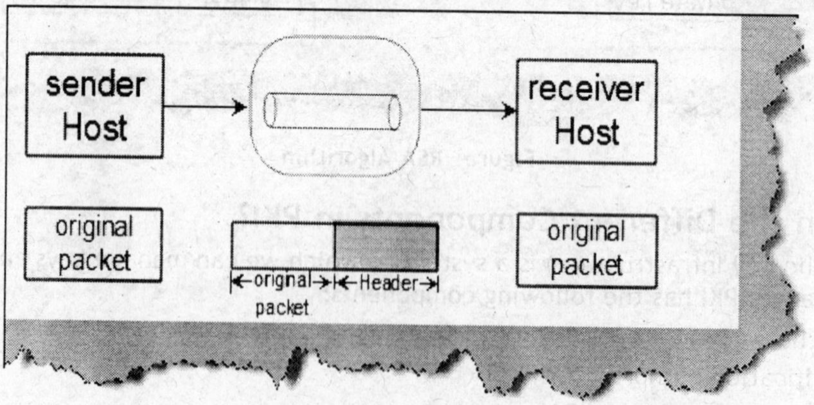

Figure: The VPN tunnel

Tunneling is the most important concept of VPN technology. It's the technique of encapsulating entire data packets. The original packet, also called the 'payload,' is appended with header information. The header provides routing information so that the packet can be successfully delivered across the network.

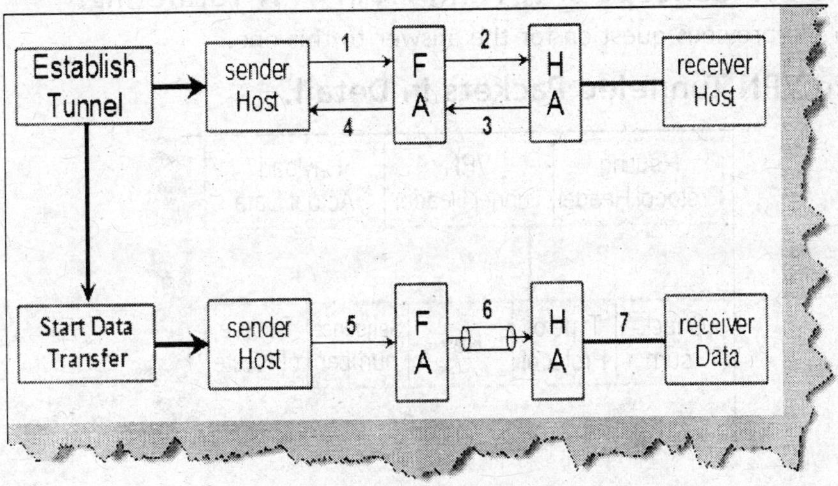

Figure: Two-Step Process for Tunnel

It's a two step process to form VPN tunnel. The first step is to authenticate and create a tunnel and the second process is to use the tunnel to start data transfer. Figure 'Detail Tunneled Packet' shows the two-step process in a more detailed manner. Before we try to understand the steps in detail, we need to understand two terminologies: HA and FA.

HA (Home Agent): This software resides at the receiver end. HA receives and authenticates the request if they come from trusted users.

FA (Foreign Agent): This software resides on the sender's end. Sender uses FA to initiate a VPN session.

Below is the sequence of events, please refer to the figure 'Detail Tunneled Packet' for the steps:

Establish Tunnel

Step 1: Client sends a connection request to FA. FA authenticates whether the request is valid by login name and password. To validate username and password, FA can use services like RADIUS server.

Step 2: If FA authenticates the request, it forwards the same to HA.

Step 3: HA verifies the request and replies with tunnel number to FA.

Step 4: FA forwards the tunnel number to the sender, and a tunnel is established for future communication.

Start Data Transfer

Step 5: Once the tunnel is established, the sender starts sending packets to FA.

Step 6: FA, using the tunnel number, creates the tunnel header and appends the same to each payload/data packet.

Step 7: On receiving the packet, HA strips of the header and forwards the packet to its original format and passes the same to the receiver.

Figure 'Two-Step Process for Tunnel' explains the same in a detailed manner.

(I) What is the Concept of HA and FA in VPN Tunneling?

Refer to the previous question for the answer to this one.

(I) Explain VPN Tunneled Packets in Detail.

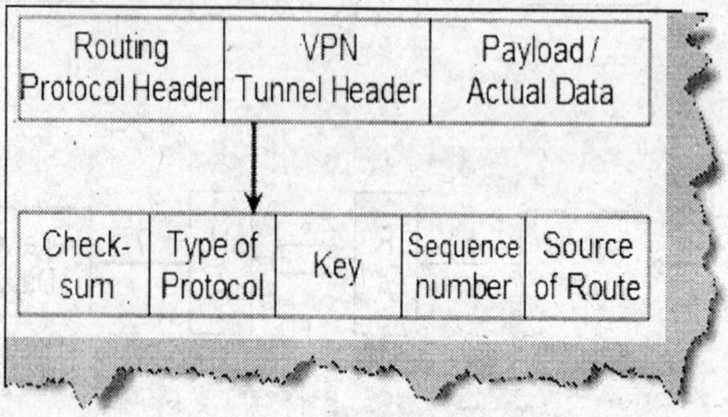

Figure: Detail Tunneled Packet

A tunneled packet is divided into three sections. Figure 'Detailed Tunneled Packet' represents the same in a pictorial fashion.

Given below is a detailed explanation of the same in a detailed manner.

Section	Description
Routing Protocol Header	This is a header field and contains the address of sender and destination address of the receiver.
VPN Tunnel Header	The header section is divided in to five sections: · **Type of Protocol**: This field gives protocol information of the original data packet. · **Checksum:** This field is used to check if the actual data was tampered or corrupted. · **Key:** This key is used to identify and authenticate the actual data source. · **Sequence Number:** This field has a number which indicates the sequence in which the packets travel. · **Source Routing:** This is an optional field which contains additional routing information.
Actual Data/Payload	This field contains the actual data which is also called 'Payload.'

(I) Explain Voluntary and Compulsory Tunnels.

Based on how they are created, there are two basic types of tunnels: compulsory and voluntary.

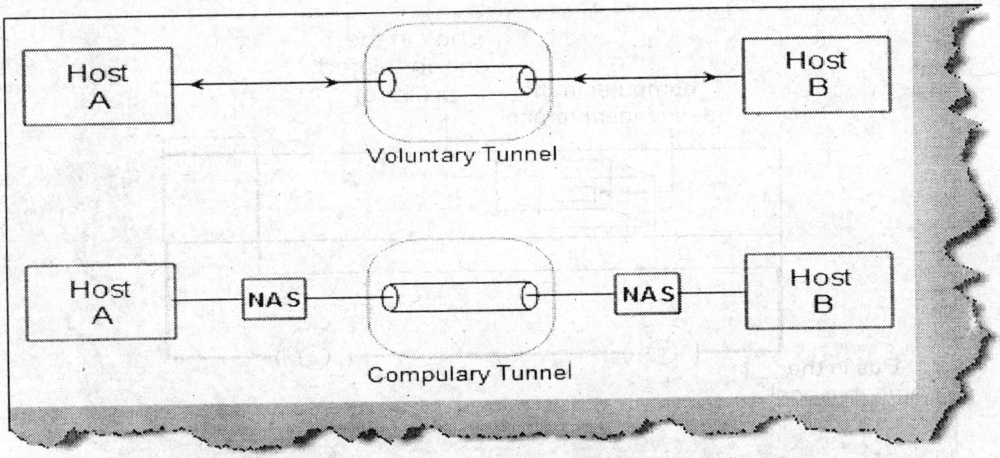

Figure: Voluntary and Compulsory Tunnels

Voluntary Tunnels: These tunnels are created at the request of the user host. So, until the initiator does not request for the tunnel they are not created. For each communicating pair host, one tunnel is created and once the communication is over, this tunnel is terminated. So the remote client that wants to setup a tunnel dials the network using dial-up connection. Once the dial-up connection is established the tunnel is setup.

Compulsory Tunnels: Compulsory tunnels are pre-configured by intermediate devices like NAS (Network Attached Storage.) So, the end-user host must compulsorily use this tunnel and not create its own, hence the term 'compulsory tunnel.'

(I) Explain Static and Dynamic Tunnels?

Static tunnels remain active regardless of data transmission, whereas dynamic tunnels are activated only when data transfer is needed. Static tunnels are also called 'Compulsory Tunnels' as mentioned earlier. Dynamic tunnels are also called 'Voluntary Tunnels' because of their short period of connectivity.

(I) Explain Encapsulating, Carrier, and Passenger Protocol.

All the three mentioned protocols in the question are basically tunneling protocols.

Carrier Protocol: These protocols are used to describe the route through which the tunnel packet will travel to the destination.

Encapsulating Protocol: These protocols encapsulate the original data/payload. PPTP, L2TP, and IPSEC are some of the types of encapsulating protocols. They are also responsible for the life-cycle of the tunnel, i.e., creation, maintenance, and termination of the tunnel.

Passenger Protocol: These protocols are the original data or the payload. PPP and SLIP are some of the examples of passenger protocols.

Figure 'Tunneling Protocol' shows the mapping of the above three protocols to the actual world. In the figure, the vehicle is the carrier protocol, the box in which the computer is taken is the encapsulating protocol and the computer itself is the passenger protocol.

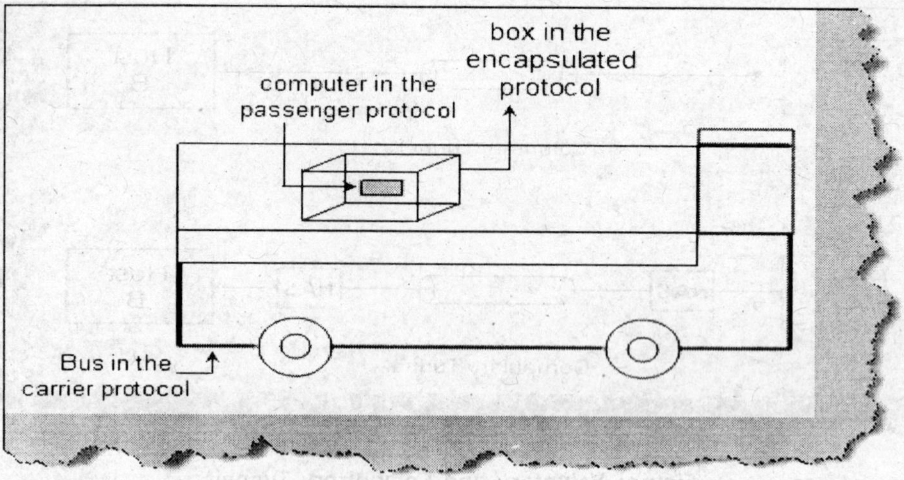

Figure: Tunneling Protocol

(A) On Which Layer Do L2F, PPTP, and L2TP Operate?

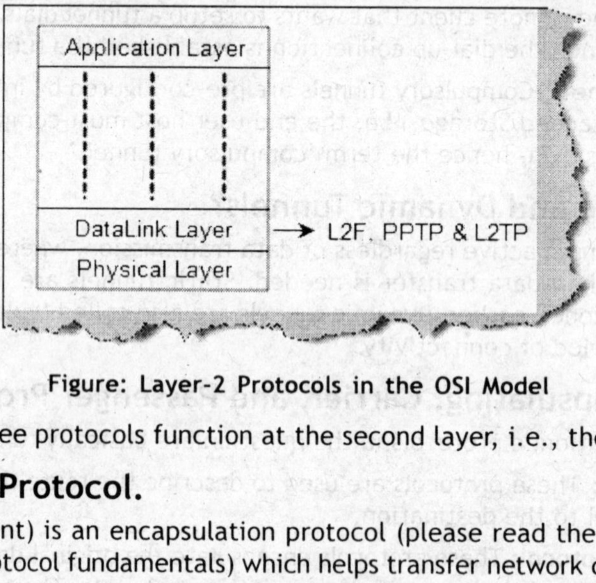

Figure: Layer-2 Protocols in the OSI Model

All the above three protocols function at the second layer, i.e., the data-link layer.

(I) Explain PPP Protocol.

PPP (Point-to-Point) is an encapsulation protocol (please read the previous questions for encapsulation protocol fundamentals) which helps transfer network data over point-to-point links.

There are three standards which PPP works on: HDLC, LCP, and NCP.

HDLC (High Level Data Link Control) encapsulates data packets. It divides the data packets into frames.

LCP (Link Control Protocol) is a standard for establishing, configuring, and testing point-to-point connection.

NCP (Network Control Protocol) is a standard for establishing and configuring network layer protocols.

(I) Explain the PPP Link Process Step by Step.

The PPP operation needs to fulfill the following conditions:

- Once the packets are encapsulated, the source sends LCP frames over P2P to the destination node.
- These frames are used to configure the link and test the establishment of the link.
- Once the destination host accepts the connection, the link is successfully established and optional parameters are negotiated.
- The source then sends NCP frames to configure the network layer.
- Once the network layer is configured, both ends start exchanging data.

Figure 'PPP Link Process' explains the concept in a more detailed manner.

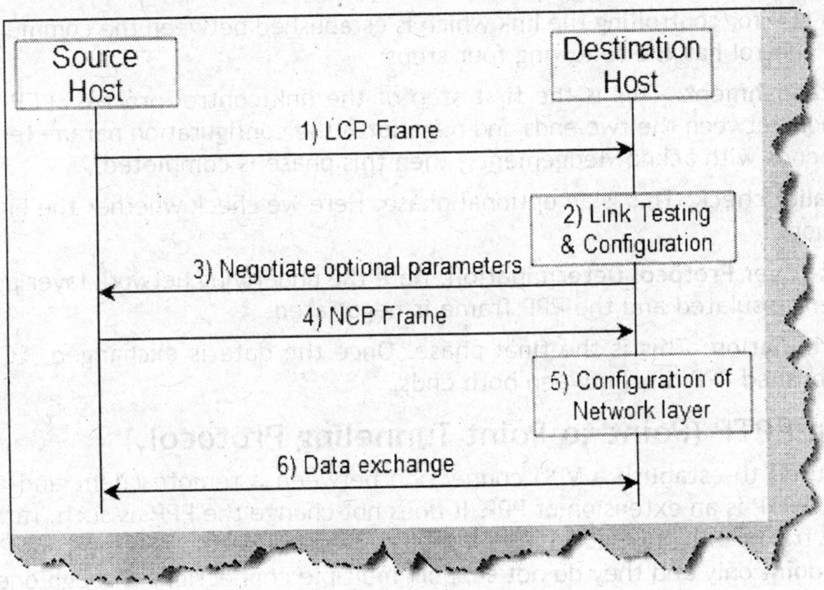

Figure: PPP Link Process

(I) Explain PPP Packet Format.

There are in all six fields in a PPP packet. Given below is a description of each field.

Flags: They indicate the beginning and the end of each frame.

Address: There is no address as such in PPP as it is point-to-point. This field has a binary sequence which represents a broadcast.

Control: This contains the binary sequence (00000011) which denotes that the frame has unsequenced data.

Protocol: This field identifies the protocol of the PPP packet.

Data: This field has the information exchanged between the source and the destination. The length of this field is variable.

FCS (Frame Check Sequence): This field had the check sequence by which we can verify the accuracy of the information received by the data section of the packet.

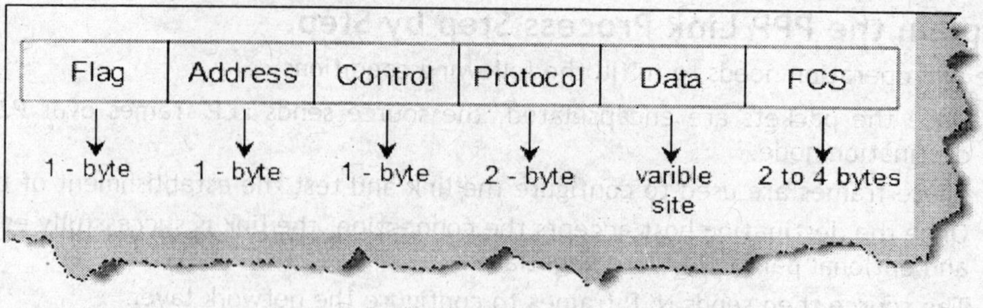

Figure: PPP Packet

(I) How Does PPP Use LCP (Link Control Process) For Link Control?

PPP uses LCP for controlling the link which is established between the communication ends. LCP link control has the following four steps:

Link establishment: This is the first step of the link control process. LCP establishes a connection between the two ends and negotiates the configuration parameters. When each end responds with acknowledgements, then this phase is completed.

Link Quality check: This is an optional phase. Here we check whether the link is ready for negotiation.

Network-Layer Protocol Determination: Here the underlying network layer protocol of the data is encapsulated and the PPP frame is negotiated.

Link Termination: This is the final phase. Once the data is exchanged, LCP terminates the established PPP link between both ends.

(I) Explain PPTP (Point-to-Point Tunneling Protocol.)

PPTP is used to establish a VPN connection between a remote client and an enterprise network. PPTP is an extension of PPP. It does not change the PPP as such, rather it defines how PPP traffic will flow across unsecured networks like the Internet. All PPTP must be point to point only and they do not support multiple connections through one connection.

There are three important components of the PPTP process:

PPTP Clients: PPTP client requests NAS server to initiate PPTP connection.

PPTP Server: PPTP are network nodes that support PPTP, and are capable of servicing requests for VPN sessions from remote and local locations.

PPTP Network Access Servers (NAS): NASs are located at the ISP. They provide Internet connectivity to the clients which dial-in using the PPTP client.

It's a three step process as showed in figure "Steps in PPTP tunnel".

Step1: First PPP client dials the NAS and establishes connection.

Step 2: User is authenticated by the NAS server.

Step 3: Data exchange starts. From the PPTP client to the NAS we have PPP connection while from the PPTP client to the PPTP server we have support of TCP + IP datagram.

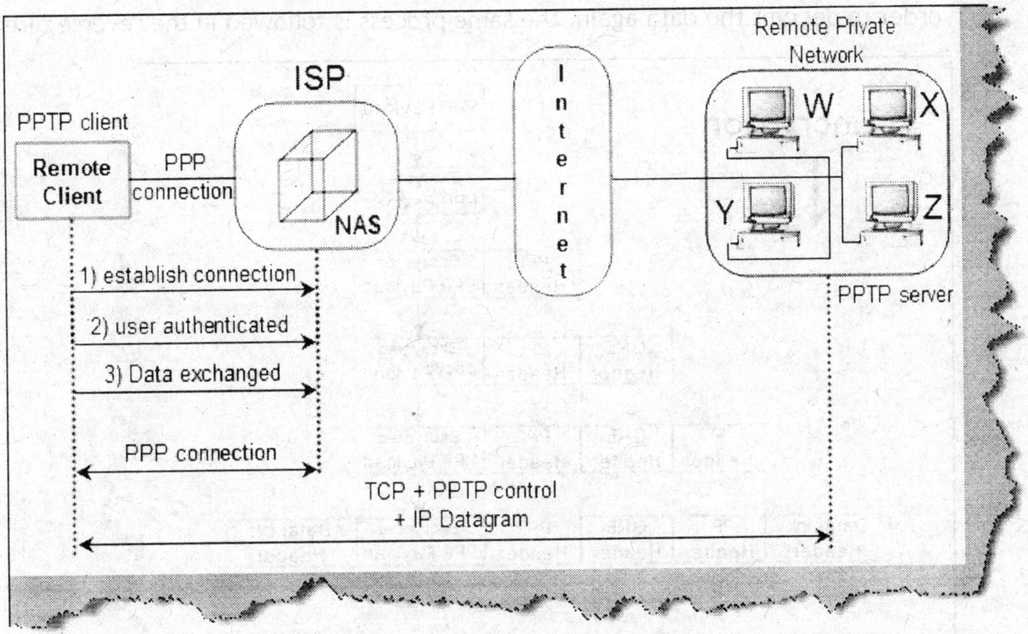

Figure: Steps in PPTP Tunnel

(A) What is GRE in PPTP?

Generic Routing Encapsulation (GRE) is a tunneling protocol to encapsulate a large variety of network layer packets inside IP tunneling packets. The original packet is the payload for the final packet. The protocol is used on the Internet to secure virtual private networks.

GRE was made by Cisco and was designed to be stateless; the tunnel end-points do not monitor the state or availability of other tunnel end-points. This feature helps service providers support IP tunnels for clients who won't know the service provider's internal tunneling architecture; and it gives clients the flexibility of reconfiguring their IP architectures without worrying about connectivity. GRE creates a virtual point-to-point link with routers at remote points on an IP internetwork.

(I) How Does PPTP Encapsulate Data?

There are multiple stages through which PPTP encrypts and decrypts data.

The figure below shows how it moves through the various stages of encryption and decryption.

- First the original information is encapsulated with PPP frame on the payload.
- The resultant PPP encrypted payload is further encrypted with GRE (the previous question explains what GRE is) and PPP header. GRE consists of an acknowledgement field and a 2-byte long payload length. PPTP sets the payload length and creates a PPTP tunnel.
- An IP header is further added to the GRE encapsulated data. The IP header contains the addresses of the source, i.e., the PPTP client and the destination server.
- As mantioned earlier, PPTP operates on the data-link layer. The IP header appended packet is further encapsulated with data-link layer header and trailer.

In order to decrypt the data again, the same process is followed in the reverse direction.

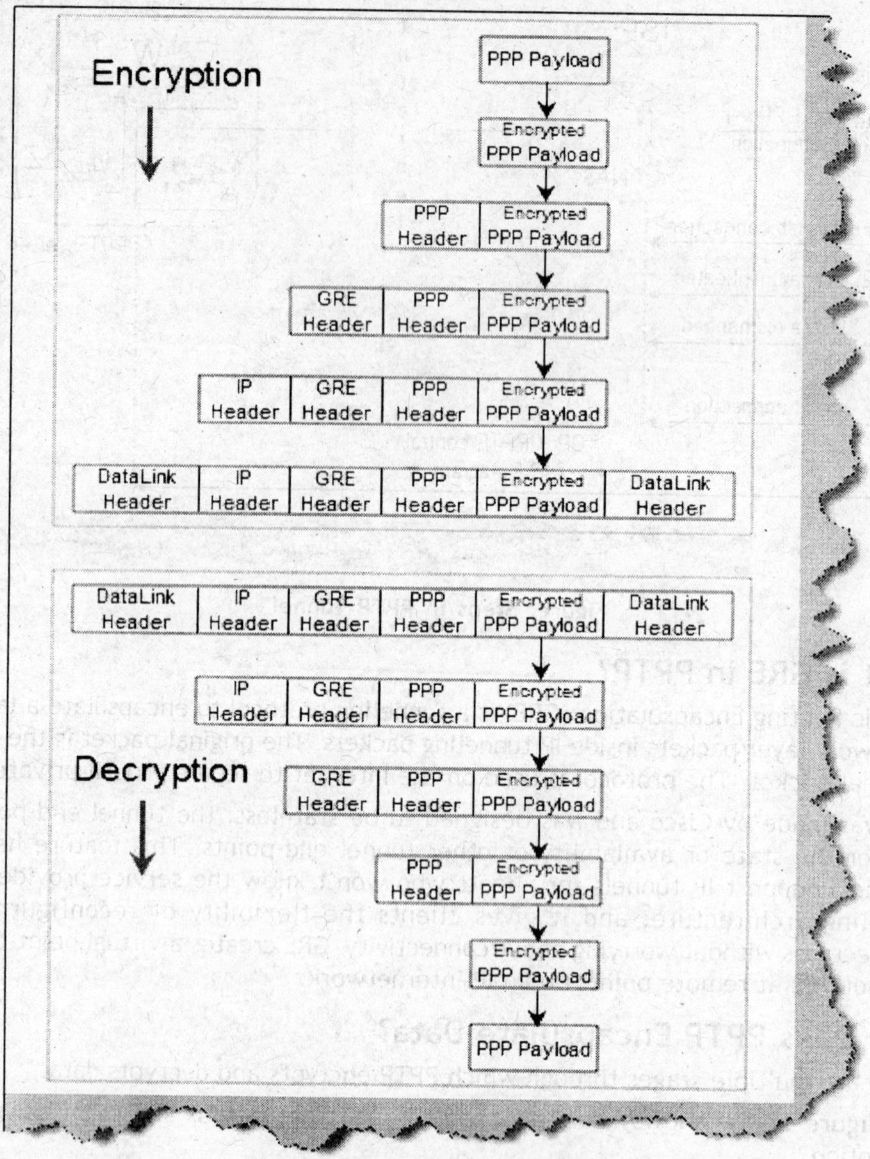

Figure: PPTP Data Encapsulation

(A) Explain CHAP.

CHAP stands for 'Challenge-Handshake Authentication Protocol.p It basically authenticates a user to an authenticating entity. It's an authentication scheme used by PPTP to validate the authenticity of the remote user. CHAP periodically checks if the end user is valid or not. This verification is done based on a shared secret key which is generated by using user's password or user ID.

Following are the steps that take place during CHAP authentication:

- The authenticating authority sends a challenge message to the peer or the user who wants to communicate.
- Peer responds with a value using a one-way hash function like MD5.
- The authenticating authority checks with its own hash value. If this matches, it allows the connection or terminates the connection.
- In between random intervals, the authenticating authority challenges the peer and completes the cycle repeatedly to ensure that there are no issues

(A) Explain PAP.

PAP, which stands for 'Password Authentication Protocol,' is a simple authentication protocol used to authenticate a user for a resource. PAP uses Point-to-Point protocol. It is a process of validating a user before accessing the resource. It sends unencrypted ASCII passwords and is, therefore, much unsecured. It's only used if the server does not have any kind of authentication mechanisms like CHAP or EAP.

(I) what Does PPTP Use for Encryption and Authentication?

Encryption

PPTP as such does not have a built-in encryption mechanism. It uses Microsoft Point-to-Point Encryption (MPPE.) MPPE is based on shared secret encryption. This shared secret key is prepared by a user ID and password with 40-bit session key using hashed algorithm. The key derived from this hashed algorithm is used to encrypt data which is transferred over the tunnel. MPPE is a 40-bit key which is too short and vulnerable to brute-force attacks. There are two options given by Microsoft:

- Make the key 128. MPPE also has 128-bit key version.
- Refresh the key after the 256th packet.

Authentication

PPTP supports two types of authentications as explained below:

MS-CHAP: This is Microsoft customized version of CHAP (you can read about CHAP in earlier questions.) The only difference is MS-CHAP is based on RC4 and DES while CHAP is based on RSA MD5 algorithm.

PAP: This has already been explained in the previous section.

(I) What is an L2F Protocol?

Once of the biggest drawbacks of PPTP was that it was based on MS-CHAP. We mentioned in the previous question how MS-CHAP was not secured because of length. So CISCO and Nortel developed a solution called as L2F which solved the below problems:

- In PPTP, one tunnel can have only one connection. In L2F you can define multiple connections in one tunnel. This leads to reduction of cost to a great extent.
- Have a secured transaction.
- Support wide range of networking protocols like ATM, FDDI, IPX, NETBEUI, and frame relay.

(A) Explain the Broad Steps of How L2F Establishes a Tunnel.

Following are the important steps which will help us create an L2F tunnel (when looking at the steps, also see figure 'L2F Tunnel' for a pictorial view):

- **Step1**: The remote user first starts a PPP connection to NAS of the ISP.
- **Step2**: If NAS of the ISP accepts the connection request, then a PPP connection tunnel is established between NAS and the end user.
- **Step 3**: User goes through an authentication process using either CHAP or PAP.
- **Step 4**: If no tunnel is enabled, then a new one is created.
- **Step 5**: After a tunnel is established, a unique Multiplex ID (MID) is allocated to the connection tunnel.
- **Step 6**: The gateway then accepts the connection request or rejects the same.
- **Step 7**: Once the user is authenticated, a virtual connection is established between the hosts.

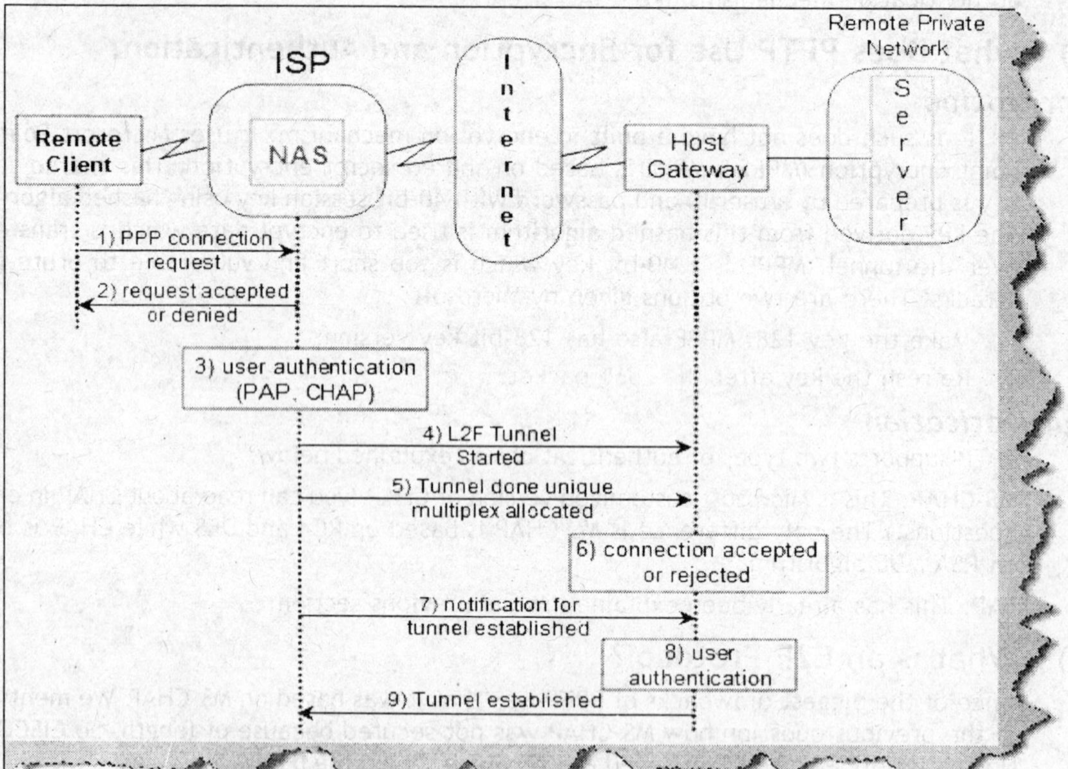

Figure: L2F Tunnel

(I) How Does the L2F Data-Tunneling Process Work?

Figure 'L2F Data-Tunneling Process' shows how the data-packet tunnel from source to destination.

(#Author: The statement 'Figure...destination' looks incomplete.)

- **Step 1**: Remote client forwards normal frames with payload and data-link layer to NAS in the ISP.
- **Step 2**: POP strips the data-link layer information and adds the L2F header and trailer to the frame which is further transferred to destination through the tunnel.
- **Step 3**: The host gateway strips the L2F header and trailer and sends the same to the destination node in the private network.

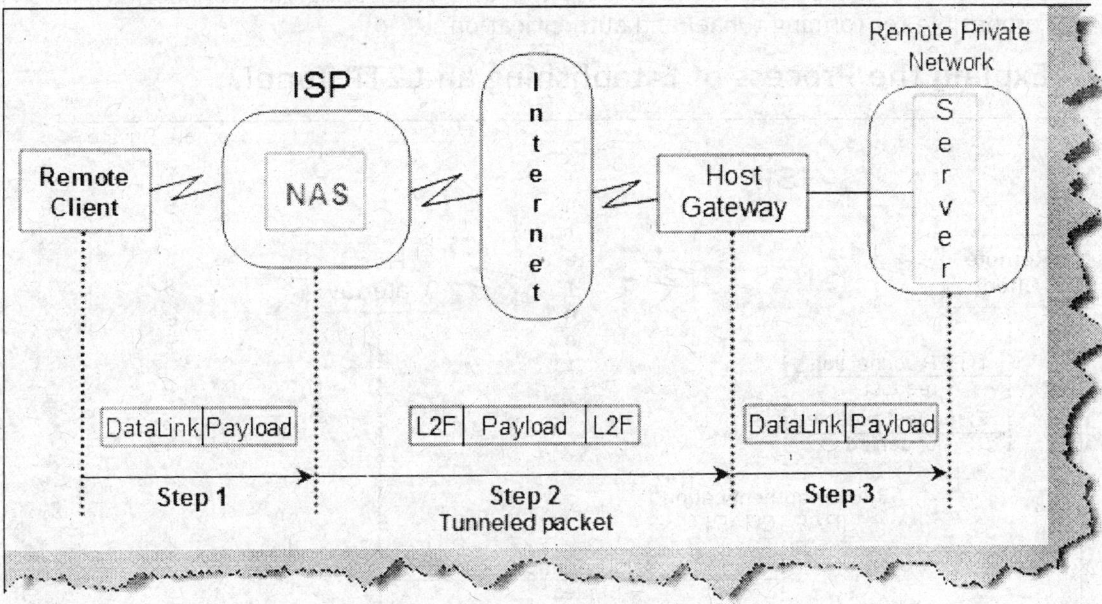

Figure: L2F Data-Tunneling Process

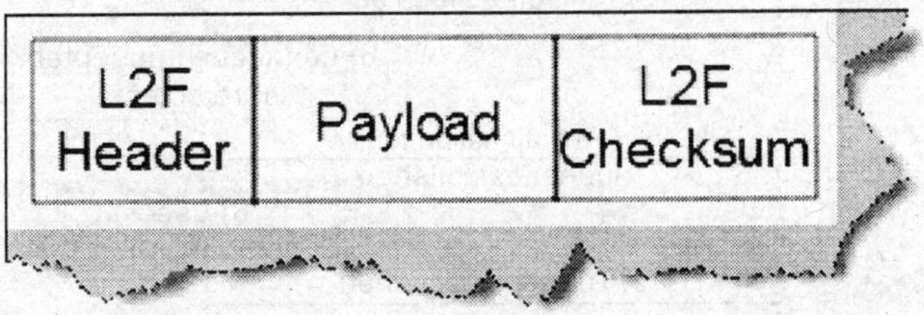

Figure: L2F Packet

(I) How is Encryption and Authentication Carried Out in L2F?

L2F uses MPPE (this has been discussed in the previous questions) for general encryption. As MPPE length is small, it is prone to brute-force attack. So L2F also uses IPSec (you can read about IPSec in the coming questions) to ensure that the data is secure during transmission.

For authentication, L2F uses CHAP and EAP.

(B) Explain L2TP.

L2TP (Layer-2 Tunneling Protocol) is the most widely used across the industry. L2TP is a combination of PPTP and L2F. L2TP provides remote access solution like L2F and provides point-to-point connectivity like PPTP.

(I) Define LAC and LNS.

L2TP Access concentrators (LAC) establishes tunnels across public networks to the LNS which is located at the host network. LAC is located at the ISP.

LNS is located at the host end. They are used to terminate L2TP connections when LAC terminates the connection. When LNS receives the request for a connection from LAC, it establishes a tunnel and authenticates the user requesting the connection. So LNS is responsible for forming tunnel and authentication.

(I) Explain the Process of Establishing an L2TP Tunel.

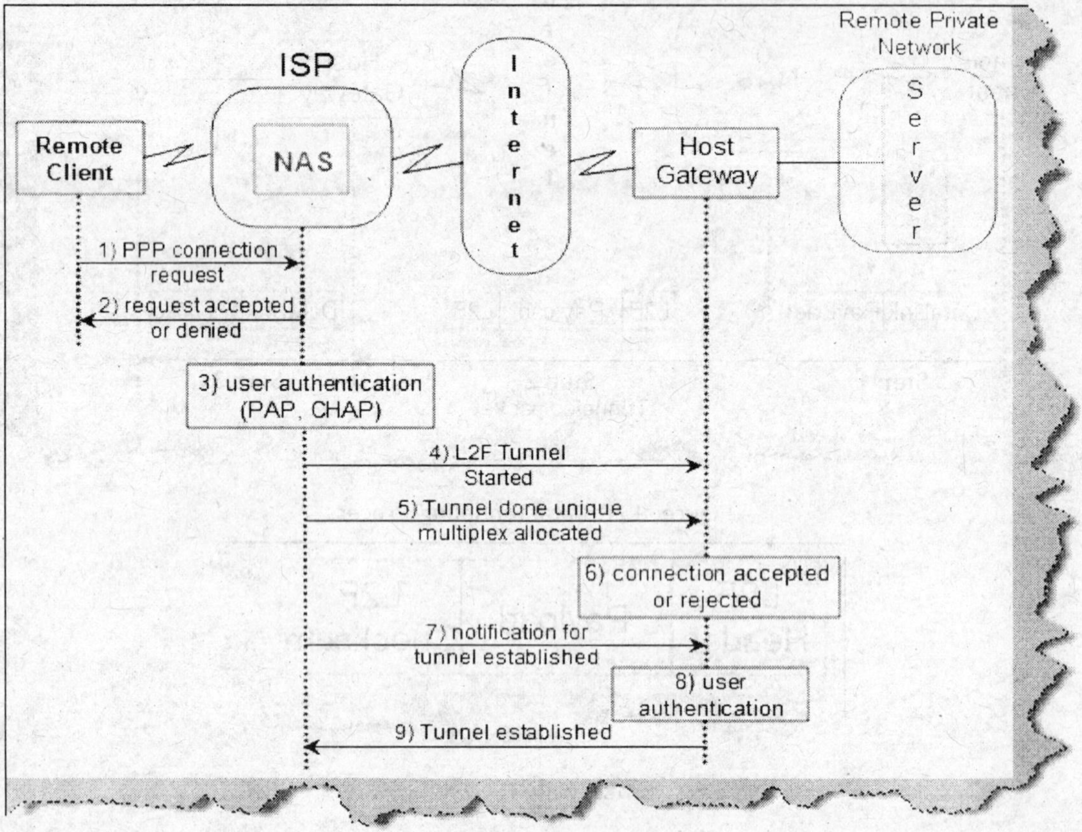

Figure: L2TP Tunnel

Given below is the step by step process of establishing an L2TP tunnel:

- Remote user sends connection request to NAS of the ISP and starts PPP connection.
- NAS accepts connection request once the user is authenticated. NAS uses PPP authentication methodology like PAP, CHAP, and EAP for authentication purpose.
- NAS then calls the LAC to establish connection between LAC and LNS.
- On getting the request, LAC established LAC-LNS tunnel over the network.
- Once the connection is established, LAC assigns a Call ID (CID) to connection and sends a notification message to LNS.

- LNS uses this information received to authenticate the end user. Once the user authenticates the end user, LNS established the tunnel.
- Once the tunnel is established data exchange can start.

(I) How is Encryption and Authentication Carried Out in L2TP?

L2TP uses PAP, EAP, and CHAP for authentication. IPSec is also on of the important ways of authentication. You can learn about IPSec in detail in the coming sections.

For data encryption, ECP (Encryption Control Protocol) is used. We can also use MPPE to encrypt.

(I) Explain What IPSec is.

IPSec is a set of protocols which provide complete security for a network. IPSec works on the IP layer. Following are the security services provided by IPSec:

- Encryption of Userdata.
- Checking the integrity of the message to ensure that it is not changed en-route.

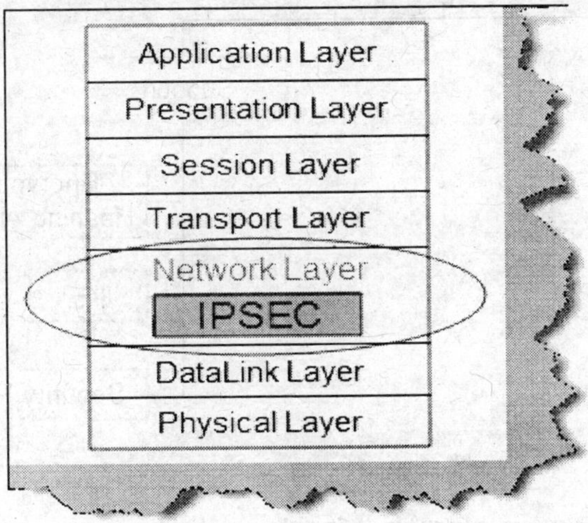

Figure: IPSec in OSI Model

IPSec is a collection of techniques and protocols to implement security in IP network. IPSec sits on the third layer of OSI, i.e., the network layer as shown in the figure 'PSec in OSI Model.' Using IPSec, a strong security mechanism is integrated with the IP Protocol itself. That's the only reason why IPSec was developed at layer-3 protocol, i.e., the network layer.

(I) Give an Overview of the Various Components in IPSec.

As mantioned earlier, IPSec is set of protocols and services. The IPSec protocol can be divided in to two sections: 'Core protocols' and 'Support.'

Core protocols consist of two core protocols AH (IPSec Authentication Header) and ESP (Encapsulating Security Payload.)

AH (IPSec Authentication Header): This protocol provides authentication services for IPSec protocols. It checks if the data was changed while traveling from source to destination.

ESP (Encapsulating Security Payload): ESP ensures the integrity of the data in the datagram.

AH and ESP can work in a stand-alone fashion, they need the **support** of other protocols and services.

Encryption and Hashing Algorithm: AH and ESP are very generic and can be attached to any encryption algorithm. This gives lot of flexibility to work with variety of algorithms and gives a choice of one suits our needs the best. IPSec uses MD5 and Secure Hash Algorithm (SHA.) These are hashing algorithms which hash the data with the key.

Security Policies: IPSec provides flexibility with different devices to decide how they want to implement security.

IKE: Internet Key Exchange (IKE) helps exchange shared keys for unlocking the encryption.

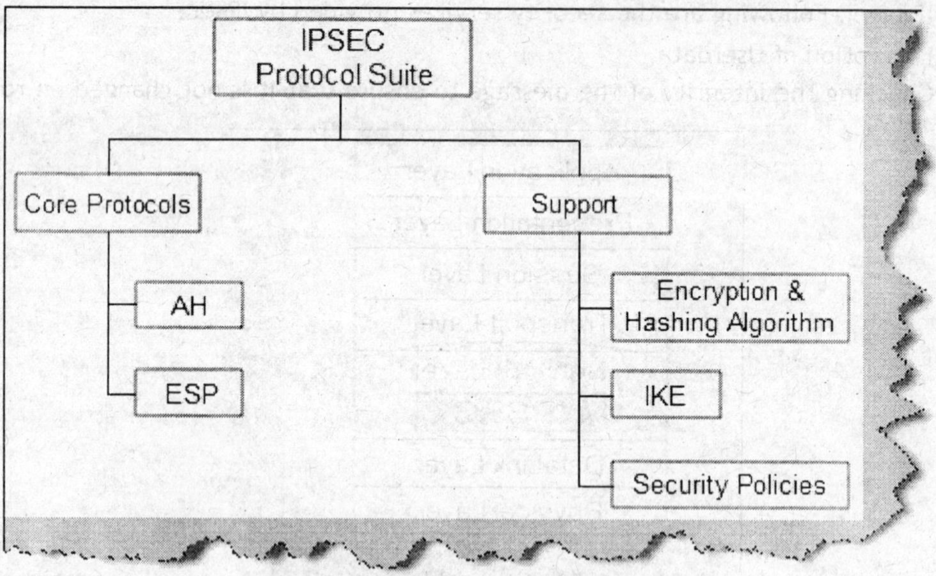

Figure: IPSec Components

(I) In IPSec, What Are SADs, SPDs, and SAs?

SPD (Security Policy Database) and SP (Security Policy): Security policy is like a rule of how to process different types of datagrams received by the device. For a particular packet, SP sees whether we need to apply IPSec. Security Policies (SPs) are stored in the SPD (Security Policy Database).

Security Associations (SAs) and Security Association Database (SAD): SA defines a set of security information rules which describes a secured connection between two devices. It can be said that it's a security contract between two devices. These contracts are contained in the SAD (Security Association Database.)

SPDs are more generic policies while SAD is more specific to a device.

(I) Explain in a Generic Manner, the Packets of IPSec.

IPSec is made of three important fields:

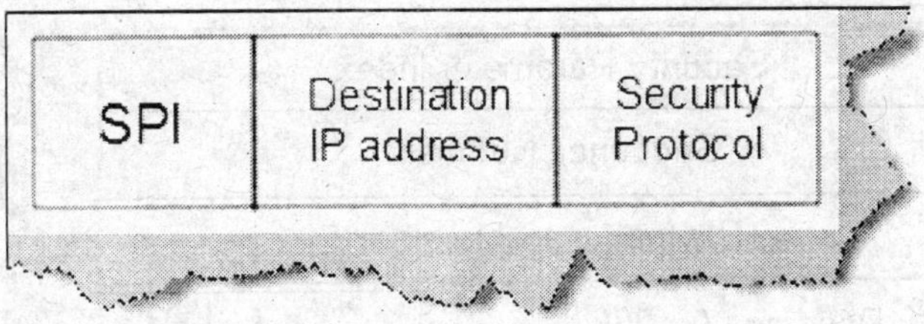

Figure: IPSec Protocol

SPI (Security Parameter Index): This is a 32-bit field which indicates the security protocol used. SPI forms the header of the security protocol and is normally selected by the end system during SA (for more on SA, read the first question) authentication.**Destination IP Address**: This is the IP address of the destination.**Security Protocol**: This represents whether it's a AH or an ESP protocol.

(A) Describe the Authentication Header (AH) Protocol.

AH protocol authenticates the origin of the IP datagram at the receiver end. So, in case the data is tampered while traveling from source to destination, this header helps identify the same.

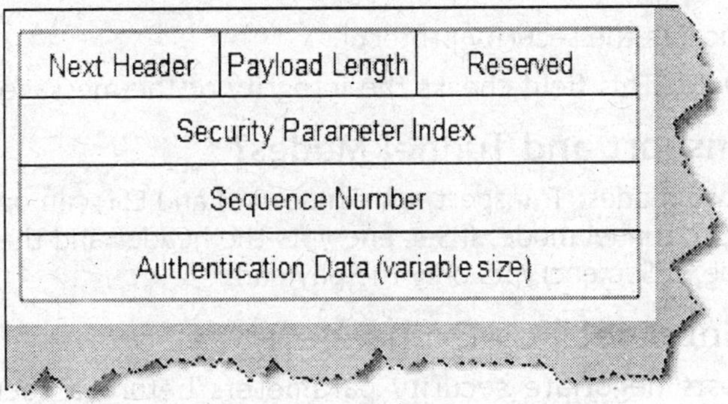

Figure: IPSec AH

Next header: Indicates the security protocol.**Payload length**: Indicates the length of the message.**Reserved**: It's a reserved field and not used as such.**SPI (Security Parameter Index)**: This field defines how different security associations (read previous questions to understand this fundamental) should be interpreted.

Sequence Number: This indicates the sequence of datagram.

Authentication Data: This field checks the integrity of the message sent.

(I) What is ESP (Encapsulating Security Payload)?

ESP encrypts the data during transport. It encrypts as defined by the SA. The encryption algorithms used by ESP is DES-CBG, IDEA, and 3DES.

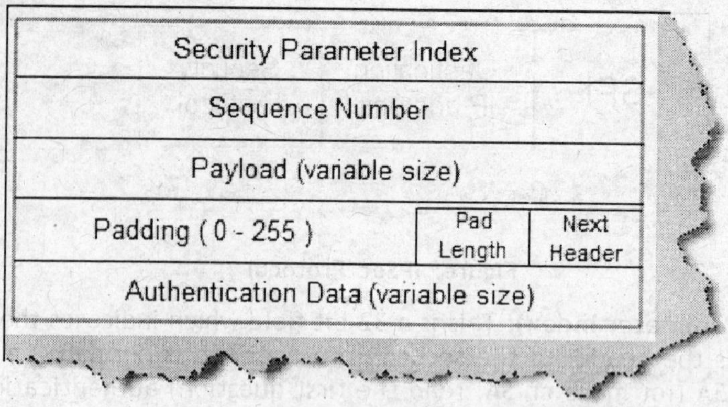

Figure: ESP

SPI (Security Parameter Index): This field defines how different security associations (read previous questions to understand this fundamental) should be interpreted. **Sequence Number:** This indicates the sequence of datagram.

Padding: If the payload is not of the required length, this field pads the same.

Pad length: This field indicates the padding length.

Next header: Indicates the security protocol.

Authentication Data: This field checks the integrity of the message sent.

(A) What Are Transport and Tunnel Modes?

IPSec operate in two modes: Transport and Tunnel. AH and ESP can operate in either these both modes. In IPSec tunnel mode, IPSec encrypts the header and the payload, whereas in the transport mode, IPSec encrypts only the payload.

(A) Explain IKE (Internet Key Exchange.)

IKE helps two hosts negotiate security parameters before a secure IPSec session is implemented.

(A) Explain the Different Phases in IKE.

We leave it on the readers to answer this question.

(A) What are the Different IKE Modes?

The different IKE modes are: Quick, Main, Aggressive, etc.

(A) Explain the Transport and Tunnel Modes in Detail With Datagram Packets.

We leave it on the readers to answer this question.

5

Protocols and Other Questions

> ***Note:*** *We have already covered some protocols in the earlier sections. In this section, we will go through some frequently asked protocols during interviews. It's very difficult to cover all protocol in depth. So we will try to cover only definitions from the interview perspective.*

(I) What is NetBIOS Protocol?

NetBIOS (Network Basic Input/Output System) is an extension of BIOS. NetBIOS is a suite of protocols. It is a session-layer protocol which provides interfaces between computers. NetBIOS consist of the following protocol suite:

- NMP (Name Management Protocol): This protocol helps us avoid duplicate names in a network. While assigning names to computers, NMP queries other computers by sending packet containing assigned names.
- NetBIOS UDP: UDP permits transfer of packets over the network. UDP packets are sent as a broadcast to all computers on the network. They do not provide session and transport services.
- DMP (Diagnostic and Monitoring Protocol): DMP provides information about the number of frames accepted or denied during any communication.
- Session Management Protocol (SMP): SMP handles duplex communication, i.e., bi-directional communication.
- Server Message Block (SMB) protocol: SMB protocol shares system resources, such as, files, printers, etc. SMB operates through TCP/IP protocol. Once a connection is established, the client can send request SMBs to perform operations, such as, read, write, etc.
- Common Internet File System (CIFS): CIFS helps clients to share documents on the Internet. It is an enhanced version of SMB protocol.

NetBIOS provides three services to the application program.

- Naming computer systems on the network.
- Transferring data between computers on a network.
- Interpreting NCB.

(B) Explain the Use of IGMP Protocol.

We always need to send information to several hosts at one time. This is achieved by IGMP (Internet Group Management Protocol.) It defines messages and formats for multicasting. Multicasting is a process of sending packets to a set of hosts which form a group. So when the packet is sent, it's sent only to that group, which in turn sends it to all hosts of that group. Multicast is implemented at the network layer. Network layer replicate packets depending on the number of host. Multicasting is implemented using UDP protocol.

A host group consists of zero or more hosts and these hosts are identified by a single IP address.

(I) What Are the Different Types of Hosts in Multicasting?

There are three types of hosts: Level 0, Level 1, and Level 2.

Level 0: These type of hosts do not support multicasting.

Level 1: These type of host can send multicast but cannot receive multicasts. If they receives multicast packets, they discard the same.

Level 2: These kind of host support full multicasting. It means that they can send as well as receive multicasting packets.

(I) Explain Ping and Tracert.

Ping and Tracert are diagnostic utilities to check and verify networks. Ping and Tracert are based on TCP/IP protocol. The ping utility verifies whether we can reach a host in a network. It also provides if we have any data loss and the delivery time the packet needs to reach the host. A ping command sends one data packet every second and prints the reply returned by that packet. Figure 'Ping Command in Action' shows how the ping command executes. (#Author: The answer says nothing about 'Tracert.')

```
C:\Documents and Settings\Administrator>ping 127.0.0.1

Pinging 127.0.0.1 with 32 bytes of data:

Reply from 127.0.0.1: bytes=32 time<1ms TTL=128
Reply from 127.0.0.1: bytes=32 time<1ms TTL=128
Reply from 127.0.0.1: bytes=32 time<1ms TTL=128
Reply from 127.0.0.1: bytes=32 time<1ms TTL=128

Ping statistics for 127.0.0.1:
    Packets: Sent = 4, Received = 4, Lost = 0 (0% loss),
Approximate round trip times in milli-seconds:
    Minimum = 0ms, Maximum = 0ms, Average = 0ms

C:\Documents and Settings\Administrator>
```

Figure: Ping Command in Action

(I) How Can You Continuously Ping an IP Address?

To ping an IP address continuously, the '-t' parameter is used.

```
C:\Documents and Settings\Administrator>ping 127.0.0.1 -t

Pinging 127.0.0.1 with 32 bytes of data:

Reply from 127.0.0.1: bytes=32 time<1ms TTL=128
Reply from 127.0.0.1: bytes=32 time<1ms TTL=128
Reply from 127.0.0.1: bytes=32 time<1ms TTL=128
Reply from 127.0.0.1: bytes=32 time<1ms TTL=128
Reply from 127.0.0.1: bytes=32 time<1ms TTL=128
Reply from 127.0.0.1: bytes=32 time<1ms TTL=128
Reply from 127.0.0.1: bytes=32 time<1ms TTL=128
Reply from 127.0.0.1: bytes=32 time<1ms TTL=128
Reply from 127.0.0.1: bytes=32 time<1ms TTL=128
Reply from 127.0.0.1: bytes=32 time<1ms TTL=128
Reply from 127.0.0.1: bytes=32 time<1ms TTL=128
Reply from 127.0.0.1: bytes=32 time<1ms TTL=128
Reply from 127.0.0.1: bytes=32 time<1ms TTL=128
Reply from 127.0.0.1: bytes=32 time<1ms TTL=128
Reply from 127.0.0.1: bytes=32 time<1ms TTL=128
Reply from 127.0.0.1: bytes=32 time<1ms TTL=128
Reply from 127.0.0.1: bytes=32 time<1ms TTL=128
```

Figure: '-t' Ping Parameter

Below are some of the frequently asked parameters of the ping command.

-a: Resolves addresses to hostnames.

-n: Specifies the number of ping request to be sent to the host.

-l: Sets the size of the data packet.

Tracert lists the path from the host computer to the final destination. In short, tracert shows the routers from the host computer to the destination. For example, the figure below shows tracert results for questpond from my home computer.

```
C:\Documents and Settings\Administrator>tracert www.questpond.com

Tracing route to questpond.com [216.185.43.181]
over a maximum of 30 hops:

  1   305 ms   298 ms   300 ms  97.233.1.2
  2   298 ms   302 ms   295 ms  220.224.134.33
  3     *      296 ms   338 ms  192.168.2.22
```

Figure: Tracert in Action

(I) How Does Tracert Actually Work?

Figure 'Tracert in Action' shows how tracert actually works. In the figure, we can see that we have two routers between the source and the destination. In the first step, the host computer on which the tracert is run sends a data packet with TTL equal to one. Once router A (i.e., the first router) gets the data packet, it decrements the TTL and sends an ICMP Type 11 message to the host computer. Once the host computer gets the ICMP Type 11 message, it again sends a data packet with TTL value 2. So now Router A decrements 1 value and Router B decrements one value and finally the packet reaches the destination host.

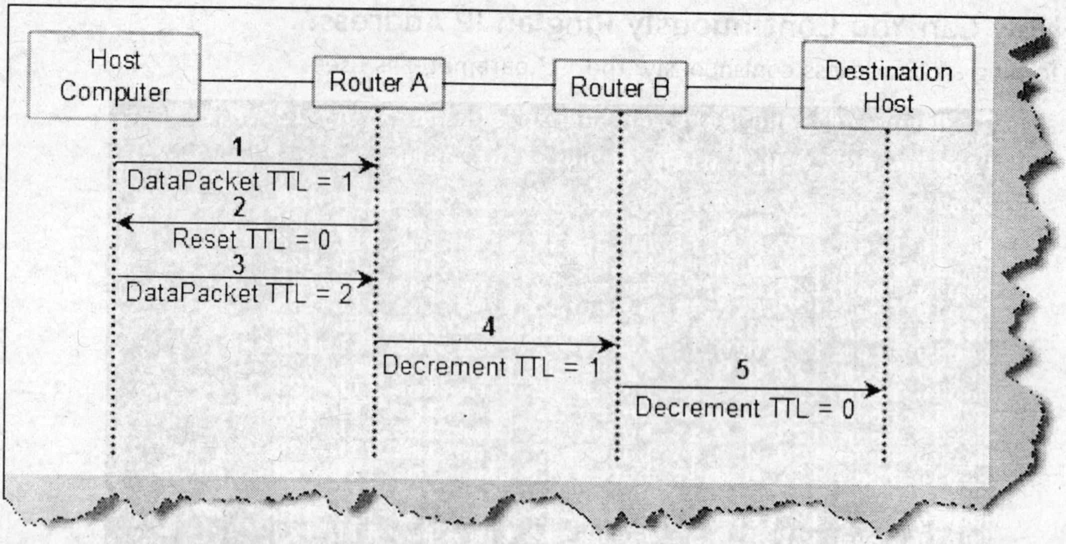

Figure: Tracert in Action

(I) What is the Use Of RTP and RTCP Protocols?

RTP (Real-Time Transfer Protocol) is used mainly to transfer audio and video over the network. In short, it's used for transmitting real-time data over the network. RTCP (Real-Time Transfer Control Protocol) monitors the transmission of the data. When the real-time traffic exceeds the bandwidth, we can have network congestion. RTP uses UDP for data transmission.

(I) Explain RTP in Detail?

We leave it on the reader to answer this question.

(I) Explain RTP Multiplexing in Detail.

We leave it on the reader to answer this question.

(I) Explain the Format of RTP and RTCP Packets.

We leave it on the reader to answer this question.

(I) Explain RSVP.

RSVP is not a protocol, but it stands on the top of other protocols and helps them determine whether the node has sufficient resources to transmit data. So RSVP requests QOS (Quality of Service) from the network on behalf of the application. This request is carried out as we travel through different nodes. At each node, RSVP attempts to make resource reservation. To make resource reservation at a node, RSVP uses two factors: Admission Control and Policy Rights. Admission control determines whether the node has sufficient resources to supply the requested QOS, and Policy Rights determine whether the packet has rights to use the resources.

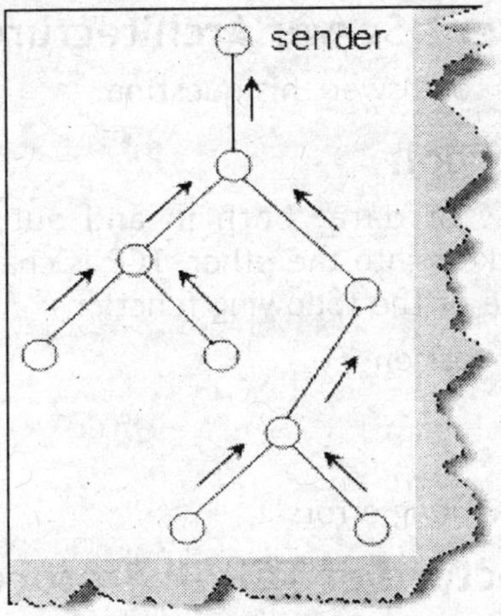

Figure: RSVP

(I) How Does RSVP Actually Work.

We leave it on the reader to answer this question.

(B) Explain RPC (Remote Procedure Calls.)

RPC enables computers to share methods, routines, and common functions on a network. Figure 'RPC: Step by Step' shows how an RPC call is made.

Step 1: Caller makes a procedure call with arguments to a remote system and waits for the results. The procedure call is made using the message-passing protocols of RPC.

Step 2: Remote host then uses the arguments and executes the method or the procedure.

Step 3: The result of the execution is then returned to the calling host/procedure.

Step 4: Once calling procedure get the results, it resumes the operation.

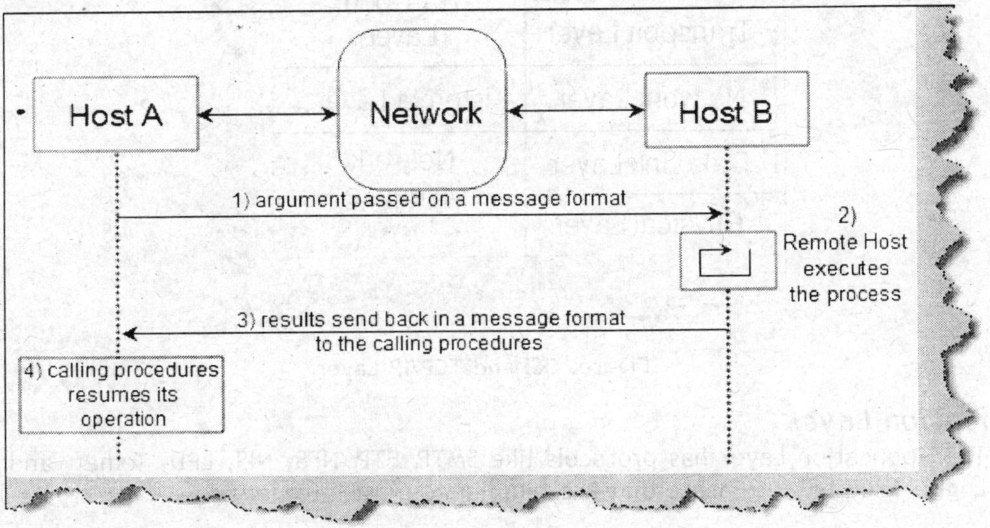

Figure: RPC: Step by Step

(I) Explain RPC and Client-Server Architecture.

We leave it on the reader to answer this question.

(B) Explain TCP/IP Protocol.

TCP/IP manage the flow of data, both in and out, over a network. Whereas IP indiscriminately gives packets into the ether, TCP is charged with making sure that they get there. TCP is in charge of the following functions:

- Starting and ending a session
- Manage packets
- Control flow
- Error detection and handling errors

(B) Explain the Architecture of TCP/IP Protocol.

TCP/IP is made up of four layers instead of the seven as compared to OSI model.

The primary difference between the OSI and the TCP/IP layer is that the Transport Layer does not guarantee delivery at all times. TCP/IP offers a more simplified protocol, User Datagram Protocol (UDP,) wherein all the layers in the TCP/IP stack perform specific duties or run applications.

The figure below shows the four layers of TCP/IP and its mapping to the OSI model.

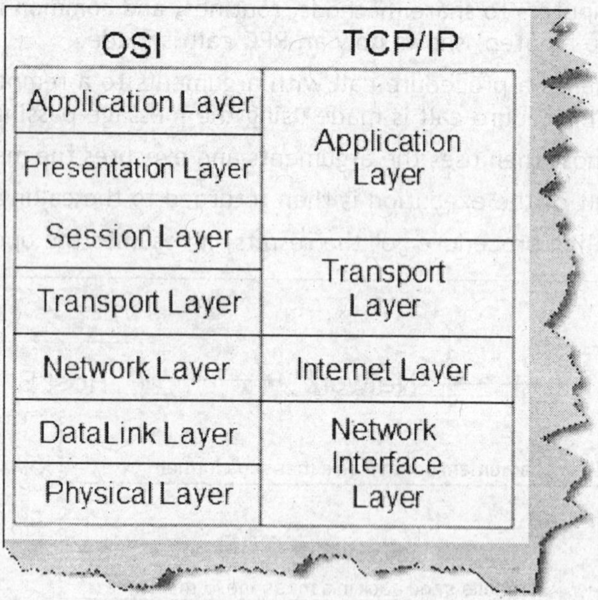

Figure: OSI and TCP/IP Layer

Application Layer

The Application Layer has protocols like SMTP, FTP, NFS, NIS, LPD, Telnet, and Remote Login. They fall into areas that are familiar to most Internet users.

Transport Layer

The Transport Layer has UDP (User Datagram Protocol) and TCP, where UDP delivers packets with almost non-existent checking, and the TCP provides delivery guarantees.

Internet Layer

The Internet Layer consists of the ICMP, IP, IGMP, RIP, OSPF, EGP, and BGP4. ICMP (Internet Control Message Protocol) is used for diagnostics and for obtaining information about IP parameters. IGMP (Internet Group Management Protocol) is used for managing multicasting. RIP, OSPF, EGP, and BGP4 are examples of routing protocols.

Network Interface Layer

The Network Interface Layer consists of ARP and RARP, and framing of data, which handle packet transmission.

(B) Explain TCP Header in Detail.

The TCP header appears as follows:

The parts of the header are detailed in the following sections.

Source Port: The source port is the numerical value indicating the source port.

Destination Port: The destination port is the numerical value indicating the destination port.

Sequence Number: The sequence number is the number of the first data octet in any given segment.

Acknowledgement Number (ACK): When the ACK bit is set, this field contains the next sequence number that the sender of the segment is expecting to receive. This value is always sent.

Data Offset: Data offset is the numerical value that indicates where the data begins, implying the end of the header by offset.

Reserved: Reserved is not used, but it must be off (0.)

Control Bits: Control bits are as follows:

U(URG): Urgent pointer field significant.

A(ACK): Acknowledgement field significant.

P(PSH): Push function.

R(RST): Reset connection.

S(SYN): Synchronize sequence numbers.

F(FIN): No more data.

Window: The window indicates the number of octets that the sender is willing to take. This starts with the packet in the ACK field.

Checksum: The checksum field is the 16-bit complement of the sum of all 16-bit words, restricted to the 1st column, in the header and text. If the result is an odd number of header and text octets, then the last octet is padded with zeros to form a 16-bit word that will checksum. Note that the pad is not sent as part of the segment.

Urgent (URG) Pointer: The URG pointer field shows the value of the URG pointer in the form of a positive offset of the sequence number from the octet that follows the URG data or points to the end of urgent data.

Options: Options may be sent at the end of a header, but must always be fully implemented and have a length that is any multiple of 8-bits. The two types of options are:

Type 1: A single octet of option-kind.

Type 2: An octet of option-kind, an octet of option-length, and the actual option-data octets. The option has a type, length and value field. The length field includes the type, option length, as well as the value fields. The value field contains the data that makes up the options being sent.

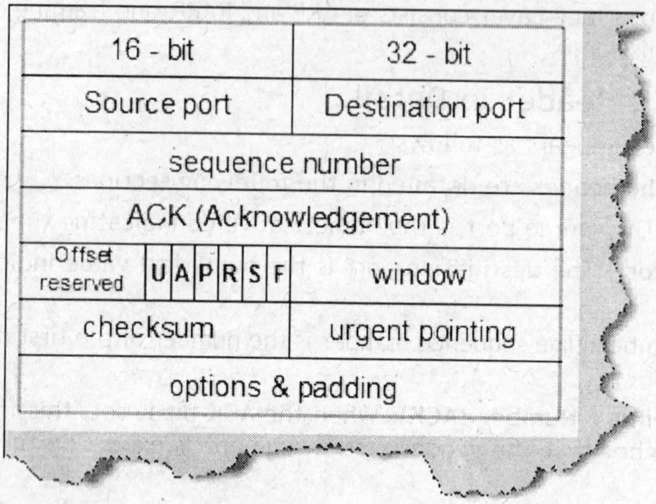

Figure: TCP Headers

(I) Explain IP Protocol.

IP manages how packets are delivered to and from servers and clients.

The IP header appears as follows:

Each field contains information about the IP packet that it carries. The descriptions in the following sections should be helpful.

Version Number

The Version Number indicates the version of IP that is in use for this packet. IP version 4 (Ipv4) is currently in widespread use.

Header Length

The Header Length indicates the overall length of the header. The receiving machine then knows when to stop reading the header and start reading data.

Type of Service

Mostly unused, the Type of Service field indicates the importance of the packet in a numerical value. Higher numbers result in prioritized handling.

Total Length

Total Length shows the total length of the packet in bytes. The total packet length cannot exceed 65,535 bytes or it will be deemed corrupt by the receiver.

Identification

If there is more than one packet (an invariable inevitability,) then the Identification field has an identifier that identifies its place in line, as it were. Fragmented packets retain their original ID number.

Flags

The first flag, if set, is ignored. If the DF (Do not Fragment) flag is set, under no circumstances can the packet be fragmented. If the MF (More Fragments) bit is turned on (1), there are packet fragments to come, the last of which is set to off (0).

Offset

If the Flag field returns a 1 (on,) the Offset field contains the location of the missing piece(s) indicated by a numerical offset based on the total length of the packet.

Time to Live (TTL)

Typically 15 to 30 seconds, TTL indicates the length of time that a packet is allowed to remain in transit. If a packet is discarded or lost in transit, then an indicator is sent back to the sending computer that the loss occurred. The sending machine then has the option of resending that packet.

Protocol

The Protocol field holds a numerical value indicating the handling protocol in use for this packet.

Checksum

The Checksum value acts as a validation checksum for the header.

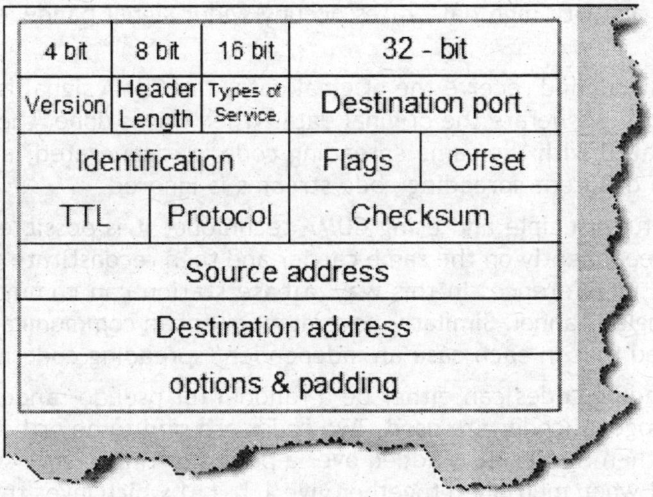

Figure: Internet Protocol

Source Address

The Source Address field indicates the address of the sending machine.

Destination Address

The Destination Address field indicates the address of the destination machine.

Options and Padding

The Options field is optional. If used, it contains codes that indicate the use of security, strict or loose source routing, routing records, and time stamping. If no options are used, then the field is called padded and contains a 1. Padding is used to force a byte value that is rounded.

(I) Explain the Concept of CDMA.

CDMA (Code Division Multiple Access) is now in widespread use for mobile or cell phone (cellular telecommunications) systems. CDMA technology is based on a form of transmission known as Direct Sequence Spread Spectrum (DSSS.) This form of transmission was originally used for the military because transmissions were difficult to detect and difficult to decipher without the correct codes. However, the possibilities of using this technology to provide a multiple access scheme for mobile telecommunications have now been utilized in a major way.

In the beginning, telecommunications organizations used either Frequency Division Multiple Access (FDMA) where different users were allocated different frequencies or Time Division Multiple Access (TDMA) where they were allotted different time slots on a channel. In the CDMA system, different users are allocated different codes to provide access to the system.

DSSS basics

The key element of CDMA is its use of DSSS. In essence, the required data signal is multiplied with what is known as a chip code data stream. This has a higher data rate than the data itself and it enables the overall signal to be spread over a much wider bandwidth. Signals with high data rates occupy wider signal bandwidths than those with low data rates.

To decode the signal and receive the original data, the CDMA signal is multiplied with the spreading code to regenerate the original data. When this is done, then only the data with that was generated with the same spreading code is regenerated, all other data that is generated from different spreading code streams is ignored

This is a powerful principle and using CDMA technique, it is possible to transmit several sets of data independently on the same carrier and then reconstitute them at the receiver without mutual interference. In this way, a base station can communicate with several mobiles on a single channel. Similarly, several mobiles can communicate with a single base station, provided that in each case an independent spreading code is used.

The CDMA spreading codes can either be a random (or pseudo-random) number, or more commonly, orthogonal codes are used. Two codes are said to be orthogonal when they are multiplied and then the result is added over a period of time. For example, a codes 1 -1 -1 1 and 1 -1 1 -1 when multiplied together give 1 1 -1 -1 which gives the sum zero. Although pseudo-random number codes can be used, there is possibility of data errors being introduced into the system.

(B) Explain the Concept of DHCP.

DHCP (Dynamic Host Configuration Protocol) is used to automatically configure a host during boot up on a TCP/IP network and also to change settings while the host is attached.

This means that you can store all the available IP addresses in a central database along with information such as the subnet mask, gateways, DNS servers etc. When the client boots, it takes all properties and applied to the clients which are connected to the DHCP server.

Below are the features provided by DHCP:

- It defines a pool of IP addresses, which are allocated to client PCs by the server. These pools are termed as scopes in DHCP terminology.
- Not only are IP addresses are applied to client, but also other configuration settings like the subnet mask, default router, DNS server, that are required to make TCP/IP work correctly.
- DHCP works across most TCP/IP routers and allocates IPs according to the subnet the request came from. Even if a PC moves from one subnet to other subnet you can still configure it.
- IP Addresses can have lease period - so an IP address that is not used for the duration of the lease is put back into the unallocated pool. This helps recover TCP/IP addresses that are no longer used.

(B) How Does DHCP Work?

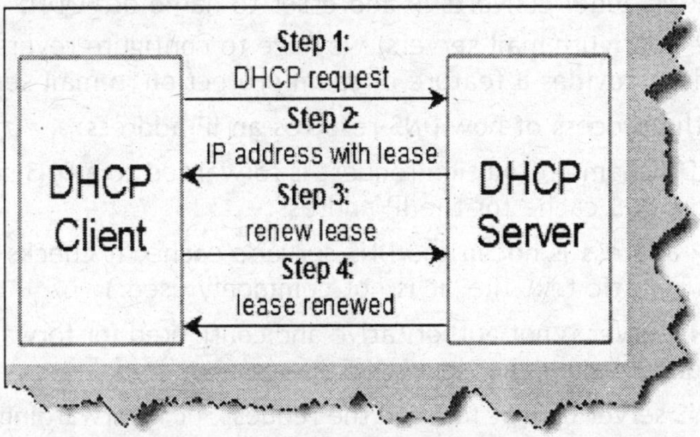

Figure: DHCP in Action

Step1: When a DHCP client first boots, it sends a packet on the network with a DHCP request. The DHCP server allocates an IP address to the PC; from one of the scopes (the pools of addresses) it has available. Each DHCP scope is used for a different TCP/IP network segment. On networks with routers that support DHCP, extra information is added to the request by the router to tell the server which networks the request came from. The DHCP server uses this information to pick an address from the correct scope.

Step2: The server replies to the client, allocating it an IP address and the required settings. But DHCP does not allocate the address permanently. It tells the client that it has 'leased' the address for a specific time period. By default, DHCP is installed with a 3-day lease period.

Step 3: When the lease expires, the client can ask the server to renew the lease. If the DHCP server does not hear from the client beyond the expiry of the lease period, it will put that address back in the pool, ready to be re-used. When the DHCP client obtains a lease on an address, it knows how long the lease period is. So it knows that it can use the address without reference to the DHCP server until the lease expires. When it does expire, it can request a renewal.

Step 4: If all the policy is in place, lease for the IP address is renewed.

(I) How Can We Configure DHCP?

Given below are the steps for configuring DHCP:

- Install Active directory services.
- Go to Start-> Settings -> Control Panel -> Add or Remove Programs -> Add/Remove Windows Components -> Select Networking services -> go to Details -> Check Box DHCP (Dynamic Host Configuration Protocol -> Click Ok -> Next -> Finish.
- Goto programs -> Admin tools -> DHCP -> then create a new scope and assign a range of IP address which will be assigned to the clients automatically.

(I) What is DNS?

DNS (Domain name server) is used to convert user-friendly names to IP addresses, and *vice-versa*. There are two zones in DNS:

1. Forward look-up zone: converts names to IP addresses.
2. Reverse look-up zone: converts IP addresses to name or FQDN.

Usually when we configure mail servers, we have to configure reverse look-up zone. This zone configuration provides a feature of spam protection in mail servers.

Given below is the process of how DNS resolves an IP address:

Step 1: When a DNS name resolution request is forwarded to a DNS server, the DNS server examines its local DNS cache for the IP address.

Step 2: If the IP address is not in the DNS server's cache, it checks its Hosts file. (Since the Hosts file is a static text file, it is not commonly used.)

Step 3: If the DNS server is not authoritative and configured for forwarding, the DNS server forwards the request to a higher-level DNS server.

Step 4: If the DNS server cannot forward the request, or if forwarding fails, the DNS server uses its Root Hints file (also known as Cache.dns.) The Root Hints file lists the 13 root DNS servers.

Step 5: The root DNS server responds with the address of a com, edu, net, or other DNS server type (depending on the request.)

Step 6: The DNS server forwards the request to the high-level DNS server, which can respond with a variety of IP addresses.

(I) How Do We Control USB Through a Network?

This is achieved by giving proper group policy rights.

(I) What Is The Difference Between Windows 2000 and Windows 2003?

The main differences between Windows 2000 and Windows 2003 are:

- In Windows 2000 we cannot rename domain, whereas in Windows 2003 we can.
- Windows 2000 supports of 8 processors and 64 GB RAM (In Windows 2000 Advance Server,) whereas Windows 2003 supports up to 64 processors and maximum of 512GB RAM.
- Windows 2000 Supports IIS 5.0, whereas Windows 2003 Supports IIS6.0.
- Windows 2000 does not support Dot net, whereas Windows 2003 Supports Microsoft .NET 2.0.
- Windows 2000 has Server and Advance Server editions, whereas Windows 2003 has Standard, Enterprise, Datacenter, and Web server Editions.
- Windows 2000 does not have any 64-bit server operating system, whereas Windows 2003 has 64-bit server operating systems (Windows Server 2003 X64 Std and Enterprise Edition.)
- Windows 2000 has the basic concept of DFS (Distributed File systems) with defined roots, whereas Windows 2003 has Enhanced DFS support with multiple roots.
- In Windows 2000, there is complexity in administering complex networks, whereas Windows 2003 is easy administration in all and complex networks
- In Windows 2000 we can create 1 million users, whereas in Windows 2003 we can create 1 billion users.
- In Windows 2003 we have the concept of volume shadow copy service which is used to create hard disk snapshots used in Disaster recovery, whereas Windows 2000 does not have this service.
- In Windows 2000 we don't have end user policy management, whereas in Windows 2003 we have a End user policy management which is done in GPMC (Group Policy Management Console.)
- In Windows 2000 we have cross-domain trust relationship, whereas in Windows 2003 we have cross-forest trust relationship.
- Windows 2000 supports 4-node clustering, whereas Windows 2003 supports 8-node clustering.
- Windows 2003 has High HCL (Hardware Compatibility List) support issued by Microsoft.
- Code name of Windows 2000 is Win NT 5.0 and code name of Windows 2003 is Win NT 5.1.
- Windows 2003 has service called ADFS (Active Directory Federation Services) which is used to communicate between branches with safe authentication.
- In Windows 2003 there is improved storage management using service File Server Resource Manager (FSRM.)
- Windows 2003 has service called Windows Share point Services (it is an integrated portfolio of collaboration and communication services designed to connect people, information, processes, and systems both within and beyond the organizational firewall.)
- Windows 2003 has improved print management as compared to Windows 2000 servers.
- Windows 2003 has telnet sessions available.
- Windows 2000 supports IPV4, whereas Windows 2003 supports IPV4 and IPV6.

(l) What are the Differences Between a Domain and a Workgroup?

Workgroup	Domain
· All computers are peers; no computer has control over another computer.	· One or more computers are servers. Network administrators use servers to control the security and permissions for all computers on the domain. This makes it easy to make changes because the changes are automatically made to all computers.
· Each computer has a set of user accounts. To use any computer in the workgroup, you must have an account on that computer.	· If you have a user account on the domain, you can log on to any computer on the domain without needing an account on that computer.
· There are typically not more than ten to twenty computers	· There can be hundreds or thousands of computers.
· All computers must be on the same local network or subnet.	· The computers can be on different local networks

6

Questions Not Covered in This Book

> **Note:** *It is simply not possible to cover all questions in one book. Below are a few questions that have been left out and we will definelty try to cover the same in the second edition. Till then, if you can think of answers to these questions, you may mail them to me at shiv_koirala@yahoo.com. We will definelty acknowledge in the second edition.*

Protocols like FTP, HTTP, UDP, and SMTP are completely left out. In the second edition these protocols will be our top priority.

The second edition will have a separate section on Wireless. Questions on Bluetooth have also been left out of this edition.

- Explain the difference between Baseband and BroadBand.
- What is the difference between terminal services and remote desktop?
- Explain RAID.
- What will you do when we have dealys in the network?
- What are some of the problems associated with operating a switched LAN?
- How do you combine TCP/IP traffic and SNA traffic on the same link?
- How do we monitor data in sockets?
- How should port numbers for servers be chosen?
- How many bytes are there in an IPX network address?
- What are the differences between MUTEX and Semaphore?
- Explain priority inversion.
- Explain MSMQ.
- What are Passive and Active FTPs?
- What is Maximum Transmission Unit (MTU?)

7

Other Books Covering Interview Question

This section was not supposed to be included in this book. But we have done it specifically to give you a fair idea of what's asked in other technologies. If you want to buy those book, you can get it from any BPB bookshop mentioned in this book's first page, or else you can mail your request to bpb@bol.net.in or bpb@vsnl.com.

.NET Interview Questions Book

Basic .NET Framework questions

- What is IL? (Twist: What is MSIL or CIL , What is JIT?)
- What is CLR?
- What is CTS?
- What is CLS(Common Language Specification ?)
- What is Managed Code?
- What is Assembly ?
- What are the Different Types of Assemblies?
- What is NameSpace?
- What is the Difference Between NameSpace and Assembly?
- If You Want to View an Assembly, How Do You Go About It ? (Twist: What is ILDASM?)
- What is Manifest?
- Where is the Version Information of an Assembly Stored?
- Is Versioning Applicable to Private Assemblies?
- What is GAC ? (Twist: What are the Situations When You Register .NET Assembly in GAC ?)
- What is the Concept of Strong Names ? (Twist: How do we Generate Strong Names? OR What is the Process of Generating String Names ? What is Use of SN.EXE ? How do we Apply Strong Names to Assembly? How do You Sign an Assembly?)

- How Do We Add and/or Remove an Assembly From GAC?
- What is Delay Signing ?
- What is Garbage Collection?
- Can We Force a Garbage Collector to Run?
- What is Reflection?
- What are the Different Types of JIT?
- What are Value Types and Reference Types?
- What are the Concepts of Boxing and Unboxing?
- What is the Difference Between VB.NET and C#?
- What is the Difference Between System Exceptions and Application Exceptions?
- What is CODE Access Security?

NET Interoperability

- How Can We Use COM Components in .NET ? (Twist: What is RCW?)
- Once I Have Developed the COM Wrapper, Do I Still Have to Register the COM in the Registry?
- How Can We Use .NET Components in COM ? (Twist: What is CCW (COM Callable Wrapper ?) What Caution Needs To Be Taken To Make Sure That .NET Components Are Compatible With COM?)
- How Can We Make Windows API Calls in .NET?
- When We Use Windows API in .NET, Is It Managed or Unmanaged Code?
- What is COM?
- What is Reference Counting in COM?
- Briefly Describe the IUKNOWN Interface.
- Explain DCOM.
- How Do We Create DCOM Objects in VB6?
- How Can DTC Be Implemented in .NET?
- How Many Types of Transactions Are There in COM + .NET?
- How Can Object Pooling Be Done in .NET?
- What Are the Types of Compatibility in VB6?

Threading

- What is Multitasking?
- What is Multithreading?
- What is a Thread?
- Does VB6 Support Multithreading?
- Can We Have Multiple Threads in One App Domain?
- Which Namespace has Threading?
- Explain in Brief How We Implement Threading?
- How Can We Change Priority ? and What Are the Levels of Priority Provided by .NET?
- What Does the Addressof Operator Do In the Background?
- How Can You Reference current thread of the method ?**(#Author: Please check the**

language of this question.)

- What's Thread.Sleep() in Threading?
- How Can We Make a Thread Sleep for an Infinite Period?
- What is Suspend and Resume in Threading?
- What is the Way To Stop a Long-Running Thread?
- How Can a Thread Be Debugged?
- What's Thread.Join() in Threading?
- What are Daemon threads ? and How Can a Thread be Created as a Daemon?
- When Working With Shared Data in Threading, How Do You Implement Synchronization?
- Can We Use Events With Threading?
- How Can We Know the State of a Thread?
- What is a Monitor Object?
- What are Wait Handles? (Twist: What is a Mutex Object?)
- What is ManualResetEvent and AutoResetEvent?
- What are ReaderWriter Locks ?
- How Can You Avoid Deadlocks in Threading?
- What's the Difference Between a Thread and a Process?

Remoting and Webservices

- What is an Application Domain?
- What is .NET Remoting ?
- Which Class Does a Remote Object Have to Inherit?
- What Are the Two Different Types of Remote Object Creation Mode in .NET?
- Describe the Basics of SAO Architecture of Remoting in Detail?
- What is the Situation in Which You Will Use Singleton Architecture in Remoting?
- What is the Fundamental of Published or Precreated Objects in Remoting?
- What are the Ways in Which a Client Can Create Objects on a Server in the CAO Model?
- Are CAOs Stateful in Nature?
- In the CAO Model, What are the Precautions to be Taken When Client Objects are Created by the 'NEW' Keyword?
- Is it a Good Design Practice to Distribute the Implementation to the Remoting Client?
- What is LeaseTime, SponsorshipTime, RenewonCallTime, and LeaseManagerPollTime?
- Which Config File Has All the Supported Channels/protocols?
- How Can You Specify Remoting Parameters Using Config Files?
- Can Non-Default Constructors Be Used With Single-Call SAOs? (Twist: What Are the Limitation of Constructors for Single-call SAOs?)
- How Can We Call Methods in Remoting Asynchronously?
- What are Asynchronous One-Way Calls?
- What is Marshalling ? and What Are the Different Kinds of marshalling?
- What is ObjRef Object in Remoting?
- What is a WebService?

- What is UDDI?
- What is DISCO?
- What is WSDL?
- What are the Different Phases of Acquiring a Proxy Object in Webservice?
- What is the File Extension of Webservices?
- Which Attribute is Used in Order to Make Sure That the Method Can Be Used as WebService?
- What Are the Steps to Create a Webservice and Consume It?
- Does Webservice Have Any State?

Caching Concepts

- What is An Application Object?
- What's the Difference Between Cache Objects and Application Objects?
- How Can We Get Access to Cache Objects?
- What Are the Dependencies in Cache? and What Are the Types of Dependencies?
- Show a Simple Code Showing File Dependency in Cache?
- What is Cache Callback in Cache?
- What is Scavenging?
- What Are the Different Types of Caching Using Cache Objects of ASP.NET?
- How Can You Cache Different Versions of the Same Page Using ASP.NET Cache Objects?
- How is Page Fragment Caching Implemented?
- What Are ASP.NET Session ? Compare ASP.NET Sessions with Classic ASP Session Variables?
- What Are the Various Modes of Storing ASP.NET Sessions?
- Is Session_End Event Supported in All Session Modes?
- What Are the Precautions That Need To Be Taken To Make Sure That StateServer Modes work properly?
- What Are the Precautions That Need To Be Taken To Make Sure That SQLSERVER Modes Work Properly?
- Where Do You Specify Session State Mode in ASP.NET?
- What Are the Other Ways In Which You Can Maintain State?
- What Are the Benefits and Limitation of Using Hidden fields?
- What is ViewState?
- Does Performance Vary for Viewstate According to User Controls?
- What Are the Benefits and Limitations of Using Viewstate for State Management?
- How Can You Use Hidden Frames to Cache Client Data?
- What Are the Benefits and Limitations of Using Hidden Frames?
- What Are the Benefits and Limitations of Using Cookies?
- What is Query String ? and What Are the Benefits and Limitations of Using Query Strings?

OOPS

- What is Object Oriented Programming?
- What's a Class?
- What's an Object?
- What's the Relationship Between Classes and Objects?
- What Are the Different Properties Provided by Object-Oriented Systems? (Twist: Explain the Different Properties of Object Oriented Systems? OR What's the Difference Between Association, Aggregation, and Inheritance Relationships?)
- How Can We Acheive Inheritance in VB.NET?
- What are Abstract Classes?
- What's an Interface?
- What is the Difference Between Abstract Classes and Interfaces?
- What is a Delegate ?
- What are Events?
- Do Events Have Return Type?
- Can Events Have Access Modifiers?
- Can We Have Shared Events?
- What is Shadowing?
- What's the Difference Between Shadowing and Overriding?
- What's the Difference Between Delegates and Events?
- If We Inherit a Class, Do the Private Variables Also Get Inherited?
- What are the Different Accessibility Levels Defined in .NET?
- Can You Prevent a Class From Overriding?
- What's The Use of the 'MustInherit' Keyword in VB.NET?
- Why Can't You Specify Accessibility Modifiers in Interfaces?
- What Are the Similarities Between Classes and Structures?
- What's the Difference Between Classes and Structures?
- What Does Virtual Keyword Mean?
- What Are Shared (VB.NET)/Static(C#) Variables?
- What is the Dispose Method in .NET?
- What's the Use of the 'OverRides' and 'Overridable' keywords?
- Where Are All .NET Collection Classes Located?
- What is an ArrayList?
- What's a HashTable? (Twist: What's the Difference Between a HashTable and an ArrayList?)
- What Are Queues and Stacks?
- What is an ENUM?
- What are Nested Classes?
- What's Operator Overloading in .NET?
- In the Sample Code Given Below, If We Create an Object of Class2, which Constructor Will Fire First?

- What's the Significance of the Finalize Method in .NET?
- Why Isn't Finalizing Not Preffered For Clean-Up?
- How Can We Suppress a Finalize Method?
- What's the Use of DISPOSE Method?
- How Do I Force the Dispose Method to be Called Automatically, As Clients Can Forget To Call the Dispose Method?
- In What Instances Will You Declare a Constructor To Be Private?

ASP.NET

- What's The Sequence In Which ASP.NET Events Are Processed?
- In Which Events Are the Controls Fully Loaded?
- How Can We Identify That The Page is PostBack?
- How Does ASP.NET Maintain State Between Subsequent Requests?
- What is Event Bubbling?
- How Do We Assign Page-Specific Attributes?
- The Administrator Wants to Make a Security Check To See Whether Anyone Has Tampered With ViewState, How Can We Ensure This?
- What's the Use of @ Register Directives?
- What's the Use of SmartNavigation Property?
- What is AppSetting Section in the 'Web.Config' File?
- Where is ViewState Information Stored?
- What's the Use of the @ OutputCache Directive in ASP.NET?
- How Can We Create Custom Controls in ASP.NET?
- How Many Types of Validation Controls Are Provided by ASP.NET?
- Can You Explain the 'AutoPostBack' Feature in ASP.NET?
- How Can You Enable Automatic Paging in DataGrid?
- What's the Use Of the 'GLOBAL.ASAX' File?
- What's the Difference Between 'Web.Config' and 'Machine.Config'?
- What's a SESSION and an APPLICATION Object?
- What's the Difference Between Server.Transfer and Response.Redirect? What's the Difference Between Authentication and Authorization?
- What is Impersonation in ASP.NET?
- Explain in Brief How the ASP.NET Authentication Process Works.
- What Are the Various Authentication Techniques in ASP.NET?
- How Does Authorization Work in ASP.NET?
- What's the Difference Between Datagrid, Datalist, and Repeater?
- From the Performance Point of View, how do they rate? **(#Author : Please check the language of this question.)**
- What's the Method to Customize Columns in DataGrid?
- How Can We Format Data Inside DataGrid?
- What is the Design Consideration to Take a Datagrid, Datalist, or Repeater?**(#Author : Please check the language of this question.)**

- What is the Difference Between ASP and ASP.NET?
- What Are the Major Events in the GLOBAL.ASAX file? and In What Order Are They Triggered?
- Do Sessions Use Cookies?
- How Can We Force All the Validation Controls to Run?
- How Can We Check Whether All Validation Controls Are Valid and Proper?
- If You Have Client-Side Validation Enabled in Your Webpage, Does That Mean Server-Side Code is Not Run?
- Which JavaScript File is Referenced For Validating the Validators At the Client Side?
- How is Client-Side Script Disabled in Validators?
- How Can I Show the Entire Validation Error Message in a Message Box on the Client Side?
- You Find That One Of Your Validation is Very Complicated and Does Not Fit In Any Of the Validators, What Do You Do?
- What is Tracing in ASP.NET?
- How Do We Enable Tracing?
- What Exactly Happens When an ASPX Page is Requested From the Browser?
- How Can We Kill a User Session?
- How Do You Upload a File in ASP.NET?
- How Do I Send an Email Message from ASP.NET?
- What Are the Different IIS Isolation Levels?

.NET Architecture

- What Are Design Patterns?
- What's the Difference Between Factory and Abstract Factory Patterns? What's an MVC Pattern? (Twist: How Can You Implement MVC Pattern in ASP.NET?)
- How Can We Implement Singleton Pattern in .NET?
- How Do You Implement Prototype Pattern in .NET? (Twist: How Can We Implement Cloning in .NET ? What is Shallow Copy ? and What is Deep Copy?)
- What Are the Situations In Which You Will Use a Web Service and Remoting in Projects?
- Give an Example of Practical Implementation of FAÇADE Patterns.
- How Can We Implement Observer Pattern in .NET?
- What is 3-Tier Architecture?
- Have You Ever Worked With Microsoft Application Blocks ? If Yes, Then Which?
- What is Service Oriented Architecture?

ADO.NET

- What is the Namespace in Which .NET Has Data Functionality Classes?
- Give a Overview of ADO.NET Architecture.
- What Are the Two Fundamental Objects in ADO.NET?
- What is the Difference Between Dataset and Datareader?
- What are the Major Difference Between Classic ADO and ADO.NET?

- What is the Use Of a Connection Object?
- What is the Use of Command Objects ? and What Are the Methods Provided By a Command Object?
- What is the Use of Data-Adapter?
- What Are the Basic Methods of Data-Adapter?
- What is a Dataset Object?
- What Are the Various Objects in Dataset?
- How Can We Connect to Microsoft Access, Foxpro, Oracle, etc?
- How Do We Connect to SQL SERVER ? Which Namespace Do We Use? How Do We Use Stored Procedure in ADO.NET ? How Do We Provide Parameters To the Stored Procedures?
- How Can We Force the Connection Object to Close After My Datareader is Closed?
- How Can I Force the Datareader to Return Only Schema of the Datastore Rather Than Data?
- How Can We Fine-Tune the Command Object When We Are Expecting a Single Row or a Single Value?
- Which is the Best Place to Store Connectionstring in .NET projects?
- What Are the Steps Involved In Filling a Dataset? (Twist: How Can We Use Data-Adapter to Fill a Dataset?)
- What Are the Various Methods Provided By the Dataset Object to Generate XML?
- How Can We Save All Data From the Dataset?
- How Can We Check Whether Some Changes Have Been Made to the Dataset Since It Was Loaded? (Twist: How Can We Cancel All Changes Done in the Dataset? How Do We Get Changed-Value Dataset?)
- How Do We Add/Remove Rows in the 'DataTable' Object of the 'DataSet'?
- What's the Basic Use of 'DataView'?
- What's the Difference Between 'DataSet' and 'DataReader'?
- How Can We Load Multiple Tables in a DataSet?
- How Can We Add Relations Between Tables in a DataSet?
- What's the Use of CommandBuilder?
- What's the Difference Between 'Optimistic' and 'Pessimistic' Locking?
- How Many Ways Are There To Implement Locking in ADO.NET?
- How Can We Perform Transactions in .NET?
- What's the Difference Between Dataset. Clone and Dataset. Copy?

SQL SERVER

- What is Normalization? What Are the Different Types of Normalization?
- What is Denormalization?
- What is a Candidate Key?
- What Are the Different Types of Joins ? and What's the Difference Between Them?
- What Are Indexes ? What is the Difference Between Clustered and Nonclustered Indexes?
- How Can You Increase SQL Performance?
- What is the Use of OLAP?

- What's a Measure in OLAP?
- What Are the Dimensions in OLAP?
- What Are the Levels in Dimensions?
- What Are Fact-Tables and Dimension-Tables in OLAP? (Twist: Can You Explain the Star Schema for OLAP?)
- What is DTS?
- What is Fillfactor? (Twist: When Does Page Split Occur?)
- What is RAID ? and How Does it Work?
- What's the Difference Between DELETE TABLE and TRUNCATE TABLE Commands?
- What Are the Problems That Can Occur If You Don't Implement Locking Properly in SQL SERVER?
- What Are the Different Transaction Levels in SQL SERVER? (Twist: What Are the Different Types of Locks in SQL SERVER?)
- What are the Different Locks in SQL SERVER?
- Can We Suggest Locking Hints to SQL SERVER?
- What is LOCK Escalation?
- What are the Different Ways of Moving Data/Databases Between Servers and Databases in an SQL Server?
- What are the Advantages of SQL 2000 over SQl 7.0?
- What is the Difference Between a HAVING CLAUSE and a WHERE CLAUSE?
- What is the Difference Between UNION and UNION ALL SQL syntax?
- How Can You Raise Custom Errors From Stored procedure?
- What is ACID Fundamental ? and What Are Transactions in SQL SERVER?
- What is DBCC?
- What is Purpose of Replication?
- What are the Different Types of Replications Supported by SQL SERVER?
- What is the BCP Utility in SQL SERVER?
- What are the Different Types of Triggers in SQl SERVER 2000?
- If We Have Multiple AFTER Triggers On the Table, How Can We Define the Sequence of the Triggers?
- What is SQl Injection?

UML

- What is UML?
- How Many Types of Diagrams Are There in UML? (Twist: Explain Briefly These Types.)
- What Are the Advantages of Using UML? (Twist: What is Modeling and Why UML?)
- What's the Sequence of UML Diagrams in Project? (Twist: How Did You Implement UML in Your Project?)
- Just a small Twist: Do I Need all UML Diagrams in a Project?
- Give a Brief Explanation of All Elements in Activity Diagrams?
- Explain the Different Elements of a Collaboration Diagram?

- Explain Component Diagrams?
- Explain All Parts of a Deployment Diagram?
- Describe Various Components in Sequence Diagrams?
- What are the Element in State-Chart Diagrams?
- Describe Different Elements in a Static-Chart Diagram?
- Explain Different Elements of a Use-Case? (Twist: What's the Difference Between Activity and Sequence diagrams?)

Project Management

- What is Project Management?
- Is Spending in IT Projects Constant Throughout the Project?
- Who is a Stakeholder?
- Explain Project Life-Cycle? (Twist: How Many Phases Are There in Software Projects?)
- Are Risks Constant Throughout the Project?
- Explain Different Software Development Life-Cycles?
- What is the Triple Constraint Triangle in Project Management?
- What is a Project Baseline?
- What is Effort Variance?
- How is a Project Management Plan Document Normally Organized?
- How do You Estimate a Project?
- What is CAR (Causal Analysis and Resolution?)
- How Do You Handle Change Request?
- What is Internal Change Request?
- What is the Difference Between SITP and UTP in Testing?
- What Are the softwares That You Have Used for Project Management?
- What Are the Metrics Followed in Project Management? (Twist: What Metrics Will You Look At In Order To See That the Project is Moving Successfully?)
- You Have People in Your Team Who Do Not Meet Their Deadlines or Do Not Perform, What Are the Actions That You Will Take? (Twist: Two of Your Resources Have Conflicts Between Them, How Will You Sort It Out?)
- How Do You Start a Project?
- How Do You Do Resource Allocation?
- How Do You Do Code Reviews?

SQL Server Interview Questions Book:

Database Concepts

- What is a Database or Database Management Systems (DBMS)?
- What's the Difference Between DBMS and RDBMS?
- What are CODD Rules?
- Is Access Database an RDBMS?
- What's the Main Difference Between ACCESS and SQL SERVER?
- What's the Difference Between MSDE and SQL SERVER 2000?

- What is SQL SERVER Express 2005 Edition?
- What is SQL Server 2000 Workload Governor?
- What's the Difference Between SQL SERVER 2000 and 2005?
- What are E-R Diagrams?
- How Many Types of Relationships Exist in Database Designing?
- Explain Fourth Normal Form.
- Explain Fifth Normal Form.
- What's the Difference Between Fourth and Fifth Normal Forms?
- Have You Heard About Sixth Normal Form?
- What is Extent and Page?
- What Are the Different Sections in Page?
- What Are Page Splits?
- In Which Files Does SQL Server Store Data?
- What is Collation in SQL Server?
- Can We Have a Different Collation for Database and Table?

SQL

- Revisiting basic syntax of SQL?**(#Author: {Please check the language of this question.)**
- What Are 'GRANT' and 'REVOKE' Statements?
- What is Cascade and Restrict in DROP Table SQL?
- What is a DDL, DML, and DCL in RDBMS?
- What Are the Different Types of Joins in SQL?
- What is 'CROSS JOIN'?
- You want to select the first record in a given set of rows? **(#Author: {Please check the language of this question.)**
- How Do You Sort in SQL?
- How Do You Select Unique Rows using SQL?
- Can You Name Some Aggregate Functions in SQL Server?
- What is the Default 'SORT' Order for an SQL?
- What is a Self-Join?
- What's the Difference Between DELETE and TRUNCATE?
- Select addresses That are between '1/1/2004' and '1/4/2004'?
- What Are Wildcard Operators in SQL Server?
- What's the Difference Between 'UNION' and 'UNION ALL'?
- What Are Cursors? and What Are the Situations You Will Use Them In?
- What Are the Steps To Create a Cursor?
- What Are the Different Cursor Types?
- What Are 'Global' and 'Local' Cursors?
- What is 'Group by' Clause?
- What is ROLLUP?
- What is CUBE?

- What's the Difference Between 'HAVING' and 'WHERE' Clauses?
- What is the 'COMPUTE' Clause in SQL?
- What is the 'WITH TIES' Clause in SQL?
- What Does 'SET ROWCOUNT' Syntax Achieve?
- What is a Sub-Query?
- What is 'Correlated Subqueries'?
- What are the 'ALL' and 'ANY' Operators?
- What is a 'CASE' Statement in SQL?
- What does the COLLATE Keyword in SQL Signify?

.NET Integration

- What Are the Steps to Load a .NET Code in SQL SERVER 2005?
- How Can We Drop an Assembly from SQL SERVER?
- Are Changes Are Made to the Assembly Updated Automatically in Database?
- Why Do We Need to Drop Assembly for Updating Changes?
- How Can We See Assemblies Loaded in SQL Server?
- How Can I See Which Files Are Linked With Which Assemblies?
- Does .NET CLR and SQL SERVER Run in Different Process?
- Does .NET control SQL SERVER ? or Is It *vice-versa*?
- Is SQLCLR Configured by Default?
- How Can CLR Be Configured for SQL SERVER?
- Is .NET feature Loaded by Default in SQL Server?
- How Does SQL Server Control .NET Run-Time?
- What's a 'SAND BOX' in SQL Server 2005?
- What is an Application Domain?
- How is .NET Appdomain Allocated in SQL SERVER 2005?
- What is the Syntax For Creating a New Assembly in SQL Server 2005?
- Do Assemblies Loaded in Database Need Actual .NET DLL?
- Does SQL Server Handle Unmanaged Resources?
- What is Multitasking?
- What is Multithreading?
- What is a Thread?
- Can We Have Multiple Threads in One App Domain?
- What is Non-Preemptive Threading?
- What is Pre-Emptive Threading?
- Explain the Threading Model in SQL Server.
- How Does .NET and SQL Server Thread Work?
- How Are Exceptions in SQLCLR Code Handled?
- Are All .NET Libraries Allowed in SQL Server?
- What is 'Hostprotectionattribute' in SQL Server 2005?
- How Many Types of Permission Levels Are There for an Assembly?

- Can You Name System Tables for .NET Assemblies?
- Are Two Versions of the Same Assembly Allowed in SQL Server?
- How Are Changes Made in the Assembly Replicated?
- Is It a Good Practice to Drop an Assembly for Changes?
- In One of the Projects, the Following Steps Were Done, Will it Work?
- What Does Alter Assembly With Unchecked Data Signify?
- How Do I Drop an Assembly?
- Can We Create SQLCLR Using .NET Framework 1.0?
- While Creating .NET UDF, What Checks Should Be Carried Out?
- How Do You Define a Function From the .NET Assembly?
- Compare T-SQL With SQLCLR?
- With Respect to .NET, is SQL SERVER Case-Sensitive?
- Does the Case-Sensitive Rule Apply to VB.NET?
- Can Nested Classes Be Accessed in T-SQL?
- Can We Have SQLCLR Procedure Input as Array?
- Can Object Datatype Be Used in SQLCLR?
- How's Precision Handled for Decimal Datatypes in .NET?
- How Do We Define INPUT and OUTPUT Parameters in SQLCLR?
- Is It a Good Practice to Use .NET Datatypes in SQLCLR?
- How Can We Move Values From SQL to .NET Datatypes?
- What is System.Data.SqlServer?
- What is SQLContext?
- Explain the Essential Steps to Deploy SQLCLR?
- How Can We Create Functions in SQL Server using .NET?
- How Do We Create Trigger Using .NET?
- How Can User Define Functions Be Created Using .NET?
- How Can User Defined Create Aggregates Be Created Using .NET?
- What is Asynchronous Support in ADO.NET?
- What is MARS Support in ADO.NET?
- What is SQLbulkcopy Object in ADO.NET ?
- How Can We Select a Range of Rows Using ADO.NET?

ADO.NET

- What Are Namespaces for ADO.NET?
- Give an Overview of ADO.NET Architecture?
- What Are the Two Fundamental Objects in ADO.NET?
- What is the Difference Between Dataset and Datareader?
- What Are the Major Differences Between Classic ADO and ADO.NET?
- What is the Use of Connection Object?
- What Are the Methods Provided by the Command Object?

- What is the Use of Data-Adapter?
- What Are the Basic Methods of Data-Adapter?
- What is a Dataset Object?
- What Are the Various Objects in Dataset?
- How Can We Connect to Microsoft Access, Foxpro, Oracle, etc?
- What's the Namespace to Connect to SQL Server?
- How Do We Use Stored Procedure in ADO.NET?
- How Can We Force the Connection Object to Close?
- I want to force the datareader to return only schema?**(#Author : Please Check the language of this question.)**
- Can We Optimize Command Object When There is Only One Row?
- Which Is the Best Place to Store Connectionstring?
- What Are the Steps Involved in Filling a Dataset?
- What Are the Methods Provided By the Dataset for XML?
- How Can We Save All Data From the Dataset?
- How Can We Check For Changes Made to the Dataset?
- How Can We Add/Remove Rows in 'DataTable' Object of the 'DataSet'?
- What's the Basic Use of 'DataView'?
- What's the Difference Between 'DataSet' and 'DataReader'?
- How Can We Load Multiple Tables in a DataSet?
- How Can We Add Relations Between Tables in a DataSet?
- What's the Use of CommandBuilder?
- What's the Difference Between 'Optimistic' and 'Pessimistic' Locking?
- How Many Ways Are There To Implement Locking in ADO.NET?
- How Can We Perform Transactions in .NET?
- What's the Difference Between Dataset. Clone and Dataset. Copy?
- What's the Difference Between Dataset and ADO Recordset?

Notification Services

- What Are Notification Services?
- What Are the Basic Components of Notification Services?
- Explain the Architecture of Notification Services?
- Which Are the Two XML Files Needed for Notification Services?
- What is Nscontrols Command?
- What Are the Situations In Which You Will Use 'Notification' Services?

Service Broker

- Why Do We Need Queues?
- What is 'Asynchronous' Communication?
- What is SQL Server Service Broker?
- What Are the Essential Components of SQL Server Service Broker?
- What Is the Main Purpose of Having Conversation Groups?

- How Can We Implement Service Broker?
- How Do We Encrypt Data Between Dialogs?

XML Integration

- What is XML?
- What is the Version Information in XML?
- What is the ROOT Element in XML?
- If XML Does Not Have a Closing Tag, Will It Work?
- Is XML Case-Sensitive ?
- What's the Difference Between XML and HTML?
- Is XML Meant to Replace HTML?
- Explain Why Your Project Needed XML?
- What is DTD (Document Type Definition ?)
- What is Well-Formed XML?
- What is a Valid XML?
- What is CDATA Section in XML?
- What is CSS?
- What is XSL?
- What Are Elements and Attributes in XML?
- Can We Define a Column as XML?
- How Do We Specify the XML Data Type as Typed or Untyped?
- How Can We Create the XSD Schema?
- How Do I Insert Into a Table Which Has XSD Schema Attached To It?**(#Author: Please check the language of this question.)**
- What is the Maximum Size for XML Datatype?
- What is Xquery?
- What are XML Indexes?
- What Are Secondary XML Indexes?
- What is FOR XML in SQL Server?
- Can I Use FOR XML to Generate SCHEMA Of a Table? and How?
- What is the OPENXML Statement in SQL Server?
- I Have a Huge XML File which we want to load in database?**(#Author : Please check the language of this question.)**
- How Can Stored Procedure Be Called Using HTTP SOAP?
- What is XMLA ?

Data Warehousing/Data Mining

- What is 'Data Warehousing?'
- What Are Data Marts?
- What Are Fact Tables and Dimension Tables?
- What is Snow Flake Schema Design in Database?
- What is ETL Process in Data Warehousing?

- How Can We do ETL Process in SQL Server?
- What is "Data Mining?'
- Compare 'Data Mining' With 'Data Warehousing?'
- What is BCP?
- How Can We Import and Export Using the BCP Utility?
- What is Bulk Insert?
- What is DTS?
- Can You Brief Us About a Data Warehouse Project That You've Worked On?
- What is an OLTP (Online Transaction Processing) System?
- What is an OLAP (On-line Analytical Processing) system?
- What Are Conceptual, Logical, and Physical Models?
- What is Data Purging?
- What is Analysis Services?
- What are CUBES?
- What Are the Primary Ways To Store Data in OLAP?
- What is META DATA Information in Data Warehousing Projects?
- What is Multidimensional Analysis?
- What is MDX?
- How Did You Plan Your Data Warehouse Project?
- What Are the Different Deliverables According to Phases?
- Explain How Analysis Service Works?
- What Are the Different Problems That 'Data Mining' Can Solve?
- What Are the Different Stages of 'Data Mining?'
- What are Discrete and Continuous Data With Reference to Data Mining?
- What is MODEL With Reference to Data Mining?
- How Are Models Actually Derived?
- What is a Decision Tree Algorithm?
- Can a Decision Tree be Implemented Using SQL?
- What is Naïve Bayes Algorithm?
- Explain Clustering Algorithm.
- Explain Neural Networks in Detail?
- What is Back Propagation in Neural Networks?
- What is Time Series Algorithm in Data Mining?
- Explain Association Algorithm in Data Mining?
- What is Sequence Clustering Algorithm?
- What Are the Algorithms Provided by Microsoft in SQL Server?
- How Do Data Mining and Data Warehousing Work Together?]
- What is XMLA ?
- What Are Discover and Execute in XMLA?

Integration Services/DTS

- What is Integration Services Import/Export Wizard?
- What Are the Prime Components in Integration Services?
- How Can We Develop a DTS Project in Integration Services?

Replication

- What's the Best Way to Update Data Between SQL Servers?
- What Are the Scenarios In Which You Will Need Multiple Databases With Schema?
- How Will You Plan Your Replication?
- What is a Publisher, Distributor, and Subscriber in 'Replication?'
- What is 'Push' and 'Pull' Subscription?
- Can a Publication Support Push and Pull at the Same Time?
- What Are the Different Models/Types of Replication?
- What is Snapshot Replication?
- What Are the Advantages and Disadvantages of Using Snapshot Replication?
- What Types of Data Will Qualify For 'Snapshot Replication?'
- What's the Actual Location Where the Distributor Runs?
- Explain in Detail How 'Snapshot Replication' Works.
- What is Merge Replication?
- How Does Merge Replication Work?
- What Are the Advantages and Disadvantages of Merge Replication?
- What is Conflict Resolution in Merge Replication?
- What is Transactional Replication?
- Explain in Detail How Transactional Replication Works.
- What Are Data Type Concerns During Replication?

Reporting Services

1. Explain How We Can Make a Simple Report in Reporting Services.
2. How Do I Specify Stored Procedures in Reporting Services?
3. What is the Architecture For 'Reporting Services ?'

Database Optimization

- What are Indexes?
- What are B-Trees?
- I Have a Table That Has a Lot of Inserts, Is It a Good Database Design to Create Indexes On That Table?
- What Are 'Table Scans' and 'Index Scans?'
- What Are the Two Types of Indexes ? Explain Them in Detail?
- What is the 'FillFactor' Concept in Indexes?
- What is the Best Value for 'FillFactor?'
- What Are 'Index statistics?'
- How Can We See the Statistics of an Index?

- How Do You Reorganize Your Index, Once You Find the Problem?
- What is Fragmentation?
- How Can We Measure Fragmentation?
- How Can We Remove Fragmented Spaces?
- What Are the Criteria You Will Look Into While Selecting an Index?
- What is 'Index Tuning Wizard?'
- What is an Execution Plan?
- How Do You See the SQL Plan in Textual Format?
- What is Nested Join, Hash Join, and Merge Join in SQL Query Plan?
- What Joins Are Good In What Situations?

Transaction and Locks

- What is a 'Database Transaction ?'
- What is ACID?
- What are 'Begin Trans,' 'Commit Tran,' 'Rollback Tran,' and 'Save Tran?'
- What Are 'Checkpoints' in SQL Server?
- What Are 'Implicit Transactions?'
- Is It Good to Use 'Implicit Transactions?'
- What is Concurrency?
- What Kind of Problems Occur When We Do Not Implement a Proper Locking Strategy?
- What Are 'Dirty Reads?'
- What Are 'Unrepeatable Reads?'
- What Are 'Phantom Rows?'
- What Are 'Lost Updates?'
- What Are the Different Levels of Granularity of Locking Resources?
- What Are the Different Types of Locks in SQL Server?
- What Are the Different Isolation Levels in SQL Server?
- If You Are Using COM+, What 'Isolation' Level is Set By Default?
- What Are 'Lock' Hints?
- What is a 'Deadlock?'
- What Are the Steps Which You Can Take to Avoid 'Deadlocks?'
- How Can I Know What Locks Are Running On Which Resource?

JAVA Interview Questions Book:

OOPS and CORE JAVA

- What is JVM (Java Virtual Machine?)
- What is JIT (Just-in-Time) Compilation?
- What is Object Oriented Programming?
- What's a Class?
- What's an Object?
- What's the Relation Between Classes and Objects?

- What Are the Different Properties Provided by Object-Oriented Systems?
- How Do You Implement Inheritance in Java?
- How Can We Implement Polymorphism in Java?
- What's an Interface ? and How Will You Go About Implementing an Interface?
- What is an Abstract Class?
- What are Abstract Methods?
- What's the Difference Between 'Abstract' Classes and 'Interfaces?'
- What's the Difference Between Static and Non-Static Fields of a Class?
- What Are Inner Classes ? and What's the Practical Implementation of Inner Classes?
- What are Packages?
- What is a Constructor in Class?
- Can Constructors be Parameterized?
- Explain Transient and Volatile Modifiers?
- What is the Use Of the 'instanceof ' Keyword?
- What Are Native Methods in Java?
- Explain Garbage Collector in Detail.
- How Does the Garbage Collector Determine Whether the Object Has to be Marked for Deletion?
- Explain the 'finalize()' Method?
- How Can We Force the Garbage Collector to Run?
- What's the Main Difference Between 'Switch' and 'If ?'
- What's the Use of the JAVAP Tool?
- What Are Applets?
- In Which Package is the Applet Class Located?
- What Are Native Interfaces in Java?
- What Are Class Loaders?
- What Are Bootstrap, Extension, and System Class Loaders?
- Explain the Flow Between Bootstrap, Extension, and System Class Loaders?
- How Can You Practically Do Dynamic Loading?
- How Can You Copy One Array Into a Different Array?
- Explain the Core Collection Interfaces?
- Explain, in Brief, the Collection Classes Which Implement the Collection Interfaces.
- What's the Difference Between Standard JAVA Array and ArrayList Class?
- What's the Use of 'ensureCapacity' in ArrayList Class?
- How Can We Obtain an Array From an ArrayList Class?
- What is 'LinkedList' Class For?
- Explain HashSet Class in Collections.
- What is LinkedHashSet Class?
- what is a TreeSet Class?
- What's the Use of Comparator Interface?

- How Can We Access the Elements of a Collection?
- What are Map and SortedMap Interfaces?
- Have You Used Any Collection Algorithm?
- Why Do We Use Collections When We Have Traditional Ways For Collection?
- Name the Legacy Classes and Interface for Collections.
- What is Enumeration Interface?
- What's the Main Difference Between ArrayList/HashMap and Vector/Hashtable?
- Are String Objects Immutable ? Explain the concept.
- What is a StringBuffer Class? and How Does It Differs From String Class?
- What is the Difference Between StringBuilder and StringBuffer Classes?
- What is Pass By Value and Pass By Reference? How Does JAVA Handle the Same?
- What Are Access Modifiers?
- What is Assertion?
- Explain the Fundamentals of Deep and Shallow Cloning?
- How Do We Implement Shallow Cloning?
- How Do We Implement Deep Cloning?
- What's the Impact of Private Constructor?
- What Are the Situations In Which You Will Need a Constructor to be Private?
- Explain Final Modifier.
- What are Static Initializers?
- If We Have Multiple Static Initializer Blocks, How is the Sequence Handled?
- Define Casting. What Are the Different Types of Casting?
- Explain Widening Conversion and Narrowing Conversion.
- Can We Assign Parent Objects to Child Objects?
- Define Exceptions.
- Explain Briefly How JAVA Exception Handling Works.
- Explain the Different Exception Types.
- Explain Checked and Unchecked Exceptions.
- Can We Create Our Own Exception Class?
- What Are Chained Exceptions?
- What is Serialization?
- How Do We Implement Serialization?
- What's the Use of Externalizable Interface?

Threading

- What's the Difference Between Thread and Process?
- What is Thread Safety and Synchronization?
- What is Semaphore?
- What Are Monitors?
- What's the Importance of Synchronized Blocks?
- How Do We Create Threads?

- What's the Difference Between Using Runnables and Extends in Threads?
- Explain Thread.sleep.
- How Can We Stop a Thread?
- What is wait() and notify()?
- Explain How Scheduling and Priority Work in Threads.
- Explain Yielding in Threading.
- What Are Daemon Threads?

JDBC

- How Does JAVA Interact With Databases?
- Can We Interact With Non-Relational Sources Using JDBC?
- Explain the Different Sections in JDBC in Detail.
- Explain Briefly How You Go About Using JDBC API in Code.
- How Do You Handle SQL Exceptions?
- If There Are More Than One Exception in SQLException Class, How Can We Go About Displaying it?
- Explain Type1, Type2, Type3, and Type4 Drivers in JDBC?
- What Are the Advantages and Disadvantages of Using JDBC-ODBC Bridge Driver?
- What Are the Advantages and Disadvantages of Using Native-API/Partially Java Driver?
- What Are the Advantages and Disadvantages of Using Net-Protocol/All-Java Driver?
- What Are the Advantages and Disadvantages of Using Native-Protocol/All-Java driver?
- Define Meta-Data.
- What is DatabaseMetaData?
- Explain 'ConnectionFactory' Class.
- I Want to Display Tables of a Database, How Do I Do It?
- Define 'ResultSetMetaData.'
- What is the Difference Between 'ResultSet' and 'RowSet?'
- Can 'ResultSet' Objects be Serialized?
- Explain the Relationship Between 'ResultSet,' 'RowSet,' 'CachedRowset,' 'JdbcRowset,' and 'WebRowSet.'
- What Are the Different Types of Resultset?
- Explain the Concept of 'PreparedStatement' Statement Interface.
- What's the Difference Between 'Statement' and 'PreparedStatement?'
- How Can We Call Stored Procedure Using JDBC?
- Explain 'CallableStatement' Interface in Detail.
- How Do You Get a Resultset Object From Stored Procedure?
- How Can We Do Batch Updates Using 'CallableStatement' Interface?
- Define Transactions.
- What is ACID in Transaction?
- What Are the Four Essential Properties of a Transaction?
- Explain Concurrency and Locking.

- What Are the Different Types of Locks?
- What Are the Different Levels of Resource on Which Locks Can Be Placed?
- Define Lock Escalation.
- What is Table-Level and Row-Level Locking?
- What Are the Problems That Can Occur If You Do Not Implement Locking Properly?
- What Are the Different Transaction Levels? (Twist: What Are the Different Types of Locks?)
- What is the Difference Between Optimistic and Pessimistic Locking?
- What Are Deadlocks?
- How Can We Set Transaction Levels Through JDBC API?
- Explain Transaction Control in JDBC?
- What Are Savepoints in a Transaction?

Servlets and JSP

- What Are Servlets?
- What Are the Advantages of Servlets Over CGI?
- Explain the Servlet Life-Cycle.
- What Are the Two Important APIs in Servlets?
- Explain 'javax.servlet' Package in Detail.
- What's the Use of ServletContext?
- How Do We Define an Application Level Scope for Servlet?
- What's the Difference Between GenericServlet and HttpServlet?
- Explain javax.servlet.http Package in Detail.
- What's the Architecture of a Servlet Package?
- Why is HTTP Protocol Called a Stateless Protocol?
- What Are the Different Ways In Which We Can Maintain State Between Requests?
- What is URL Rewriting?
- What Are Cookies?
- What Are Sessions in Servlets?
- What's the Difference Between getSession(true) and getSession(false)?
- What's the Difference Between 'doPost' and 'doGet' Methods?
- Which are the Different Ways in Which You Can Communicate Between Servlets?
- What is the Functionality of a 'RequestDispatcher' Object?
- How Do We Share Data Using 'getServletContext () ?'
- Explain the Concept of SSI.
- What Are Filters in JAVA?
- Explain Briefly How You Go About Implementing Filters Using Apache Tomcat? (Twist: Explain Step-by-Step How To Implement Filters.)
- What's the Difference Between Authentication and Authorization?
- Explain Briefly the Directory Structure of a Web Application?
- Explain a JSP Page Life-Cycle.

- What is EL?
- How Does EL Search For an Attribute?
- What Are the Implicit EL Objects in JSP?
- How Can We Disable EL?
- What is JSTL?
- Explain Briefly the Different Types of JSTL Tags.
- How Can We Use Beans in JSP?
- What is the <jsp:forward> Tag For?
- What Are JSP Directives?
- What Are Page Directives?
- What Are Include Directives?
- Explain Taglib Directives.
- How Do JSP Engines Instantiate Tag Handler Classes Instances?
- What's the Difference Between JavaBeans and Taglib Directives?
- What Are the Different Scopes an Object Can Have in a JSP Page?
- What Are the Different Implicit Objects of JSP?
- What Are the Different Authentication Options Available in Servlets?
- Explain How We Can Practically Implement Security on a Resource.
- How Can We Practically Implement Form-Based Authentication.
- How Do We Authenticate Using JDBC?
- Explain JDBCRealm.
- Explain How We Configure JNDIRealm.
- How Do You Implement Caching in JSP?

EJB

- What is EJB?
- What Are the Different Kinds of EJBs?
- You Are Designing th Architecture For a Project, How Do You Decide Which Architecture You Should Use? Session, Entity, or Message-Driven Bean?
- Explain 'EJBHome' and 'EJBObject' in EJB.
- Can a Client Directly Create Objects of Session or Entity Beans?
- Explain the Concept of Local Interfaces.
- What Are the Limitations of Using Local Objects?
- Which Application Server Have You Used for EJB?
- Explain the Method Of Practically Developing and Deploying EJB Components.
- What is Passivation and Activation in EJB?
- Can Beans That Are Involved in Transaction Have 'Passivation' Process?
- How Does the Server Decide Which Beans to Passivate and Activate?
- In What Format is Conversational Data Written to the Disk?
- Explain Briefly, the Life-Cycle for Stateless and Stateful Beans.

Struts

- What's MVC Pattern?
- Define Struts.
- Explain the Directory Structure For a Struts Folder in brief.
- Give an Overview of How a Struts Application Flows. (Twist: What Are Action and Action Form Classes in Struts?)

XML and Web Services

- What is XML?
- What is the Version Information in XML?
- What is ROOT Element in XML?
- If XML Does Not Have a Closing Tag, Will it Work?
- Is XML Case-Sensitive?
- What is the Difference Between XML and HTML?
- Is XML Meant to Replace HTML?
- Explain Why Your Project Needed XML.
- What is DTD (Document Type Definition?)
- What is Well-Formed XML?
- What is a Valid XML?
- What is CDATA Section in XML?
- What is CSS?
- What is XSL?
- What Are Elements and Attributes in XML?
- What Are the Standard Ways of Parsing an XML Document?
- In What Scenarios Will You Use a DOM Parser and a SAX Parser?
- What is XSLT?
- Define XPATH?
- What is the Concept of XPOINTER?
- What is a Web Service?
- What is DISCO ?
- What is SOAP?
- What is WSDL?
- Explain UDDI.
- Explain JAXP.
- What is an XML Registry?
- What is JAXR?
- What is JAXM?
- Explain How JAXM Messaging Model Works.
- Explain JAX-RPC Internationalization.
- Explain i18n and l10n.
- Explain Internationalization and Localization.

- What is Locale?
- How Do We Display Numbers, Currency, and Dates according to proper Locale Format?
- What Are Resource Bundles?
- How Do We Load a Resource Bundle File?
- How Can We Do Inheritance in Resource Bundles?

JNI

- What is Native Interface in JAVA?
- Describe In Brief the Steps Required to Implement Native Interfaces in Java.
- Can JNI Be Used For VB6, C#, or VB.NET directly?
- What Are JNI Functions and Pointers?
- How Does the Garbage Collector Know Which JNI Objects Are No More Used? (Twist: What Are the Different Types of References for JNI Supports?/Twist: How Do You Delete Global Objects?)
- How Does the Native Language (C or C++) Understand Data Types in JAVA?
- Explain Exception Handling in JNI?
- What Are the Limitations for the 'JNIEnv' Pointer in Multithreading Scenarios?
- What Are the Advantages and Disadvantages of using 'JNI?'

Architecture

- What Are Design Patterns?
- What is the Difference Between Factory and Abstract Factory Patterns?
- What is MVC pattern? (Twist: How Can You Implement MVC Pattern in Servlets and JSP?)
- How Can We Implement Singleton Pattern in JAVA?
- How Do You Implement Prototype Pattern in JAVA? (Twist: How Do You Implement Cloning in JAVA? What Are Shallow copies and Deep copies?)
- Give an Example of the Practical Implementation of FAÇADE Patterns?
- How Can We Implement Observer Pattern in JAVA?
- What is 3-Tier Architecture?
- What is Service-Oriented Architecture?
- What is Aspect Oriented Programming?

Project Management

- What is Project Management?
- Is the Spending on IT Projects Constant Throughout the Project?
- Who is a Stakeholder?
- Explain a Project Life-Cycle? (Twist: How Many Phases Are There in a Software Project?)
- Are Risks Constant Throughout the Project?
- Explain Different Software Development Life-Cycles?
- What is Triple Constraint Triangle in Project Management?
- What Are Project Baselines?
- What is Effort Variance?
- How is a Project Management Plan Document Normally Organized?

- How Do You Estimate a Project?
- What is CAR (Causal Analysis and Resolution ?)
- What is DAR (Decision Analysis and Resolution ?)
- What is a Fish-Bone Diagram? (Twist: What is an Ishikawa Diagram?)
- What is the Pareto Principle? (Twist: What is the 80/20 Principle?)
- How Do You Handle Change Request?
- What is an Internal Change Request?
- What is the Difference Between SITP and UTP in Testing?
- Which Software Have You Used for Project Management?
- What Are the Metrics Followed in Project Management? (Twist: What Metrics Will You Look At In Order To See That the Project is Moving Successfully?)
- You Have People in Your Team Who Do Not Meet Their Deadlines or Do Not Perform. What Are the Actions You Will Take? (Twist: Two Of Your Resources Have Conflicts Between Them, How Will You Sort It Out?)
- What is Black-Box Testing and White-Box Testing?
- What's the Difference Between Unit Testing, Assembly Testing, and Regression Testing?
- What is the V-Model in Testing?
- How Do You Start a Project?
- How Do You Do Resource Allocation?
- How Will You Do Code Reviews?
- What is CMMI?
- What Are the Five Levels in CMMI?
- What is Continuous and Staged Representation?
- Can You Explain the Process Areas?
- What is Six Sigma?
- What is DMAIC and DMADV?
- What Are the Various Roles in Six Sigma Implementation?
- What Are Function Points? (Twist: Define the Elementary Process in FPA?)
- What Are the Different Types of Elementary Processes in FPA?
- What Are the Different Elements in Functions Points?
- Explain GSC and VAF in Function Points.
- What Are Unadjusted Function Points? and How Are They Calculated?
- Explain the Steps in Function Points?
- What is the FP Per Day in Your Current Company? (Twist: What is Your Company's Productivity Factor?)
- Do You Know How to Use Case points?
- What is COCOMO I, COCOMOII, and COCOMOIII?
- What is the SMC Approach of Estimation?
- How Do You Estimate Maintenance Project and Change Requests?

UML

- What is UML?
- How Many Types of Diagrams Are There in UML? (Twist : Explain Briefly All Types of Diagrams in UML?)
- What Are the Advantages of Using UML? (Twist: What is Modeling? and Why UML?)
- What is the Sequence of UML Diagrams in projects? (Twist: How Did You Implement UML in your Project?/ Just a Small Twist: Do I Need All UML Diagrams in a Project?)
- Explain Briefly All Elements in Activity Diagrams.
- Explain the Different Elements of a Collaboration Diagram.
- Explain Component Diagrams.
- Explain All Parts of a Deployment Diagram.
- Describe the Various Components in a Sequence Diagram.
- What Are the Element in State-Chart Diagrams?
- Describe the Different Elements in Static-Chart Diagrams?
- Explain the Different Elements of a Use Case? (Twist: What is the Difference Between Activity and Sequence Diagrams?)

Software testing Interview Questions Book

Software Testing Basics

- In Which Software Life-Cycle Phase Does Testing Occur?
- Explain the PDCA Cycle, and Where Does Testing Fit Into It?
- What is the Difference Between White-Box, Black-Box, and Gray-Box Testing?
- Define Defect?
- What is the Difference Between Defect and Failure?
- What Are the Broad Categories of Defects?
- What is the Difference Between Verification and Validation?
- How Does Testing Affect Risk?
- Does an Increase in Testing Always Mean Good For the Project?
- As a Manager, What Process Did You Adopt to Define Testing Policy?
- Should Testing Be Done Only After Build and Execution?
- Are the Number of Defects More in the Design Phase or Coding Phase?
- What Kind of Inputs Do We Need From the End User to Start Proper Testing?
- What is the Difference Between Latent and Masked Defect?
- A Defect Which Could Have Been Removed During the Initial Stage is Removed in Later Stages, How Does it Affect Cost?
- In Testing, Can You Explain the Concept of Work-Bench?
- What's the Difference Between Alpha and Beta Testing?
- Explain the Concept of Defect Cascading?
- Explain How One Defect Leads to Other Defects?
- Explain What Usability Testing Is.
- What Are the Different Strategies of Rollout to End Users?

- Explain Requirement Traceability and Its Importance?
- What is the Difference Between Pilot and Beta Testing?
- How Will You Do a Risk Analysis During Software Testing?
- How do you Conclude Which Section is Most Risky in your Application?
- What Do Entry and Exit Criteria Mean in a Project?
- On What Basis is the Acceptance Plan Prepared?
- What's the Relationship Between Environment Reality and Test Phases?
- What Are Different Types of Verifications?
- What's the Difference Between Inspections and Walkthroughs?
- Can You Explain Regression Testing and Confirmation Testing?
- What Do You Mean By Coverage? and What Are the Different Types of Coverage Techniques?
- How Does Fundamentally a Coverage Tool Work?
- What is Configuration Management?
- Explain the Concept of Baseline in Software Development.
- What Are the Different Test-Plan Documents in Projects?
- How do Test Documents in a Project Span Across the Software Development Life-Cycle?
- Explain Inventories.
- How Do You Do Analysis and Design for Testing Projects?
- Explain Calibration.
- Which Test Cases Are First Written? White Boxes or Black Boxes?
- Explain Co-Habiting Software.
- What Different Impact Ratings Have You Used in Your Project?
- Explain What a Test Log is.
- Explain SDLC (Software Development Life-Cycle) in Detail.
- Explain the Waterfall Model.
- Explain the Big-Bang Waterfall Model.
- Explain the Phased Waterfall Model.
- Explain Iterative Model, Incremental Model, Spiral Model, Evolutionary Model, and V-Model?
- Explain Unit Testing, Integration Tests, System Testing, and Acceptance Testing.
- What's the Difference Between System and Acceptance Testing?
- Which is the Best Model?
- What Group of Teams Can Do Software Testing?

Testing techniques

- Explain Boundary Value Analysis.
- What is BV in Software Testing?
- Explain Equivalence Partitioning.
- Explain How State Transition Diagrams Can Be Helpful During Testing.
- Explain Random Testing.

- Explain Monkey Testing.
- What is Negative and Positive Testing?
- Explain Exploratory Testing.
- What Are Semi-Random Test Cases?
- Explain the Concept of Orthogonal Arrays?
- Explain Pairwise Defect Fundamental.
- Explain the Concept of Decision Tables.
- How Did You Define Severity Ratings in Your Project?

Software Process

- What is a Software Process?
- What Are the Different Cost Elements Involved in Implementing Processes in an Organization?
- What is a Model?
- What is Maturity Level?
- Explain the Concept of Process Area in CMMI?
- Explain the Concept of Tailoring.

CMMI

- What is CMMI? and What's the Advantage of Implementing CMMI in an Organization?
- What's the Difference Between Implementation and Institutionalization?
- What Are the Different Models in CMMI?
- Explain Staged and Continuous Models in CMMI.
- Explain the Different Maturity Levels in Staged Representation.
- Explain Capability Levels in Continuous Representation.
- Which Model Should We Use? and In What Scenarios?
- How Many Process Areas Are There in CMMI? and How Are They Classified?
- What's the Difference Between Every Level in CMMI?
- What Different Sources Are Needed to Verify the Authenticity for CMMI Implementation?
- Explain the SCAMPI Process?
- How is Appraisal Done in CMMI?
- Which Appraisal Method Class is the Best?
- Explain the Importance of PII in SCAMPI.
- Explain the Implementation of CMMI in One of the Key Process Areas?
- Explain All Process Areas With Their Goals and Practices?
- Explain the Different Process Areas?

Six Sigma

- What is Six Sigma?
- Explain the Different Methodologies for the Execution and Design Process in Six Sigma?
- What Do Executive Leaders, Champions, Master Black-Belt, Green-Belts, and Black-Belts Mean?
- What Are the Different Kinds of Variations Used in Six Sigma?

- Explain the Concept of Standard Deviation.
- Explain the Concept of Fish-Bone/Ishikawa Diagram.
- Explain QFD.
- Explain FMEA.
- Explain X-Bar Charts.
- Explain Flowcharting and Brainstorming.

Metrics

- What is Meant by Measure and Metrics?
- Explain the Number of Defects Measure.
- Explain the Number of Production Defects Measure.
- Explain Defect Seeding.
- Explain DRE.
- Explain Unit and System-Test DRE.
- How Do You Measure Test Effectiveness?
- Explain Defect Age and Defect Spoilage.

Automated Testing

- What Are Good Candidate For Automation in Testing?
- Does Automation Replace Manual Testing?
- Which Automation Tools Have You Worked With? and Can You Explain Them in Brief?
- Explain How Load Testing Conceptually Works for Websites.
- Explain How You Performed Load-Testing.
- What Does a Load-Test Summary Report Contain?
- Explain the Concept of Data-Driven Testing?
- Explain Table-Driven Testing?
- How Can You Perform Data-Driven Testing Using Automated QA?

Testing Estimation

- What Are the Different Ways of Carrying Out Black-Box Testing?
- Explain TPA Analysis.
- Briefly Explain Function Points.]
- Explain the Concept of Application Boundary.
- Explain the Concept of Elementary Process.
- Explain the Concepts of Static and Dynamic Elementary Processes.
- Explain the Concepts of FTR, ILF, EIF, EI, EO, EQ, and GSC.
- How Can You Estimate the Number of Acceptance Test Cases in a Project?
- On What Basis Does TPA Work?
- How Did You Do Estimation For Black-Box Testing?
- How Did You Estimate White-Box Testing?
- Is There a Way to Estimate Acceptance Test Cases in a System?

8

References

- The TCP/IP Guide by Charles M. Kozierok; No Starch Press; © 2005.
- Networking Foundations by Patrick Ciccarelli and Christina Falukner; Sybex; © 2004.
- Network Routing Basics: Understanding IP Routing in Cisco Systems by James Macfarlane; John Wiley & Sons; © 2006.

Other titles of interest......

by SHIVPRASAD KOIRALA

.NET
INTERVIEW QUESTIONS
ISBN : 81-8333-147-5
Pages: 388

SOFTWARE TESTING
INTERVIEW QUESTIONS
ISBN : 81-8333-236-6
Pages: 212

SQL SERVER
INTERVIEW QUESTIONS
ISBN : 81-8333-103-3
Pages: 228

JAVA/J2EE
INTERVIEW QUESTIONS
ISBN : 81-8333-173-4
Pages: 320

NETWORKING
INTERVIEW QUESTIONS
ISBN : 81-8333-243-9
Pages: 216

C# AND ASP.NET
PROJECTS
ISBN : 81-8333-217-X
Pages: 228

Notes